LINCOLN CONNECTIONS

Aspects of City and County since 1700

A Tribute to Dennis Mills

Edited by Shirley Brook, Andrew Walker and Rob Wheeler

Published by
THE SOCIETY FOR LINCOLNSHIRE HISTORY AND ARCHAEOLOGY
2011

LINCOLN CONNECTIONS

First published by The Society for Lincolnshire History and Archaeology 2011
© The Society for Lincolnshire History and Archaeology

ISBN 978 0 903582 42 1

British Library Cataloguing in Publication Data
A CIP catalogue record for this book is available from the British Library

All rights reserved

No part of this publication may be reproduced or transmitted in any form or by any means, electronic or mechanical, including photocopying, recording or any information storage and retrieval systems, without permission in writing from the publisher.

Front cover
The April Horse Fair on Lincoln's High Street, c.1905
(Courtesy of Maurice Hodson)

Back cover
Skellingthorpe: the Christ's Hospital plan, 1847
(NB East is at the bottom)
[LAO TLE 43/4]

Production editors: Ken Redmore and Catherine Wilson

Designed by Nigel Kingston

Printed in the United Kingdom by F W Cupit (Printers) Limited
Horncastle, Lincolnshire

CONTENTS

List of Abbreviations and General Acknowledgements — 4

Introduction: *Rob Wheeler* — 5

Dennis Mills
    A Short Biography: *Rob Wheeler* — 8
    An Appreciation: *Nigel Goose* — 10
    A Bibliography: *Shirley Brook* — 12

Notes on Contributors — 16

1: 'Inexhaustible Themes for Study and Speculation'
    Michael Drury and the recording of Lincoln's buried archaeology: *Michael J. Jones* — 19

2: The Building of Skellingthorpe Reservoir: *Rob Wheeler* — 31

3: The Sibthorps of Canwick
    The rise and fall of a dynasty: *Michael Trott* — 43

4: North Lincolnshire's Country Carriers: *Dan Ellin* — 59

5: The Alehouses of Kesteven
    Control of the trade of licensed victualling 1755-1831: *Wendy Atkin* — 75

6: 'The Development of Rural Settlement Around Lincoln' Revisited
    with special reference to farm buildings and loans for improvement: *Shirley Brook* — 91

7: Fairs and Markets
    Challenging encounters between the urban and rural in Lincolnshire c.1840-1920: *Andrew Walker* — 107

8: Visions of Victorian Lincoln
    The production of an urban image 1846-1900: *Denise McHugh* — 124

9: Towards the Late Twentieth Century and Beyond
    Rural and urban change and the task of the historian: *Andrew J. H. Jackson* — 136

LIST OF ABBREVIATIONS

BL	British Library
CRO	Cornwall Record Office
DRO	Devon Record Office
HRO	Hertfordshire Record Office
JBAA	*Journal of the British Archaeological Association*
JRASE	*Journal of the Royal Agricultural Society of England*
KU	Keele University
LAO	Lincolnshire Archives
LC	*Lincolnshire Chronicle*
LE	*Lincolnshire Echo*
LRSM	*Lincoln, Rutland and Stamford Mercury*
MLE	*Mark Lane Express*
NDRO	North Devon Record Office
ORO	Oxford Record Office
RCP	Royal College of Physicians
TNA	The National Archives

The place of publication of books is London unless otherwise stated.

GENERAL ACKNOWLEDGEMENTS

Acknowledgements are due first and foremost to Dennis Mills, who has inspired all of us. To Joan Mills we are grateful for assistance in ways too numerous to mention. Miriam Smith, who edits *The Lincoln Enquirer* (the newsletter of the Survey of Lincoln) and Ken Redmore, of the Society for Lincolnshire History and Archaeology, assisted with compiling the bibliography; Jayne Knight helped with typing it. Maurice Hodson gave important help with photographs.

Turning to illustrations generally, Figures 1.1, 1.5, 4.4, 4.5, 4.7 and 4.8 are from the Local Studies Collection, Lincoln Central Library, and reproduced by courtesy of Lincolnshire County Council; Figure 6.7 is reproduced with the permission of the Diocese of Lincoln and Lincolnshire Archives. The figures in Chapter 2 and the back cover are reproduced with the permission of Lincolnshire Archives. Not least, we are grateful to the staff of Lincoln Central Library and the Lincolnshire Archives for all the help and advice they have provided to many of the contributors.

INTRODUCTION

Rob Wheeler

After a brief biography and an appreciation of Dennis Mills's academic output, we start with one of his latest interests, Lincoln's nineteenth-century sewerage schemes: Mick Jones describes Michael Drury's observations of archaeology uncovered during the laying of sewers and other construction work. He examines Drury's career and discusses his motivation for making such a record and what it reveals about his competence as an archaeologist.

A prerequisite for any modern system of sewerage was a supply of piped water. My own contribution describes how the main reservoir for that scheme came to be transformed into an ornamental lake for Hartsholme Hall, how it delayed the publication of the second edition of Padley's map of Lincoln (another recent interest of Dennis) and how the solicitor Richard Carline benefited from it.

When the sewers were at last laid, their contents were pumped to a sewage farm at Canwick. That village and the Sibthorp family of Canwick Hall have long been the subject of Dennis's investigations. Michael Trott here explores the careers of some of the earlier generations of that family and their approaches to ensuring that the family prospered.

To many, *connections* implies transport. The likes of the Sibthorps would scarcely have deigned to enter one, but the humble carrier's cart was the mainstay for the local movement of produce and people. Dan Ellin explores the nature of that trade and how it changed in the course of the nineteenth century.

Carriers, like grander forms of road transport, made use of licensed premises. Queueing in the rain at a bus stop was not our ancestors' lot. Wendy Atkin explores how the number of alehouses in Kesteven changed in the later eighteenth and early nineteenth centuries, and how successful central government was in controlling those numbers. Interestingly, the fall in numbers appears to bear relatively little relationship to legislative activity.

A village's prosperity, as well as the income of the dominant landowner, was based on the profitability of its farming. Investment in improvement could enhance that profitability, but where the land was part of a settled estate, in the legal sense of that phrase, the current generation might have difficulty finding the capital to finance improvements. Shirley Brook describes the system of Land Improvement Loans, and how their records can assist modern historians and those interested in farm buildings. She uses them to confirm Dennis's more tentative conclusions about the factors influencing dispersal of settlement from villages' historic centres.

Just as the boundary between villages and their fields was becoming more blurred, so was the boundary between urban Lincoln and its rural hinterland. Andrew Walker examines one aspect of this interface, looking at the various markets and fairs that took place in Lincoln and how the City authorities sought to regulate and control them. The concern of the respectable classes at the intoxication which accompanied these events can be compared with the concerns underlying the government legislation on alehouses described by Wendy Atkin: the offence might vary from age to age but the villain was still the demon drink. The major fairs gradually turned into pleasure fairs as the twentieth century dawned, so the role of the 'statutes' in providing a rare opportunity for rural visitors to engage in boisterous revelry continued under another guise.

Lincoln also attracted visitors of a different sort. Many thousands from all social classes came to Lincoln to improve their minds by viewing Lincoln's historic sites; they too also wanted a good day out. Denise McHugh analyses the way Lincoln sold itself as a tourist destination, looking particularly at the role of the guide book and what it suggested visitors should look at. The authors and publishers of most of these guide books have already been encountered in Mick Jones's chapter. Denise offers a different perspective on how they selected their content.

Finally, Andrew Jackson extends Dennis's work on open and closed villages, showing how this aspect of their history has affected their character right up to the present day. Residents of the villages around Lincoln should see their built environment in a new light, just as Andrew Walker's chapter should make them more conscious of the mental constructs they use to relate to the City and to those of their neighbours who are still engaged in the world of agriculture.

Connections recur in the most surprising ways. The carriers' carts that took rural folk to market lost customers as the agricultural labourer started to turn up at 'statutes' on his new-fangled bicycle. With that, and the transformation of villages near Lincoln (and, increasingly, across the county) into dormitory settlements, we are into a world which Dennis could write about from personal experience. We are all part of history, but only a few have the ability to discern what is important. Dennis is one of those few.

*After retiring from the Open University,
Dennis undertook some heritage interpretation work for
North Kesteven District Council.*

DENNIS MILLS
A Short Biography
Rob Wheeler

Dennis Mills is the son of a gardener and grew up in the estate village at Winthorpe, near Newark, and then at Canwick outside Lincoln. One of his grandfathers was a small farmer at Scothern[1] who, by hard work and a canny business sense, was able to buy his own farm at Thurlby by Bassingham. Rural society was already changing under the influence of the internal combustion engine and the shadow of the approaching war but it still retained its traditional structure. Dennis was thus one of the last of that select group of academic geographers who could write about traditional rural society with the benefit of personal experience as well as academic rigour. As just one small example of how that affected his outlook, in considering the practices of a rural registrar of births and deaths in the mid-nineteenth century, he drew on his own experience to pose questions like how those registering births and deaths would have known where to find the registrar and what his office hours were.

After reading geography at Nottingham, with National Service looming, he chose to join the Royal Navy, for no better reason than that he had seen a little of the Army and Air Force and might as well see how the Senior Service conducted itself. The navy must have been a little unsure what to do with a graduate in a non-technical subject. They might have made a 'schoolie' (an Education Branch officer) of him, but the Cold War was getting hotter, there was a massive requirement for Russian translators, and so they sent him to the Joint Service School for Linguists. He thus became one of that select group of *kursanty* who have so influenced the academic and artistic worlds.[2] After service in Germany, observing a different pattern of rural society, as well as putting his Russian to good use in the service of military intelligence, he returned to Nottingham as a Demonstrator and Temporary Assistant Lecturer.

At this point, fortune may have seemed to turn her back: the temporary post came to an end without anything permanent turning up, and Dennis became a schoolteacher. Nevertheless, it provided an opportunity to take a part-time external PhD from Leicester. It was in this period also that he met his wife Joan, whose subsequent support has meant so much to him, academically as well as domestically. A subsequent move to Melbourn Village College introduced him to that well-documented village which provided the material for a rich vein of research. Three years as a senior lecturer at Ilkley College followed, after which he joined the Open University, first as a staff tutor, then as a senior lecturer within the central academic staff. That made it possible for him and his wife Joan to move house closer to their home turf, as a result of which Dennis became involved with SLHA's publication programme, chairing its History of Lincolnshire committee and himself editing the *Twentieth Century Lincolnshire* volume.

Dennis's first papers stemmed more from his knowledge of the Russian language than from any deep interest in Russian geography. Besides, Russian geography must have been a rather awkward academic interest at that date, when so much of the relevant material was secret. His first publication on English geography was a division of Kesteven into characteristic regions, a piece of work still used to this day. It drew on his Nottingham MA but did not open up any new lines of investigation. The field of work for which he became best known, the extension of the traditional open/closed classification of English villages in the eighteenth and nineteenth centuries, started with his Leicester PhD, but then drew on the wealth of material he had uncovered relating to Melbourn, and led to a dozen papers between 1972 and 1988.

A 1978 paper on the techniques of house repopulation may have seemed a mere diversion at the time but was enthusiastically received by the growing band of amateur local historians, people who needed advice on the potential and quirks of the key sources for eighteenth- and nineteenth-century social history and a demonstration of how those sources could be used. This linked in to the activities of the Cambridge Group for the History of Population and Social Structure. In due course it led to a series of papers and books on the Census Enumerators' Books, on Land Tax Assessments and on trade directories. There must be thousands of local historians who have never read a word of Dennis's papers on open and closed villages but who regularly turn to these useful aids whenever they encounter some new oddity in these sources.

Dennis's involvement with the Cambridge Group continued after his retirement from the Open University in 1985. Indeed, freed from the burdens of teaching and administration, Dennis's output of papers grew considerably. One difference was that he was now able to pursue topics that he found interesting, without worrying about whether they would be viewed favourably in academic circles. He wrote extensively on the village of Canwick and the Sibthorp family. He took an interest in the history of his old school. In fact, it was a wish for a base map on which to plot the residences of the subscribers to this school that served as the germ from which grew the project to republish all of Padley's large-scale Lincoln maps. He wrote on hermaphrodites - which may seem a remarkable jump in interests to those unaware that a hermaphrodite or 'moffrey' is a farm cart that can be converted to a wagon. Most recently, an interest in the large-scale map produced in 1848 by the engineer George Giles to set out his proposals for providing Lincoln with a system of underground sewerage has led to further work on that phase of Lincoln's long-running sewerage controversy and on the career of George Giles himself. Much of this work has been aimed at a relatively wide audience, but it has all been characterised by extensive research and a punctilious concern to tie in with existing work in related domains.

Not the least of the benefits Dennis has conferred on Lincolnshire historical work has been his encouragement of researchers from a wide range of backgrounds. A natural teacher, he has the gift of posing productive questions that can test or transform a hypothesis. He has always set himself exacting standards and he encourages others to live up to them, but in a gracious manner that exhorts rather than commands. By this means, his influence will live on long after his last paper has come off the press.

Notes

[1] Dennis Mills, 'The small farm, with special reference to Victorian Lincolnshire', *Lincolnshire Past and Present*, 24 (Summer, 1996) pp.7-11.

[2] Geoffrey Elliott and Harold Shukman, *Secret Classrooms* (2002).

DENNIS MILLS
An Appreciation
Nigel Goose

I first met Dennis Mills in Cambridge where I studied as a postgraduate from 1976 to 1979. From time to time I would steel myself to enter the hallowed portals of the Cambridge Group for the History of Population and Social Structure (CAMPOP), then housed at 27 Trumpington Street, and I made sure I was present when Dennis Mills came to talk about his work on Melbourn in Cambridgeshire. At that time community reconstruction (now more commonly called 'micro-history') was very much in vogue: Alan Macfarlane's *Reconstructing Historical Communities* was published by Cambridge University Press in 1977, and I used to discuss the progress of Macfarlane's Earls Colne and Kirkby Lonsdale projects, over a glass or two in the bar of Wolfson College, with Charles Jardine - then acting as his computing adviser. Jardine, as I recall, was convinced that, in time, the project would come to fruition. How impressive, then, that Dennis Mills - a lone researcher without dedicated computing support or the infrastructure that the Cambridge Group provided - should be embarking on a similarly time-consuming, challenging and ambitious project, at the forefront of current research in social and economic history. Dennis was given a rather rough ride at CAMPOP that day, in particular for keeping only a single card index rather than the six or seven that the spokesman for the Cambridge Group felt to be a minimum, but he defended himself well, vigorously flying the flag for the lone researcher. And, of course, his project came to fruition very shortly thereafter, in the form of his *Lord and Peasant in Nineteenth-Century Britain.* In reviewing the book, Harold Perkin noted that Dennis had resurrected the English peasantry from the oblivion to which they had been consigned by Macfarlane's overly strict definition of the term 'peasant', and had also 'drawn timely attention to an alternative tradition in the English countryside which rescues the rural "freeborn Englishman" from Marx's contempt for "the idiocy of rural life"' (*Victorian Studies,* 25 [1982], pp.382-4). Eric Jones similarly praised the book for its effective demonstration of how an elaboration upon the open/close village dichotomy could give shape to the study of nineteenth-century rural social structure, but also celebrated the fact that this was 'an enjoyable book written in a relaxed style far from the constipated prose of so much social science history' (*Journal of Economic History,* 41 [1981], pp.436-7).

It was some considerable time before our paths crossed again, and I cannot remember at this remove exactly how the contact was made, but on this occasion it was Dennis's generosity, not merely his scholarship, that was so clearly demonstrated. I was preparing my first study based upon the 1851 census for the Berkhamsted region of Hertfordshire, and was desperately in search of comparative analyses to give my results some context. Dennis had been working on census material for many years, of course, but I was completely unaware that he had been assiduously collecting rural data - until, that is, a tabulation arrived through the post one day providing a breakdown of gender ratios, marital status and age profiles for a wide selection of rural villages, encompassing 18,490 individuals, and providing a 'rural norm' against which I could compare my regional results. It was given freely, without qualification or insistence upon attribution, as an act of generosity and support for a fellow researcher with similar interests in nineteenth century population and social structure. Subsequently Dennis sent me the 5.25 inch disks on which the data was stored, compiled by his son on a BBC computer in a code that, to this day, no-one has been able to crack. I have kept them, in the hope that one day I will be able to return the favour, and render them accessible once again.

My third vignette arises from my role as editor of *Local Population Studies,* a position I took on in 1999 and continue to enjoy today. The Editorial Board of *Local Population Studies* also acts as the publications committee of the Local Population Studies Society, and from time to time the society publishes 'supplements' to the journal, which are in fact full-blown and free-standing books on a topic of interest to the journal's readership. One of my colleagues on the Board drew my attention to Dennis's work on rural trade directories, at the time (and perhaps still) a source that had attracted insufficient attention from local historians. After some exchange of correspondence I travelled to Branston in Lincolnshire to visit Dennis at his home, and in the course of an afternoon we had ironed out any remaining wrinkles, clearing the path to the publication of the study which appeared shortly thereafter as *Rural Community History from Trade Directories* (Aldenham, 2001). On this occasion, not only was I impressed by Dennis's hospitality, but also his ease of manner and his professionalism.

As the list of publications included in this volume testifies, Dennis has published extensively on the economy and society of eighteenth- and nineteenth-century England and, throughout his career, has retained a particular interest in, and love for, his home county of Lincolnshire. So fitting it is, then, that this celebration of his work to mark his eightieth birthday should be published under the auspices of the Society for Lincolnshire History and Archaeology. But if Dennis is demonstrably, through his work both on Melbourn and upon Lincolnshire, a 'local historian', he is a local historian of all England, for his innumerable contributions have shed light upon so many features of eighteenth- and nineteenth-century economy and society, and have invariably transcended the local setting within which they have been based. This, of course, is what all good local history does. At the same time, Dennis has wrestled with the sources, and has performed an additional service in helping colleagues - both professional and non-professional - make better use of the census, land tax assessments, rural trade directories, and other sources besides. In both his substantive and his source-based work, he has effectively straddled the professional-amateur divide, in the process making important contributions to both. As I hope my personal recollections have demonstrated, he has done this with imagination and energy, with generosity and professionalism - and with modesty too. I'm sure he will continue to do so for many years to come.

University of Hertfordshire
October 2010

A BIBLIOGRAPHY

Shirley Brook

The place of publication of books is London unless otherwise stated.

(with J. P. Cole and J. C. Crossley) 'Recent Soviet atlases', *Geographical Journal*, 122 (1955), 282-84

'The USSR: A reappraisal of Mackinder's Heartland Concept', *Scottish Geographical Magazine*, 72 (1955), 144-53

(with J. P. Cole) *English Guide to the Soviet Geographical Atlas for Teachers in Middle Schools* (Nottingham, 1956)

'Regions of Kesteven devised for the purposes of agricultural history', *Lincolnshire Architectural and Archaeological Society, Reports and Papers*, 7.1 (1957), 60-82

'Population and Settlement in Kesteven (Lincs.) c.1775 - c.1885', MA Thesis, University of Nottingham (1957)

'Lincolnshire farming regions', *East Midland Geographer*, 9 (1958), 41-43

'A bibliography of post-war work relating to the geography of Lincolnshire', *Lincolnshire Architectural and Archaeological Society Reports and Papers*, 7.2 (1958), 175-83

'Enclosure in Kesteven', *Agricultural History Review*, 7 (1959), 82-97

'The development of rural settlement around Lincoln, with specific reference to the eighteenth and nineteenth centuries', *East Midland Geographer*, 11 (1959), 3-15. Republished in *English Rural Communities: The Impact of a Specialised Economy*, edited by D. R. Mills (1973), 83-97

'The poor laws and the distribution of population, c.1600-1860, with special reference to Lincolnshire', *Transactions and Papers of the Institute of British Geographers*, 26 (1959), 185-95

'Land Ownership and Rural Population: With Special Reference to Leicestershire in the Mid-19th Century', PhD Thesis, University of Leicester (1963)

The Early History of Meldreth (Melbourn, Cambridgeshire, 1965)

'English villages in the eighteenth and nineteenth centuries: A sociological approach. Part I: The concept of a sociological classification', *Amateur Historian*, 68 (1965), 271-78

'English villages in the eighteenth and nineteenth centuries: A sociological approach. Part II: A survey of the main types of source material', *Amateur Historian*, 7.1 (1966), 7-13

'Integration (of Geography) with the humanities', *Times Educational Supplement,* 25 May, 1967, 1804

The English Village (1968)

'Middle school teachers' training in Geography', *Times Educational Supplement,* 28 March, 1969, 1028

'The geographical effects of the Laws of Settlement in Nottinghamshire: an analysis of Francis Howell's Report, 1848', *East Midland Geographer*, 5.1-2 (1970), 31-38. Republished in *English Rural Communities: The Impact of a Specialised Economy,* edited by D. R. Mills (1973), 182-191

(with Andrew Learmonth et al.) *Political, Historical and Regional Geography* (Bletchley, 1972)

'Francis Howell's Report on the operation of the Laws of Settlement in Nottinghamshire, 1848', *Transactions of the Thoroton Society of Nottinghamshire,* 76 (1973 for 1972), 46-52

(ed.) *English Rural Communities: The Impact of a Specialised Economy* (1973)

(with Ray Thomas and John Collins) *The Spread of Cities* (Milton Keynes, 1973)

'The christening custom at Melbourn, Cambs', *Local Population Studies,* 11 (1973), 11-22. Republished in *Population Studies from the Parish Registers,* edited by Michael Drake (Matlock, 1982), 36-47

'The peasant tradition', *Local Historian,* 11 (1974), 200-06

'Starting points for local history teachers', *Times Educational Supplement,* 15 February, 1974, 65

(with Andrew Learmonth and Brendan Connors) *Population Resources and Technology* (Milton Keynes, 1975; repr. 1976)

'A social and demographic study of Melbourn, Cambridgeshire, c.1840', *Archives,* 12 (1976), 115-20

'An economic, tenurial, social and demographic study of an English peasant village', Social Science Research Council, HR 3932 (1977)

'The peasant culture', *New Society,* 7 April, 1977, 10-12

'The quality of life in Melbourn, Cambridgeshire, in the

period 1800-50', *International Review of Social History,* 23 (1978), 382-404

'The residential propinquity of kin in a Cambridgeshire village, 1841', *Journal of Historical Geography,* 4 (1978), 265-76

'The technique of house repopulation: experience from a Cambridgeshire village, 1841', *Local Historian,* 13 (1978), 86-97

'The Court of Arches and church rates disputes as sources of social history', *Bulletin of Local History East Midland Region,* 14 (1979), 1-11

Aspects of Marriage: An Example of Applied Historical Studies (Milton Keynes, 1980)

Lord and Peasant in Nineteenth Century Britain (1980)

'The false widows of Melbourn: A cautionary census tale', *Journal of the Cambridgeshire Family History Society,* 3.1 (1981), 3-5

(with Carol G. Pearce) *Census Enumerators' Books: An Annotated Bibliography of Published Work Based Substantially on 19th Century Census Enumerators' Books* (Milton Keynes, 1982)

'The significance of land tax assessments', *Local Historian,* 15 (1982), 161-65

'Rural industries and social structure: Framework knitters in Leicestershire, 1670-1851', *Textile History,* 13 (1982), 183-203

(ed. with J. Gibson) *Land Tax Assessments* c.1690-c.1950 (Plymouth, 1983; repr. with minor amendments and additions Plymouth, 1984)

'Family background: The significance of family and demographic history for the general historian', *Times Educational Supplement,* 9 April, 1982, 27

(with Brian M. Short) 'Social change and social conflict in nineteenth-century England: the use of the open-closed village model', *Journal of Peasant Studies,* 10.4 (1983), 253-62. Reprinted in *Class, Conflict and Protest in the English Countryside, 1700-1800,* edited by Mick Reed and Roger Wells (1990), 90-99

A Guide to Nineteenth-Century Census Enumerators' Books (Milton Keynes, 1984)

(with Philip Aslett *et al.*) *Victorians on the Move: Research in the Census Enumerators' Books 1851-1881* (Buckingham, 1984)

'The nineteenth century peasantry of Melbourn, Cambridgeshire', in *Land, Kinship and Lifecycle,* edited by Richard M. Smith (Cambridge, 1985), 481-519

(*et al.*) 'Sustaining rural communities', in *The Changing Countryside,* edited by John Blunden and Nigel Curry (1985), 162-202

(ed. with Michael Turner) *Land and Property: the English Land Tax 1692-1832* (Gloucester, 1986)

'Early land tax assessments explored, 1: Rutland, Cambridgeshire and Lincolnshire', in *Land and Property: the English Land Tax 1692-1832,* edited with Michael Turner (Gloucester, 1986) 189-203

'Survival of early (pre 1780) land tax assessments', in *Land and Property: the English Land Tax 1692-1832,* edited with Michael Turner (Gloucester, 1986) 219-234

'Country matters', *History Today,* 36 (1986), 5-7

(with Carol Pearce) 'Researching in the Victorian censuses: A note on a computerized, annotated bibliography of publications based substantially on the census enumerators' books', *Quarterly Journal of Social Affairs,* 2.1 (1986), 55-68

'A Lincolnshire guide to the nineteenth century censuses', *Lincolnshire History and Archaeology,* 22 (1987), 25-29

'Peasants and conflict in nineteenth-century rural England: a comment on two recent articles', *Journal of Peasant Studies,* 15.3 (1988), 395-400. Reprinted in *Class, Conflict and Protest in the English Countryside, 1700-1800,* edited by Mick Reed and Roger Wells (1990), 115-20

'A "directory" of Lincolnshire medical men in the late eighteenth century: Two original sources', *Lincolnshire History and Archaeology,* 23 (1988), 59-62

(with Carol Pearce) *People and Places in the Victorian Census: A review and Bibliography of Publications Based Substantially on the Manuscript Census Enumerators' Books, 1841-1911,* Historical Geography Research Series, 23 (Bristol, 1989)

(ed.) *Twentieth Century Lincolnshire,* History of Lincolnshire Series, 12 (Lincoln, 1989)

'The revolution in workplace and home', in *Twentieth Century Lincolnshire,* (ed.) History of Lincolnshire Series, 12 (Lincoln, 1989), 18-36

(with Joan Mills) 'Occupation and social stratification revisited: The census enumerators' books of Victorian Britain', *Urban History Year Book* (1989), 63-77

The Knights Templar in Lincolnshire (Sleaford, 1990; rev. edn. Sleaford, 2009)

(with Ruth Tinley) 'The people of Swinderby in 1771 and 1791: A study in population mobility', *Lincolnshire History and Archaeology,* 26 (1991), 7-11

'The rise and fall of the English village: or rural planning and technological change', *Lincolnshire Past and Present,* 3 (Spring, 1991), 18-21

'Village history in the Scopwick area', *Lincolnshire Past and Present*, 9 (Autumn, 1992), 15

(ed. with P. Baumber) *Kirkby Green and Scopwick: Historical Sketches of two Lincolnshire Parishes* (Scopwick, 1993)

(ed. with Jeremy Gibson and Mervyn Medlycott) *Land and Window Tax Assessments* (Birmingham, 1993; 2nd edn. Birmingham, 1998; updated Bury, 2004)

'County Seats of the Gentry', in *An Historical Atlas of Lincolnshire,* edited by Stewart Bennett and Nicholas Bennett (Hull, 1993; repr. Chichester 2001), 106-07

'Dispensaries and hospitals to 1937', in *An Historical Atlas of Lincolnshire,* edited by Stewart Bennett and Nicholas Bennett (Hull, 1993; repr. Chichester, 2001), 128-29

(with Michael Drake) 'The census, 1801-1991', in *Studying Family and Community History, Nineteenth and Twentieth Centuries, 4, Sources and Methods: A Handbook,* edited by Michael Drake and Ruth Finnegan (Cambridge, 1994), 25-56

'Community and nation in the past: perception and reality', in *Time, Family and Community: Perspectives on Family and Community History,* edited by Michael Drake (Oxford, 1994), 261-85

(with Ruth Tinley) 'Population turnover in an eighteenth-century Lincolnshire parish in comparative context', *Local Population Studies,* 52 (Spring, 1994), 30-38

'Heritage and historians', *The Local Historian,* 24.4 (1994), 225-28

'The founding fathers of the City School, Lincoln', *Lincolnshire Past and Present,* 21 (Autumn, 1995), 7-8

(with Kevin Schurer) *Local Communities in the Victorian Census Enumerators' Books* (Oxford, 1996)

'The Fawcetts of Lincolnshire and the development of the medical profession', in *Lincolnshire People and Places: Essays in Memory of Terence R. Leach (1937-1994),* edited by Christopher Sturman (Lincoln, 1996), 162-67

(with Joan Mills) 'The holy well and conduit, Canwick', *Lincolnshire Past and Present,* 23 (Spring, 1996), 3-5

'The small farm with special reference to Victorian Lincolnshire', *Lincolnshire Past and Present,* 24 (Summer, 1996), 7-11

(with Michael Edgar and Andrew Hinde) 'Southern historians and their exploitation of Victorian censuses', *Southern History,* 18 (1996), 61-86

(with Joan Mills) 'Prehistoric barrows in the Witham valley at Canwick', *Lincolnshire Past and Present,* 29 (Autumn, 1997), 3-5

(with Joan Mills) 'Farms, farmers and farm workers in the nineteenth century census enumerators' books: a Lincolnshire case study', *Local Historian,* 27 (1997), 130-43

(with Joan Mills) 'A case study at Canwick of the enduring influence of monastic houses', *Lincolnshire History and Archaeology,* 33 (1998), 47-54

'More information on the Fawssett family of Holbeach, Horncastle, Louth etc', *Lincolnshire Past and Present,* 33/34 (Autumn/Winter, 1998), 24

'Trouble with farms at the Census Office: An evaluation of farm statistics from the censuses of 1851-1881 in England and Wales', *Agricultural History Review,* 47 (1999), 58-77

(with Paul Hudson) 'English emigration, kinship and the recruitment process: Migration from Melbourn in Cambridgeshire to Melbourne in Victoria in the mid-nineteenth century', *Rural History,* 10 (1999), 55-74

'Wigford in the nineteenth century', in *Wigford: Historic Lincoln South of the River,* edited by P. R. Hill, Survey of Lincoln Series, 1 (Lincoln, 2000) 26-29

(with Maurice Hodson) 'A Lincoln scene about a century ago', *The Lincoln Enquirer,* 1 (October, 2000)

Rural Community History from Trade Directories (Aldenham, 2001)

'An "edge-land": the development of the Witham valley east of Canwick Road', in *Aspects of Lincoln: Discovering Local History,* edited by Andrew Walker (Barnsley, 2001), 134-46

(with Joan Mills and Michael Trott) 'New light on Charles de Laet Waldo-Sibthorp, 1783-1855', *Lincolnshire History and Archaeology,* 36 (2001), 25-37

'A common question: were Wigford, Canwick and Bracebridge part of a single early estate?', *Lincolnshire Past and Present,* 44 (Summer, 2001), 7-11

'Proposed historical atlas of Lincoln 1610-1920', *The Lincoln Enquirer,* 4 (April, 2002), 2

A Walk Round Canwick, the Lincolnshire Estate Village of the Sibthorps: with Enclosure Map of 1787 (Branston, 2003)

'Brayford Villa: where was it, what was it, when was it?', *Lincolnshire Past and Present,* 51 (Spring, 2003), 3-7

'Where was it?', *The Lincoln Enquirer,* 5 (April, 2003), 4

(with Rob Wheeler) *Historic Town Plans of Lincoln, 1610-1920,* Lincoln Record Society, 92 (Woodbridge, 2004)

'Defining community: a critical review of "community" in Family and Community History', *Family and Community History,* 7.1 (2004), 5-12

'A "Tech" school for Victorian Lincoln', *Family and Community History,* 7.2 (2004), 129-40

'The Lincoln atlas', *The Lincoln Enquirer,* 7 (November, 2004), 3-4

The People of the Steep Hill Area of Lincoln About 1900: An Illustrated Social Study (Lincoln, 2005)

(with Timothy H. M. Clough) *The 1712 Land Tax Assessments and the 1710 Poll Book for Rutland,* Rutland Local History and Record Society Occasional Publication, 7 (Oakham, 2005)

'"Recollections" of the Romans in Canwick village', *Lincolnshire Past and Present,* 59 (Spring, 2005), 3-6

(with Rob Wheeler) 'Some peregrinations of Lincoln race course', *Lincolnshire Past and Present,* 60 (Summer, 2005), 6-12

'Recusancy and declining gentry fortunes: evidence relating to the Forsetts of Lincolnshire', *Recusant History,* 27.3 (2005), 321-32

'Lowering Cross Cliff and Canwick Hills', *The Lincoln Enquirer,* 8 (May, 2005), 4-6

'Population, 1801-1901', in *Monks Road: Lincoln's East End Through Time,* edited by Andrew Walker, Survey of Lincoln Series, 2 (Lincoln, 2006) 16-17

'Pregion's progress: The life and times of a Lincolnshire yeoman family, 1570 to 1773', *Lincolnshire History and Archaeology,* 41 (2006), 7-17

'William Watkin's house and the Lincoln Register of Plans and Buildings', *Lincolnshire Past and Present,* 63 (Spring, 2006), 3-6

'Canwick (Lincolnshire) and Melbourn (Cambridgeshire) in comparative perspective within the open-closed village model', *Rural History,* 17.1 (2006), 1-22

'Housing at the turn of the twentieth century', *The Lincoln Enquirer,* 11 (November, 2006), 2-3

'Titus Kime, entrepreneur of Mareham le Fen 1848-1931, and the Eldorado Potato Boom of 1903-1904', in *All Things Lincolnshire,* edited by Jean Howard and David Start (Lincoln, 2007) 139-150

'The Cow Paddle, Lincoln, 1855: a plan, a cemetery, a boiling copper and a furnace', *Lincolnshire Past and Present,* 67 (Spring, 2007), 7-10

(with Rob Wheeler) 'Interpreting the 1:2500 County Series', *Sheetlines,* 78 (April, 2007), 45-48

'Cartographic Treasures', *The Lincoln Enquirer,* 12 (April, 2007), 3-5

(with Rob Wheeler and Matthew Woollard) 'Some comparative perspectives on two early-Victorian registrars of births and deaths in rural Lincolnshire in the context of national legislation' *Local Population Studies,* 79 (Autumn, 2007), 8-22

'The building of Monson Street', *The Lincoln Enquirer,* 13 (November, 2007), 4-6

'Recording and interpreting moffreys: hermaphrodite cart/wagons of Eastern England', *Folk Life: Journal of Ethnological Studies,* 46 (2007-8), 99-122

'Monson Street courts and clearances', *The Lincoln Enquirer,* 14 (May, 2008), 2-5

'Rasen Lane', in *Uphill Lincoln I: Burton Road, Newport and the Ermine Estate,* edited by Andrew Walker, Survey of Lincoln Series, 5 (Lincoln, 2009) 51-54

'Population growth in North Lincoln', in *Uphill Lincoln I: Burton Road, Newport and the Ermine Estate,* edited by Andrew Walker, Survey of Lincoln Series, 5 (Lincoln, 2009) 58-59

'Public health, environment and surveying', *Social History of Medicine,* 22.1 (2009), 153-63

'A "Valentine" - no not that sort!' *The Lincoln Enquirer,* 17 (November, 2009), 4-5

'Local studies in sanitary reform - the importance of the engineering aspect, Lincoln 1848-50', *Local Historian,* 39.3 (2009), 207-17

'St Giles' Avenue', in *Uphill Lincoln II: The North-Eastern Suburbs,* edited by Andrew Walker, Survey of Lincoln Series, 6 (Lincoln, 2010) 44-46

'Where were George Giles and Motherby Hill?', *The Lincoln Enquirer,* 19 (November 2010), 2-5

Additional item

A substantial body of material entitled 'Parish History - Doing A Parish History' was written by Dennis Mills in 2001 for the Lincolnshire County Council website: http://www.lincolnshire.gov.uk/section.asp?docid=27161&ovt=1

Forthcoming

(titles may be subject to alteration)

Miasma, contours and politics: sanitary engineering in early Victorian Lincoln, Society for Lincolnshire History and Archaeology, 2011

(with Joan Mills) *Traditional Farming in Branston,* Branston History Group

'The Coder Special branch of the Royal Navy in the 1950s', *Intelligence and National Security*

NOTES ON CONTRIBUTORS

Wendy Atkin gained a Certificate in Local and Regional History (University of Nottingham, 1990), a BA (Hons) in Regional and Local History (University of Hull, 1994) and was awarded a PhD by the Department of History, University of Nottingham in 2008. Her interest in local history was encouraged and supported by Dennis Mills from the 1980s, when she became interested in computerising the census returns for Sleaford. Her particular interests include inns and alehouses, the profession of attorney-at-law, and the development of Sleaford in the late-Georgian period.

Shirley Brook pursues research interests that centre on the rural landscape and its buildings. She studied part-time for a Certificate in Local History (University of Nottingham, 1990) and a BA (Hons) in Local and Regional History (University of Hull, 1994). A Postgraduate Research Scholarship from the University of Hull led to a doctoral thesis, *The Buildings of High Farming: Lincolnshire Farm Buildings 1840-1914* (University of Hull, 2005), which examined nineteenth-century agricultural improvement in Lincolnshire. She is currently a Visiting Tutor for the BA (Hons) in Heritage Studies at Bishop Grosseteste University College, Lincoln.

Dan Ellin obtained a degree in English and History from the University of Lincoln and an MA in Historical Studies from the same university in 2010. In January 2011 he was awarded the Lincoln Record Society Prize for the best dissertation in MA Historical Studies. He is currently hoping to win a scholarship to undertake his PhD. His main interests are the social and cultural history of the nineteenth and twentieth centuries, including local history and military aviation history. In the near future he hopes to publish the results of his recent research on RAF Bomber Command's treatment of neuropsychiatric casualties and of aircrew found to be LMF or 'lacking in moral fibre' during the Second World War.

Nigel Goose is Professor of Social and Economic History at the University of Hertfordshire. His early research focussed upon early modern English provincial towns, and he has published extensively in that field. While he continues to work on early modern themes - particularly immigration, poverty and philanthropy - he now also researches and publishes on population, economy and society in nineteenth-century England. His recent books include *Women's work in industrial England* (2007) and *A history of Doughty's Hospital, Norwich, 1687-2009* (2010).

Andrew Jackson is Senior Lecturer in Heritage Studies and History at Bishop Grosseteste University College Lincoln. He studied history and geography at Swansea, and then took the MA in English Local History at Leicester. PhD research in geography at University College London brought him in to contact with the work of Dennis Mills and the possibilities of using the open and closed settlement model for studying the twentieth century. Andrew was born in Exeter, and moved from Devon to Lincolnshire in 2007. Much of his current research focuses on the experience of these two predominantly rural as well as coastal counties.

A native of South Yorkshire, **Michael J. Jones** studied Classics and then undertook research in Roman archaeology at the University of Manchester. He has since spent almost all his professional life in Lincoln, for over twenty years directing the city's Archaeology Unit before becoming City Archaeologist in 2000. His primary research interests are in the Roman and Early Medieval periods, and he has written several books and excavation reports on aspects of Lincoln, as well as many articles. He holds honorary positions at Bishop Grosseteste University College in Lincoln and the University of Nottingham. He is keen to promote the interest and value of Lincoln's heritage to the local community and visitors alike. He is an active member of the Society for Lincolnshire History and Archaeology, of which he is currently President. He also chairs the Survey of Lincoln Project.

Denise McHugh first became interested in the history of Lincoln when researching a PhD on late Victorian county towns. She has published a chapter on urban governance in *Who Ran the Cities? City elites and urban power structures in Europe and North America 1750-1940,* edited by Ralph Roth and Robert Beachy. Denise's research interests include provincial British city centres in the nineteenth and twentieth centuries and the impact of empire in Victorian England. Denise is an Associate Lecturer with the Open University and is an Honorary Research Fellow at the Centre for Urban History at the University of Leicester.

Following retirement from British Coal, **Michael Trott** was able to pursue an interest in the nineteenth-century Church by researching the controversial cleric Richard Waldo Sibthorp who was born at Canwick. It was when visiting the parish church there that he was advised to contact Dennis Mills who freely shared his knowledge of the Sibthorp family and provided much encouragement. The resultant biography, which earned Michael his PhD, was published in 2005. He is now researching the writings of the Victorian historian and theologian Thomas William Allies.

Andrew Walker is currently Vice Principal at Rose Bruford College in Kent. He completed his PhD at the University of Sheffield and worked for many years at the University of Lincoln, latterly as Head of the Lincoln School of Humanities and Performing Arts. He has research interests in nineteenth- and twentieth-century local history and is currently working on social and cultural articulations of local belonging. He first came into contact with, and was inspired by, the work and enthusiasms of Dennis Mills during the late 1980s whilst exploring census enumerators' books in his doctoral research at the University of Sheffield on the development of several nineteenth-century South Yorkshire mining villages.

Rob Wheeler gained a D Phil in mathematics and followed a career in the scientific civil service, but now has time to follow his historical interests. The careers of Lincoln land surveyors in the nineteenth century are a particular interest, as is cartographic history more generally. He has edited two volumes for the Lincoln Record Society: *Maps of the Witham Fens,* and (jointly with Dennis Mills) *Historic Town Plans of Lincoln, 1610-1920.* He has for some years been Honorary Secretary of the Charles Close Society for the study of Ordnance Survey maps.

CHAPTER 1

'INEXHAUSTIBLE THEMES FOR STUDY AND SPECULATION'
Michael Drury and the recording of Lincoln's buried archaeology

Michael J. Jones

Dennis Mills's systematic enquiry into aspects of the various Lincoln sewerage schemes has been characteristically productive in a number of ways. Although this topic reflects only one avenue among his many researches into social and economic aspects of the city and its surrounding area, it does represent pioneering work in terms of the historical value of the sequence of sewer maps, including their potential in terms of engineering history.[1] This chapter considers the record of archaeological features noted by Lincoln architect and surveyor Michael Drury during the construction of the Lincoln sewers in 1877-8 from an archaeologist's perspective. There is cause to wonder both why Drury bothered to undertake the extra burden and at how competent he proved to be. Not only, then, does this piece concern itself with the significance of his record, but it also explores the social milieu of Drury's endeavours as a member of the professional classes in the late nineteenth century.

This essay is only possible because Drury's manuscript survives intact in the Local Studies Collection at Lincoln Central Library, along with that of a paper he later gave describing some of the discoveries.[2] The manuscript's existence may not have been known to antiquarians in the half-century or so after it was written, but at a later date the library had it bound, probably at Tom Baker's request. Baker, who had been inspired as a child to take an interest by his architect father, was already the city's most prominent resident archaeologist. He was employed within the city's Library and Museum Service.[3] A note in his distinctive hand appears on the inside of the binding, indicating that the manuscript had been deposited with the Museum at an unknown date, and that no map had been found. Tom Baker subsequently made it known to Ian Richmond along with much of the other evidence on Roman Lincoln that he had collected, to be used in Richmond's classic paper produced to coincide with the visit of the Royal Archaeological Institute in that year (1946).[4]

It is notable, then, that it was not Drury's work on the findings made during the construction of the sewers that was quoted by Sir Francis Hill in the opening chapter of his *Medieval Lincoln* (1948) that dealt with 'The Roman Pattern', but a brief account by J. S. Padley.[5] Padley was an acquaintance, or possibly a relative, of Drury's family. Drury and Son printers, probably by then in the hands of Drury's uncle John Would Drury, had published a *History of Lincoln* in 1816; it contained an illustration by J. S. Padley. Drury's father Edward Bell Drury later acted as publisher of Padley's report on a proposed canal between the rivers Witham and Ancholme in 1828.[6] Padley was primarily a surveyor, with a major role in managing the county's drainage system, and a mapmaker. The significance of his remarkable series of maps for our understanding of the expanding Victorian city was realised by Mills, and they have since been made available for general study.[7] Padley's awareness of the antiquarian ethos is also demonstrated by his presentation of a Roman sword and pottery to the Mechanics' Institution in 1845.[8]

Both Padley and Drury took an active interest in recording ancient remains that were coming to light as a result of the acceleration in Lincoln's renewed growth and development. They belonged to a generation later than the gentleman-scholars, many of them members of the clergy, who had constituted the previous antiquarians.[9] The distinguished antiquarian, E. J. Willson (1787-1854), was also an architect and surveyor by training. He was the author of the 1816 *History of Lincoln* mentioned above, and must have witnessed the beginnings of this change. Advances in science and technology gave a greater appreciation and understanding of scientific and technical matters, including drainage and geology. In the mid-nineteenth century, archaeology was still seen as a respectable pursuit suitable for the gentry and clergy. The week-long meeting of the recently-founded Archaeological Institute in Lincoln in 1848, in which E. J. Willson played a prominent role, was an important occasion in social terms as well as scientific.[10]

The professions had advanced considerably in terms of numbers and importance by the time that the (by then Royal) Archaeological Institute met again in the city in 1880. Its rival organisation, the British Archaeological Association (hereafter BAA), also held a meeting in the city, in the summer of 1889. A key address at the BAA conference was given by Charles Roach Smith, a pioneer in recording the remains revealed by development in the city of London from as early as 1836.[11] Roach Smith spoke regretfully of the deaths of E. J. Willson and Arthur Trollope since his last visit as long ago as the 1848 conference, when he must have been a young man. (He was himself to die in the year following the BAA meeting). He thanked the then mayor (the architect William Watkins) for his good offices, and declared that Lincoln deserved its own museum, an ambition not realised until 1906. At that 1889 event, in what turned out to be the last year of his life too, Drury gave a report on his findings.[12] By then, archaeological techniques had also moved on.[13]

Michael Drury and his architectural career

Drury was born in Lincoln on 28 July 1831, one of six children of Edward Bell Drury and his wife Millicent (née Partridge). They lived, at least for a while, at 6 Sincil Street. The parish records for the family in the late eighteenth and nineteenth centuries indicate that the Drurys' local parishes were historically either St Peter-at-Arches, St Mary-le-Wigford, or St Benedict, in the commercial heart of the city, areas where the population grew more than tenfold in the course of the nineteenth century.[14] There was a literate, bookish streak within the family. Drury's grandfather John, originally from Newark, had been a printer and bookbinder. One of Edward's older brothers, John Would Drury, followed in his father's footsteps as a printer and publisher, while another brother, James, also sold books in the premises on the High Street.[15] With perhaps too little scope in Lincoln for another brother to establish a successful enterprise, Edward apparently moved to Stamford as a young man. There he took over the 'New Public Library', and met and supported the poet John Clare, then at an early stage in his career.[16] He subsequently returned to Lincoln, and ran a bookseller's, printing, and publishing business from near to the Stonebow. He edited the *Lincoln Gazette* for several years, from 1836 until it ceased publication in 1841.[17] He also became a prominent radical (Whig) in the city. After he died in 1843, when Drury was not yet 12, Millicent continued to live in the same house until at least 1856, but appears to have left by 1863.[18]

At the age of nineteen Drury was already articled to a distinguished Southwell-born architect, W. A. Nicholson (1803-53), who ran one of the few practices in the city at the time. There may have been a family link: Mrs Nicholson's maiden name was the same as a family into which Drury's aunts married.[19] The Nicholson practice (jointly with Henry Goddard for the period 1839-46) undertook many repair and construction projects for churches in the county, including extensions to St Peter at Gowts' in 1852-3 (incomplete at the time of Nicholson's death and one of Drury's first projects). It designed a number of important public buildings in the city, including the Wesleyan Chapel (1837), the Union Workhouse (1838), the west range of the Corn Exchange (1847), the extension to the county prison at the Castle (1846), St Peter-in-Eastgate school (1852), the North District National School, now the Castle Hotel, (1852); and possibly St Mark's Railway Station (1846).[20] These public schemes were often the subject of intense competition.[21] Some of the new structures were in classical style, others in the increasingly fashionable Gothic, using both brick and stone. The design of, and materials used in, the two schools recall the Tudor revival style of Pugin's St Anne's Bedehouses, completed in 1848.

Figure 1.1
13 Silver Street, Drury's family home after his first marriage

Figure 1.2
Michael Drury
(by courtesy of Anne Wallbank)

In 1857, at Hackthorn church, Drury married Mary Jane Carlisle, a contemporary who had been born at Eagle. They lived at 13 Silver Street *(Figure 1.1)*, a three-storey house on its south side immediately east of Free School Lane, purchased in September 1856 at a cost of £1100, for which he needed a mortgage of £800.[22] Two servants were also in residence in 1861.[23] Drury *(Figure 1.2)* could now describe himself as an 'Architect Surveyor'. He was certainly in practice by 1856, when his nearby office was listed as being at 1 Bank Street, on the east side of the junction with Silver Street, where Mrs Nicholson continued to reside.[24] This, and the fact that Drury completed the extensions at St Peter at Gowts' church, seem to suggest that he took over the practice and business accommodation after his mentor Nicholson died in 1853, at the age of 49. At the time, the company was busy with all manner of major projects. Any family link might have been of some help in securing Drury's advance, but it is also true that there would have been few local candidates.

Henry Goddard had meanwhile established himself in new premises on High Street, and helped to train William Watkins, who was operating in his own right by 1867 and who became highly successful.[25] By this date, Drury had become a prominent member of civic society. He had been appointed surveyor to Lincoln Corporation, as well as surveyor to the 'Lunatic Asylum' (at The Lawn). As will be seen, he also became an important member of the Diocesan Architectural Society.

In spite of this success, he had soon to undergo professional and personal upheavals. His wife Mary died in February 1871, and the house on Silver Street was sold in October to John George Williams, a 'gentleman', for the sum of £1130, little more than Drury had paid for it fifteen years earlier.[26] In the following year he was living at the Lincoln Club (later the Albion Hotel, and more recently the Barbican Hotel) at 5 Portland Place, on St Mary's Street, another building designed by the practice. He had by now joined up with the architect William Mortimer, whose successive residences at 16 The Park and later - succeeding the initial owner - at Walnut House (again designed by Drury and Mortimer) near to the top of Motherby Hill, reflect the company's commercial success.

Drury married his second wife, Rose (née Cohen), who was eight years his junior, in 1873. After two sons had died in infancy while they were resident in Portland Place, their daughter Dorothy Agnes was born on 20 November 1878. In 1877, Michael and Rose had moved to Foss Lodge *(Figure 1.3)*, a sizeable detached house designed by Drury on the north side of the Fossdyke canal at the junction with Carr Street. It has since been demolished, but was adjacent to what is now Arthur Taylor Street. The house had three storeys, with five bedrooms and a separate stable block.

Figure 1.3
Foss Lodge, Drury's second family home

(Lincoln Urban Sanitary Authority, register of plans for streets and buildings, application no.2440 (approved 28.08.1894): by courtesy of City of Lincoln Council)

In 1874, Mrs Nicholson left her previous address above the offices at 1 Bank Street for a house designed by the practice at the corner of Eastgate and James Street, on which she had her initials inscribed. Coincidentally, this building is currently the home of an architectural practice. She was no longer there by 1877. Drury and Mortimer also left 1 Bank Street at about the same time, and moved to new offices at 'Palfrey Chambers', immediately to the east on Silver Street, a three-storey building that they also designed.[27] Their former offices in the corner property were redeveloped, after a few years' delay: the initial scheme, by the former Mayor Francis 'Blood Mixture' Clarke, did not go ahead. As St Edmond's Chambers, it received a second permission in 1877 for a development for J. S. Webb. Along with Palfrey Chambers, and the premises of Charles Akrill (of Akrill's *Lincoln Directories*), next door to the east, it stood until 1963, before being demolished.

The partnership with Mortimer broke up in 1879. An economic depression beginning about that time meant that there was now probably less work around. The city's population increase in the 1880s was smaller than in previous decades and there was, as a result, more competition for architectural contracts.[28] Goddard and Son were appointed Ecclesiastical Surveyors to the Dioceses of Lincoln and Southwell. Mortimer set up new offices in the Oddfellows Hall on Unity Square. Drury's response was to diversify into acting as an agent and valuer for the Perpetual Investment Building Society, and subsequently also as Surveyor for the Starr Bowkett Building Societies.[29] New partners joined the residue of Drury's firm. They subsequently included G. E. B. Padley, a son of J. S. Padley who acted as a solicitor and insurance agent.

Michael Drury died at home on 6 February 1890, at the age of fifty-eight, from inflammation of the lungs that developed suddenly after he caught a chill. The death notice in the local newspaper referred to him as 'a man of genial temperament and kindly disposition'.[30] He was buried in Canwick Road cemetery, where, as his tombstone *(Figure 1.4)* records, he had designed the chapels, and where his second wife Rose followed him in 1906. She had moved from their large house soon after his death: in 1894, it was occupied by the florist William Buffham, who had become its owner by the time the photograph of the house was taken.[31]

Figure 1.4
Michael and Rose Drury's tomb in Canwick Road cemetery, with the chapel that he designed in the background

(M. J. Jones)

By the same date, the only trace of Drury's former architectural practice at their Silver Street premises was the firm Smith-Woolleys and Ingram, Land Agents and Surveyors.

Unlike two other prominent local architects of the century, E. J. Willson and William Watkins, Drury did not rise sufficiently to be elected mayor: perhaps he simply did not live long enough, or perhaps by his later years he had ceased to be so prominent in local society. His architectural work had included a number of churches, several in the city and locality, including St Peter at Gowts' (mentioned above - perhaps his first church job). Among the others, Mint Street Baptist Church (1870-1), unusually in Italian Romanesque style, was a completely new building, but there were also extensions and rebuildings: All Saints, North Hykeham (1858), SS Peter and Paul, Reepham (1862), the chapel of St Helen's church, Boultham (1864), and a thorough restoration of St Michael, South Hykeham (1869).[32]

He is also documented as having designed the northern gates of the Arboretum (1872).[33] The cemetery chapels on Canwick Road were a product of his sole practice, as well as other churches further afield. In addition, there was a new wing at the County Hospital, then on Drury Lane (1855). The Lincoln Club on St Mary's Street, another Neo-Romanesque structure, and Drury's temporary home, was built in 1867, at a cost of £7000. In due course, it had about 300 members drawn from the gentry. In addition, there were numerous commissions for residential buildings, among them much workers' housing, in particular off lower High Street, along Burton Road, and in the West End. The growth of the city's engineering firms created a huge demand, and during their partnership in the decade from 1870 Drury and Mortimer were responsible for designing over 500 such houses and almost 200 tenements.[34] Lincoln was already growing fast, but the few decades that followed the arrival of the railways in 1846-8 were a time of especially rapid expansion for Lincoln, with plenty of work for the construction industry and rising incomes.

Victorian urban society and the advance of the professions

Fortunately for him, Drury's professional life coincided with the period of Lincoln's greatest urban growth and with the related professionalisation of both architecture and engineering, phenomena made possible by industrialisation. The Institute of British Architects was established in 1834, and the royal charter was received in 1837. Its original membership of a few hundred grew by several hundred each decade. Many other similar bodies were set up in the middle of the century, including the Amalgamated Society of Engineers in 1850, and improvements were made in various activities on the basis of technological advances.[35] In Lincoln, a Mechanics' Institution (sic) for 'the cultivation of the arts and sciences' was established in 1833 following a petition signed by a large number of influential people.[36] They included Edward Bell Drury. Another characteristic of urban society was the growth of voluntary societies, mainly attracting middle-class members and run by leading figures, one response to a fast-changing world.[37] The professionals provided most of the original social thinkers of the era, and their influence increased over time.[38]

In architecture, the influence of the Cambridge Camden Society, inspired by A. W. N. Pugin, a Roman Catholic, and notable figures such as John Ruskin, encouraged a revival of the Gothic style.[39] Gothic became dominant, overtaking the popularity of neo-classical forms from the 1840s.[40] The Classical style was still commonly used for certain structures, notably nonconformist chapels, for which there was a huge building programme, and to some extent by political Liberals. Churchgoing - and nonconformists actually outnumbered Anglicans - as well as moderation and 'good works' were seen as essential elements of the 'civil society' that characterised the urban middle classes. Visible attendance, along with other social rituals facilitated by contemporary municipal developments, allowed the elite to show off their status. They wished to be seen as hard-working, respectable and trustworthy, as well as 'cultured'.[41] Although Lincoln's leading families were more conservative than in the larger cities, civic values were promoted, partly through participation in voluntary societies and other local groups, engendering close personal contacts.[42] The professional ideal was 'service in terms of human happiness and improvement'.[43] Part of that service was to provide workers' houses fit for habitation.

The Lincoln antiquarian tradition

One local response to these developments in society was the formation of the Lincolnshire Topographical Society. Its honorary officials and council included several of the great and good, amongst whom was Dr E. P. Charlesworth, the moving spirit behind the foundation in 1820 of the Asylum (now The Lawn), and the mathematician George Boole, then still working in Lincoln. Prominent among them was the Castle Surveyor E. J. Willson whose activities have been discussed above. Willson was already a prolific recorder of and writer on ancient remains and collector of antiquities. He had designed several Roman Catholic chapels in the area, most in the Gothic style. It was Willson with whom A. C. Pugin, father of A. W. N. Pugin, had some contact on his visits to Lincoln.[44] Willson also collaborated with the senior Pugin on written works on Gothic architecture (but did not become a member of the Cambridge Camden Society). It was appropriate, therefore, that Willson should give the opening address at the inaugural meeting of the Topographical Society (later published in its Papers), defining the scope of the Society's planned activities.

Among the other members, apart from the philanthropic Bromheads and some of the Tennysons, were W. A. Nicholson and J. S. Padley. Nicholson delivered papers about Gothic architecture in Lincoln as well as an influential article encouraging the detailed recording of ancient remains uncovered by development.[45] He noted his regret at not having made more systematic records when early structures had been revealed during his fifteen previous years in the city, and reported that much had been destroyed with only brief and ephemeral accounts. As the city's urban renewal continued, finds were still being made on an 'almost daily' basis. His accounts record the discovery of the south wall of the Roman city, and demonstrate an understanding of buried silts for defining the earlier course of the river nearby. Nicholson hoped that the Society would become a medium for recording the evidence of 'the former condition of the city and its suburbs', and advised the Society's members to take every opportunity in future.

In spite of its association with these influential figures, however, the volume containing some of the papers delivered in 1841-2 was the only one ever published. The Society only survived for a few years, but there were soon moves to establish bodies with similar aims, and its replacement was the Architectural and Archaeological Society for Lincolnshire and Nottinghamshire.[46] The Archaeological Institute's summer meeting in the city in 1848, in the organisation of which Willson was supported by Nicholson among others, increased local awareness and appreciation further.[47] By 1852, the local group had eventually settled on the name the 'Lincoln Diocesan Architectural Society': one of its primary objects was the study and practice of church architecture. Nicholson was made an honorary member. It was primarily an Anglican organisation, with few Roman Catholic or Methodist members. E. J. Willson, already in his last years, did not join. There was strong Anglican disapproval of dissenters: Drury's original design for the new cemetery chapels was criticised for not separating the two more clearly, and modifications had to be made to give the Anglican element more distinction.[48]

From the mid-1850s, and for several decades thereafter, the Society's moving spirit was the Rev. Edward Trollope, a local clergyman of Lincolnshire origins, supported by his antiquarian brother, Captain Arthur Trollope.[49] Previously based in Louth, the Society's offices were moved in 1857 to a new base in Lincoln. The choice of Drury's offices for that base was one that would have moved him further up the social ladder. The new Society's arrival in the city was a high-profile event. Its representatives were greeted by an address from the mayor, recorded in full in the Minute Book of the City Council for 19 May that year.[50] The minutes of the subsequent Council meeting, held on 16 June, incorporated a gushing response on behalf of the Society.

Drury served on the Committee, and held the offices of Curator and Sub-Librarian.[51] Edward Trollope became editor of its proceedings (the Reports and Papers), which covered a range of antiquarian interests, and about a hundred new members joined in the next year, including Alfred Tennyson. Trollope was also an energetic promulgator of the need to publish archaeological discoveries and to preserve historic monuments, and in due course received awards and promotions for his endeavours and efficiency. He served for a while as Archdeacon of Stow (1867-77), with responsibility for church buildings in part of the diocese. There were other social links. A silver cup survives in the possession of one of Drury's descendants; its inscription records its presentation to Michael Drury by Arthur Trollope as the Prize Cup for the First Lincolnshire Rifle Volunteers No.2 Company.[52]

Drury's role in such a prominent group as the Lincoln Diocesan Architectural Society would no doubt have helped his business, for many churches required restoration or rebuilding, as well as reinforcing his high social standing. The example of the Spalding Gentlemen's Society illustrates the extra social status that membership of such male-orientated associations could bring to the professional elite.[53] By 1877, Drury was a Life Member of the Architectural Society, along with several peers and senior members of the clergy, and the architect Henry Goddard, but he did not appear in the members' list for 1889; perhaps other priorities demanded more of his time and energy.

Roman Lincoln: the state of knowledge in 1877 and the growing Victorian city

The pace at which the city and its suburbs were developing meant that the flood of archaeological discoveries was relentless. The outline of the Roman city had been known since before William Stukeley produced his map in 1722, but more discoveries were constantly being made. The Archaeological Institute's 1848 conference had provided an opportunity not just for an exhibition of artefacts but also a visit to the Roman sewers beneath Bailgate shops.[54] The growth of the city accelerated after the arrival of the railways in 1846, and archaeological discoveries with it. The installation of a drain across the High Street in 1847 in conjunction with the Great Northern Railway revealed the stone 'blocks' of the ancient road, with various deposits beneath: a precursor of Drury's observations.[55] New buildings were not confined to those areas where industrial buildings and associated residences were rising, but included public facilities, market buildings, churches and retail shops. Some of these developments were large enough to reveal remains of sufficient scale to be interpreted, and they took place in different parts of the city. The construction of an extension to the county gaol at the castle in 1845 uncovered an impressive mosaic, probably belonging to an aristocratic residence in the upper city. Ground-works for new housing at The Park in 1859 brought up sculpted and decorated stones that had been incorporated into the rebuilt wall of the lower Roman city. Further housing on Monson Street, off lower High Street, built at about the same time, was found to overlie a cemetery containing the tombstones of Roman legionaries. These discoveries also entailed the destruction both of stone monuments, some of them until then remarkably preserved (such as the city wall on Broadgate, standing eighteen feet high), and associated Roman and later deposits whose value was not then recognised.

The Lincoln sewerage scheme

The burgeoning town also needed a better infrastructure and essential services, something that Lincoln Corporation was notoriously slow to provide. The delay had much to do with the composition of the council, where the enlightened voices of the medical profession, supported by the wealthier classes, were outnumbered, or overawed, by threats from the lesser traders - the so-called 'Shopocracy' - a common characteristic of Victorian cities.[56] Some of these were also the small landlords who put up the poor-quality housing that was a contributory factor in the spread of water-borne infections. They tended to be against increasing the rates, fearful of the effect it might have on their own scarcely profitable businesses.

The sorry tale of the City's lingering response to the series of Public Health Acts passed from 1848, which allowed local authorities to borrow for such projects against the rates, has been documented by both Hill and Mills.[57] A scheme was drawn up in 1849 by the notable engineer George Giles and presented to the Corporation. Giles's report included a section on the local surface geology, featuring an illustration provided 'through the kind assistance of W. A. Nicholson'. This had been sourced from a presentation to the Lincolnshire Topographical Society by W. Bedford and published, for the second time, in its sole volume, of the substance of which Drury would have been made aware.[58] Copies of the maps accompanying Giles's report also survive, and have been the subject of valuable studies by Mills.[59] Unfortunately, the scheme's cost, at about £30,000, was considered too expensive by the majority of the Council. It would have added about eight pence to rates for the next thirty years. Although the leading industrialists and clergy were in favour, several further initiatives, in which as city surveyor Drury would have had a significant role, were rejected. An indication of those in favour of a scheme (205 in all) is made clear by a document whose significance has only just been realised, in the form of a petition to the Local Government Board in 1874, a few months after new proposals were voted down.[60] Among the names listed were many clergy and professionals, including the architects F. H. Goddard and William Watkins.

It had the desired effect in due course. National government ordered the Corporation to provide sewerage for the city, and, in September 1876, the contract was eventually signed. It was to cost over £63,000, more than twice the proposal of 1849, but the town and its population had grown considerably since then. It was complete by 1881. A surviving map of this scheme was drawn up part way through the work, as the first contractor had become bankrupt. It was, of course, this scheme that Drury carefully monitored, and in the course of its progress made archaeological records.

Michael Drury's account and its significance

As noted in the introduction to this chapter, Michael Drury's account takes the form of his original manuscript, in an Akrill's exercise book, but the date of its compilation (1888) appears to be a decade later than his observations. Perhaps the surviving manuscript is something that was prepared from his site notes as a basis for an archive record as well as for his 1889 talk to the Lincoln meeting of the British Archaeological Association.[61] He was to live for less than a year after the Association's meeting, and the notes appended to his article were prepared by others.

The account clearly demonstrates an awareness of stratification, not only in terms of the local geology but also of archaeological deposits. For instance, the discrepancy in the depth of accumulation between the St Botolph's area of High Street (less than six feet) and that at St Mark's (about thirteen feet), and even more so near to the Stonebow (about twenty feet), is remarked on and explained. One element of the build-up was what he referred to as a 'concreted causeway', which he (correctly) concluded was of Roman date. In the St Mark's area, where this causeway was about five feet thick, he deduced that its thickness was necessary to carry the road over a lower-lying, damper area *(Figure 1.5, 1.6)*. The accuracy of his observation was corroborated in 1977 when excavations on the former site of St Mark's church revealed that the land had been drained and the level raised in the second century prior to its development.[62] In addition, Drury noted that the difference in the amount of subsequent accumulation over the causeway reflected that there had been more intensive occupation at St Mark's than at St Botolph's. He also remarked that the level at St Mary's Guildhall had not risen so much, since this medieval building was still in use.

The 'muddy mass', three or four feet thick, below the causeway is ascribed to the pre-Roman period, perhaps as an ancient path. In spite of the recent discovery of prehistoric timber causeways at Fiskerton and other sites in the Witham Valley[63], this seems unlikely. A more likely interpretation would be that this was a lower bedding for the causeway, possibly a matting of dumped reeds and/or timber, of Roman date. It might have been associated with the Roman legionary occupation. Drury was,

Figure 1.5
One of the illustrations in Drury's account, showing the different depths of stratigraphy in High Street

however, perceptive enough to recognise that the rising ground in the area of St Mary-le-Wigford appeared to represent an earlier island, one of three so far identified in what was a much greater expanse of water than is the case today. It is now accepted that there was previously another, more southerly, course of the river, and that the late Iron Age house found in 1972 was located on the island. Drury also suggested that the island was artificial, similar to those containing prehistoric lake dwellings. Although probably mistaken in this belief, Drury's citing of the parallel indicates that he had consulted specialists or had read himself the two recently-published syntheses of lake dwellings in Scotland and Ireland: those at Glastonbury were not investigated until the following decade.[64]
His reference to his prehistoric ancestor as 'the semi-savage native' probably reflects the consensus view of the time!

Similarly, it is difficult to be confident about the date of the row of large timber piles that Drury recorded in the area from the Cornhill to the north side of the river. Again, a Roman date seems most likely, but an earlier or later one is not impossible. A similar feature (also noted during sewer works) in Norwich is provisionally dated to the tenth century.[65] Re-excavation and dendrochronological dating would resolve the problem. The same section-drawing would suggest that the original northern edge of the river lay well to the north of the lower Roman defences and the Stonebow. This hypothesis needs to be tested by excavations to establish the exact line and elevation. The large block of stone noted to the south of St Benedict's church, if accurately recorded, at an astonishing twelve feet long, and found beneath the grave soil, may well have indicated part of a Roman dock - but if so, is the only evidence for such a structure so far upstream. He also concluded correctly that the 'peaty mud' beneath the streets of Newland and Guildhall Street suggested that they were 'relatively recent' (i.e. medieval).

Monitoring the sewer trenches as they proceeded northwards into the walled Roman city, Drury noted elements of some large ancient structures. These, together with the evidence from later research, suggest that the frontage of the main Roman street in the Lower Roman city was occupied principally by public buildings.[66] The 'cavern-like apertures, in concreted masses', found beneath the medieval graves near to St Martin's church could indicate the sub-basement of a large Roman structure, such as a classical temple. It is possible that the early church here re-used its foundations. Further up the hill, he identified locations where the natural clay, or, higher up, ironstone or limestone, was close to the ground level, which was due in part to the need to maintain the Medieval level (for instance by the Jew's House and the upper south gate) and also as a result of terracing operations. Two parallel walls, one of them fifteen feet thick, were recorded near to Christ's Hospital Terrace. Drury suggested that these represented a major Roman terrace, an idea accepted by Richmond and likened by him to Tarragona, capital of one of the Spanish provinces.[67] A mosaic found at shallow depth on Spring Hill (then 'Asylum Road' - perhaps he was on his way to a meeting at the hospital) was probably the same as that found by chance in 1983 and subsequently excavated along with the adjacent site.[68] To the east of the cathedral on the hilltop, several quarries were identified, with possible paths surviving as islands between them. Fragments of the Roman and medieval east gates and associated roads were also recorded. Here Drury estimated Roman accumulation five feet thick, sealed by three feet of the 'fragmentary ruins' of the 'great and populous Danish and Saxon city', and followed by another two feet 'accretion subsequent to Norman times'. This had produced an 'accumulation of ten feet of debris and rubbish caused by successive and repeated destruction of the city during the period of 1600 years': a fairly accurate interpretation of the way the archaeological deposits have accumulated.

There follow brief sections on other previously noted Roman remains both within the walled city and other finds from the extra-mural area. The first of these mainly concentrated on the line of the main north-south Roman sewer and street above it, drawing reasonable inferences about the accumulation of later deposits around the Bailgate colonnade exposed by the sewer trenches. Drury's account of new discoveries does not, however, cover the trenches dug in the areas to east or west of the main north-south route: it is possible that he considered that construction work here would not be so productive - although it did apparently reveal more finds.[69] Another possible explanation is that the economic depression and the break with Mortimer in 1879 - possibly linked events - meant that he had to devote more time to business. His notebook contains a further section on discoveries (by others) outside the walls, including the 'rock cliff' - presumably the edge of the limestone outcrop - noted along Lindum Terrace, and a list of other recent finds made during construction work, including some in the 1880s. The map that accompanied the original manuscript has not survived along with the report, but is unlikely to be much different from that published in the 1889 conference proceedings. This indicates the locations to which he refers in his account, including those of the other Roman remains listed in the paper.

Conclusions

The era in which Drury operated was marked by the emergence of both professional ethics and technical expertise, while the members of these new professions were subject to social and economic pressures. These factors both equipped Michael Drury to grasp the significance of the archaeological deposits exposed in the trenching for the new sewer scheme and encouraged him to go to the effort of making records. He had absorbed much of his value-system in turn from his literate family and from his subsequent mentors W. A. Nicholson and Edward Trollope. The opening paragraph of his account noted that the strata 'frequently attracted [his] attention', and that he 'could not refrain from speculating on the meaning of such extraordinary phenomena'. In introducing his paper to the British Archaeological Association, he noted that the sewer trenches had 'disclosed layers of made soil... the undisturbed result of human agency... and providing inexhaustible themes for study and speculation'.[70] Obviously his intellect was excited by the idea of the rich evidence that survived below ground for the city's past, and by the exhilaration that accompanies the deciphering of complex stratigraphy. Those involved in such activity will understand that thrill. His manuscript noted that he 'regretted much [his] ability to give more than a passing glance'. In truth, he achieved a great deal, perhaps as much as could be hoped for from a busy professional. We can only be thankful that he identified with a relatively new

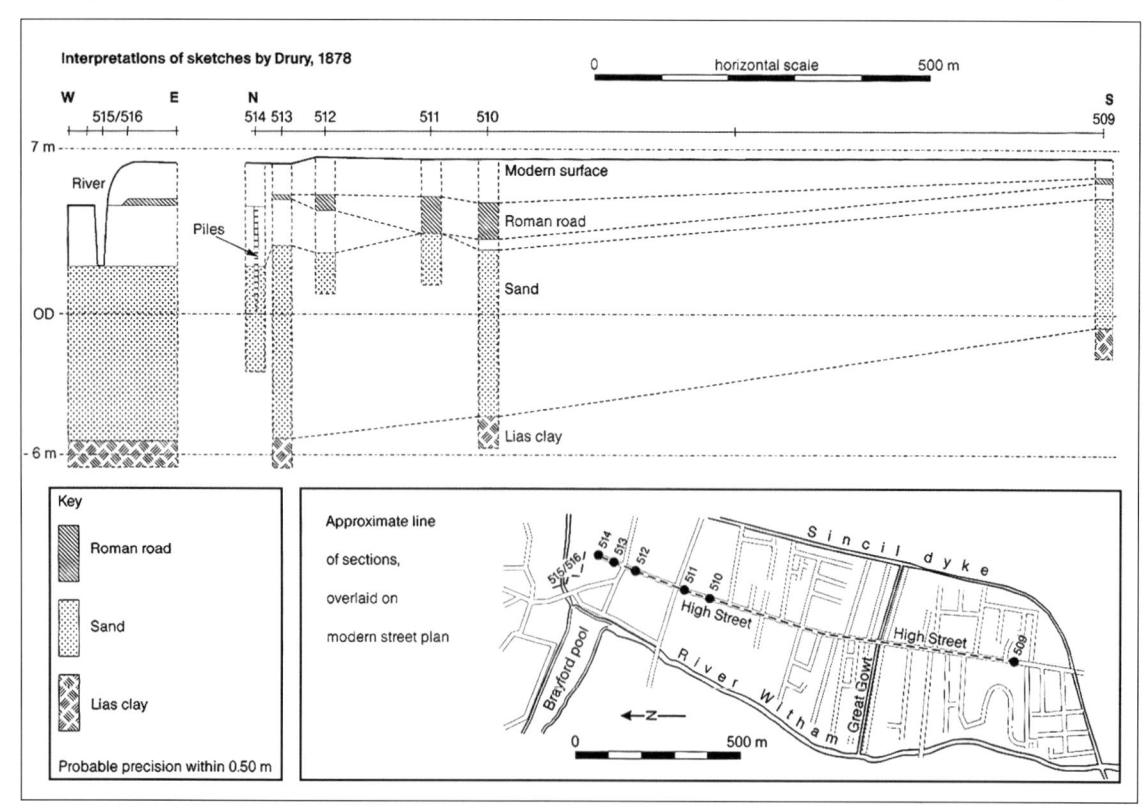

Figure 1.6
Diagram showing the locations on lower High Street where Drury recorded remains of the Roman Road and causeway, and its varying depth

(copyright English Heritage/NMR)

and enlightened tradition that considered such matters of cultural significance. As the inheritors of their endeavours, we in our turn have a duty both to rescue a record of the past and to hand on an intellectual tradition to the future. Dennis Mills's achievements have proved an inspiration in this respect.

Notes

[1] For example, Dennis Mills, 'Local studies in sanitary reform: the impact of the engineering aspect, Lincoln, 1848-1850', *The Local Historian,* 39.3 (2009), pp.207-17.

[2] Michael Drury, 'Notes on the excavations for sewer works at Lincoln'. Unpublished MS. (1888). Local Studies Collection, Lincoln Central Library; Michael Drury, On a concrete causeway, supposed to be Roman, at Lincoln, *Journal of the British Archaeological Association* (hereafter *JBAA*), 46 (1890), pp.221-6.

[3] F. T. Baker, 'A lifetime with Lincolnshire Archaeology: looking back over 60 years', *Lincolnshire History and Archaeology,* 20 (1985), pp.5-14.

[4] I. A. Richmond, 'The Roman city of Lincoln', and 'The four coloniae of Roman Britain', *Archaeological Journal,* 103 (1946), pp.25-68.

[5] F. Hill, *Medieval Lincoln* (Cambridge, 1948), p.11, n.2, quoting J. S. Padley, *Fens and Floods of Mid-Lincolnshire* (1882), p.11.

[6] Lincolnshire Archives Office (hereafter LAO), L.LINC. O94 Drury.

[7] D. R. Mills and R. C. Wheeler, *Historic Town Plans of Lincoln 1610-1920* (Woodbridge, 2004).

[8] *Lincoln, Rutland, and Stamford Mercury,* 12 Sept. 1845, p.3.

[9] Dorothy Owen, 'The development of historical studies in Lincolnshire', in *Some Historians of Lincolnshire,* edited by Christopher Sturman, Occasional Papers in Lincolnshire History and Archaeology 9 (Lincoln, 1992), pp.7-12; Rosemary Sweet, *Antiquaries: the Discovery of the Past in Eighteenth-Century Britain* (2004), p.49.

[10] Neville Birch, 'The "Archaeologians"' visit to Lincoln', in *Lincolnshire People and Places; Essays in Memory of Terence R. Leach (1937-1994),* edited by Christopher Sturman, (Lincoln, 1996), pp.170-75; 'Memoirs illustrative of the history and antiquities of the County and City of Lincoln', *Proceedings of the Archaeological Institute of Great Britain and Ireland 1848* (1850).

[11] C. Roach Smith, 'Notes on Roman Antiquities at Lincoln, during the Lincoln Congress', *JBAA,* 46 (1890), pp.53-7; David Gaimster, 'The Art of Recording', in *Making History: Antiquaries in Britain 1707-2007* edited by David Gaimster, Sarah McArthy and Bernard Nurse (2007), pp.201-07.

[12] Drury, 'On a concrete causeway'.

[13] Christopher Evans, 'The birth of modern archaeology', in *Making History,* pp.185-99.

[14] F. Hill, *Victorian Lincoln* (Cambridge, 1974), Appendix I, p.306.

[15] Personal Communication (hereafter pers. comm.) Anne Wallbank; William White, *History, Gazetteer and Directory of Lincolnshire 1842* (Sheffield).

[16] The story of their encounters is told in vivid detail in Frederick Martin, *The Life of John Clare* (1865), esp. pp.71-98.

[17] F. Hill, *Victorian Lincoln,* pp.9, 39, 54.

[18] William White, *History, Gazetteer and Directory of Lincolnshire 1856* (Sheffield), p.122; *Akrill's City of Lincoln Directory 1863.*

[19] pers. comm. Anne Wallbank.

[20] Nikolaus Pevsner and John Harris, *Buildings of England: Lincolnshire.* Revised by Nicholas Antram (1989), Index to Artists, p.863, *s.v.* 'Nicholson W. A.'; I am grateful to Arthur Ward for further information.

[21] David Brock, 'The competition for the design of Sleaford Sessions House, 1828', in *Architectural History,* 27 (1984), pp.344-55. It is clear from this study that losing candidates could still make a good impression on the committee of gentry making decisions on contracts, and be awarded subsequent projects.

[22] *Akrill's City of Lincoln Directory 1857;* LAO Hill 42/3/3-5.

[23] 1861 Census.

[24] William White, *History, Gazetteer and Directory of Lincolnshire 1856* (Sheffield), p.127.

[25] Sibyl Burgess *et al, The Victorian Façade: W. Watkins and Son, Architects, Lincoln, 1859-1918* (Lincoln, 1990).

[26] LAO Hill 42/3/4.

[27] The location is shown on the Sewer Connection Map (LAO AWA 19/20); cf. Beryl George, 'Rediscovered: Lincoln's lost sewerage petition', *Lincolnshire Past and Present,* 82 (Autumn, 2010), pp.14-19.

[28] F. Hill, *Victorian Lincoln,* pp.203-5; Kate Hill, 'The middle classes in Victorian Lincoln', in *Aspects of Lincoln,* edited by Andrew Walker (Barnsley, 2001), pp.88-100, esp. p.92.

[29] Akrill, Ruddock and Keyworth's *City of Lincoln Directory 1885,* pp.16, 61.

[30] pers. comm. Anne Wallbank. The exact source of the news cutting that Anne Wallbank has inherited is uncertain. The *Lincoln, Rutland, and Stamford Mercury* published a simple death notice on 14 February, 1890.

[31] Akrill, Ruddock and Keyworth's *City of Lincoln Directory 1894.*

[32] Pevsner, *Lincolnshire,* p.859, *s.v.* 'Drury, Michael', and 'Drury and Mortimer'.

[33] City Council Minute Book, June 1872; LAO L1/1/1/10.

[34] This information and many other details contained in this article are derived from the City Building Registers, applications to the urban sanitary authority of Lincoln Corporation, and have been kindly supplied by John Herridge. Precise figures are not possible, as some applications do not specify the number of houses.

[35] K. T. Hoppen, *The Mid-Victorian Generation, 1846-86* (Oxford, 1998), pp.40-45; 416; Kate Hill, 'The middle classes in Victorian Lincoln'.

[36] The minute book of its establishment and first meetings survives in the Local Studies Collection at Lincoln Central Library. It was printed by J. W. Drury. 'Mechanics' Institute' was the name usually given to such organisations but in Lincoln's case it was the 'Mechanics' *Institution*'. There was often confusion over this. See for example Mills and Wheeler, *Historic Town Plans:* Dewhirst and Nichols (p.39) reference it as *Institute* whereas Padley (p.98) gives it as *Institution*.

[37] R. J. Morris, 'Voluntary societies and British urban elites, 1780-1850: an analysis', *The Historical Journal*, 26.1 (1983), pp.95-118; R. J. Morris, 'Clubs, societies and associations', in *The Cambridge Social History of Britain 1750-1950. Volume III: Social Agencies and Institutions*, edited by F. M. L. Thompson (Cambridge, 1990), pp.406-19.

[38] Harold Perkin, *The Rise of Professional Society: England since 1880* (revised edition, 2002), p.xxii.

[39] *'A Church as it should be'. The Cambridge Camden Society and its influence*, edited by Christopher Webster and John Elliott, (Stamford, 2000); Rosemary Hill, *God's Architect: Pugin and the Building of Romantic Britain* (2007).

[40] Tristram Hunt, *Building Jerusalem. The Rise and Fall of the Victorian City* (2004), pp.104-27.

[41] Hunt, *Building Jerusalem,* pp.128-85; Simon Gunn, *The Public Culture of the Victorian Middle Classes; Ritual and Authority in the English Industrial City 1840-1914* (Manchester, 2000).

[42] Kate Hill, 'The middle classes in Victorian Lincoln', pp. 97-9.

[43] Harold Perkin, *The Origins of Modern English Society 1780-1880* (revised edition, 1985), pp.252-339.

[44] R. Hill, *God's Architect,* pp.53-4.

[45] W. A. Nicholson, 'The advantage of recording the discovery of local antiquities', *A Selection of Papers relative to the County of Lincoln read before the Lincolnshire Topographical Society, 1841-2* (1843), pp.87-90.

[46] F. Hill, 'The early days of a society', *Lincolnshire History and Archaeology,* I (1966), pp.57-63; see now also Nicholas Bennett, *'Wonderful to Behold': A Centenary History of the Lincoln Record Society 1910-2010,* Lincoln Record Society, 100 (2010), pp.4-5.

[47] *Proceedings of the Archaeological Institute of Great Britain and Ireland 1848* (1850).

[48] F. Hill, 'Early days', p.59; F. Hill, *Victorian Lincoln,* pp.159-60.

[49] Terence R. Leach, Edward Trollope and the Lincoln Diocesan Architectural Society, in *Some Historians of Lincolnshire,* edited by Sturman, pp.13-26.

[50] City Council Minute Book: LAO L1/1/1/10.

[51] William White, *History, Gazetteer, and Directory of Lincolnshire 1872* (Sheffield), p.80.

[52] pers. comm. Anne Wallbank.

[53] Chris Renn, 'Keeping the flame burning: the revival of the Spalding Gentlemen's Society from 1889 to 1911', *Lincolnshire History and Archaeology,* 42 (2007), pp.29-39.

[54] Birch, 'The Archaeologians'.

[55] F. Hill, *Medieval Lincoln,* pp.10-11.

[56] Hunt, *Building Jerusalem,* pp.292-312; K. Hill, 'The middle classes in Victorian Lincoln', pp.92-3.

[57] F. Hill, *Victorian Lincoln,* pp.160-71; see also Mills, 'Local studies in sanitary reform'.

[58] William Bedford, 'An account of the strata of Lincoln, from a recent survey, commencing north of the Cathedral, and descending to the bed of the river', *The Magazine of Natural History,* New Series 3 (1839), pp.553-56; William Bedford, 'The Geology of Lincoln', *Lincolnshire Topographical Society papers 1841-2,* pp.15-28.

[59] Dennis Mills, 'Public health, environment and surveying', *Social History of Medicine,* 22.1 (April 2009), 153-63.

[60] Beryl George, 'Rediscovered', regarding LAO Misc Don 640/2.

[61] Drury, 'On a concrete causeway'

[62] Kate Steane *et al*, *The Archaeology of Wigford and the Brayford Pool.* Lincoln Archaeological Studies, 2 (Oxford, 2001), pp.224-6.

[63] Naomi Field and Mike Parker Pearson, *Fiskerton: An Iron Age Timber Causeway with Iron Age and Roman Votive Offerings* (Oxford, 2003).

[64] Francis Pryor, *Britain BC. Life in Britain and Ireland before the Romans* (2003), pp.395-406.

[65] Brian Ayers, *Norwich: 'A Fine City'* (Stroud, 2003), p.167.

[66] Michael J. Jones, 'The lower walled city in the colonia era', in *The City by the Pool,* edited by David Stocker, Lincoln Archaeological Studies, 10 (Oxford, 2003), pp.82-93.

[67] Richmond, 'The Roman City of Lincoln', pp.42-3.

[68] Jones, 'The lower city', p.92, with fig.7.72.

[69] Finds of coins were noted in *Akrill, Ruddock and Keyworth's Lincoln Directory 1894,* Introduction.

[70] Drury, 'On a concrete causeway', p.221.

CHAPTER 2

THE BUILDING OF SKELLINGTHORPE RESERVOIR

Rob Wheeler

The city of Lincoln entered the Victorian age lacking either a supply of clean water or an efficient system for the disposal of sewage. The former was remedied by the formation in 1846 of a Lincoln Water Company; there was no call on the city's own funds and there was no controversy. A modern sewerage system was proposed as early as 1849 but the cost to the city would necessarily be substantial and it would be more than 30 years before it was constructed.

The water company's own records do not survive and this paper does not attempt any overall account of its operation but focuses rather on the early history of its reservoir. This might seem an excessively narrow topic, even though the reservoir may well have been unique in serving also as an ornamental lake for a substantial country house. However, the real interest of the account lies in the involvement of two men from Lincoln's professional classes, both of whom were stretching the bounds of their professional activities in a manner which today might cause the raising of eyebrows.

The first of these was J. S. Padley (1792-1881), the surveyor. Brought up in humble circumstances, he had gained experience as an unofficial assistant on the Ordnance Survey of Lincolnshire, 1819-21. He later assisted William Hayward, the Surveyor of County Bridges for the Parts of Lindsey, being recognised in this role by Quarter Sessions, then made Hayward's deputy, and finally succeeded to the post on Hayward's death in 1825. On the basis of this position, he gained clients in and around Lincoln and became the leading surveyor there.

There were no formal educational or professional barriers to becoming a surveyor, and Padley appears to have achieved his position through a mixture of ambition, the determination to do a good job, an ability to get on with a wide range of people, and sheer natural ability. His ambition was not confined to the surveying profession. An earlier paper has described his attempts to make a name for himself as an antiquary.[1] In 1829 he promoted a bridge across the Trent at Dunham, putting forward a plan which was almost a copy of one currently being built by the engineer George Leather at Hunslet.[2] He had been cheerfully adapting his predecessor's plans for minor bridges in Lindsey and quite probably did not realise that the engineering profession disapproved of such blatant plagiarism. In due course, Leather was appointed engineer for the project and declined any suggestion that Padley should have a continuing role. As it happens, that was not the end of Padley's involvement: after the bridge's completion, he leased the tolls in 1834 for three years, gambling on an increase in traffic. He almost certainly made a loss on the transaction. Meanwhile, in 1836, he was unsuccessfully seeking an appointment as an assistant tithe commissioner.[3] A collection of family letters from 1839 to 1842 (when Padley's first wife died) give an impression of a busy and successful professional who stays in Regent Street when giving evidence to House of Lords committees. Two of his sons are at Cambridge, or about to go up, and seem set fair for successful careers in the church.[4]

The second of the professional men to play a prominent part in this story was Richard Carline. His paternal grandfather was a Lincoln man who had married into the Hayward family. His father was in business in Shrewsbury as an architect, builder and monumental mason.[5] Richard Carline had returned to Lincoln to practise as a solicitor, initially in partnership with Charles Hayward. He appears to have concentrated on estate management, rather than in progressing criminal or civil cases. He succeeded Hayward as Steward of Christ's Hospital's manor of Skellingthorpe, serving from 1837 until his death in 1863.[6] His role went much further than presiding in manorial courts: he served as the local agent for Christ's Hospital (for this was the London Christ's Hospital, not the Lincoln one), advising on the suitability of applicants for tenancies, on the reorganisation of farms and the management of woodland. A letter of 17 February 1844 suggests that he acted in a similar manner for both the Sibthorp estates and likewise for both the Ellison estates.[7] It is clear that Christ's Hospital took an active interest in how their estate was managed. Their own land surveyor would visit periodically and he attended the formal Views conducted by the Hospital's Treasurer and Clerk. Carline's relations with the Clerk, George Trollope, were cordial; the Treasurer, William Gilpin, was in effect his client. Carline would stay at the Treasurer's house when in London and would send the occasional basket of game by coach as an expression of his gratitude, but his normal contact for business matters was the Clerk.

He was active in local politics and Hill[8] regards him as the most far-seeing of the men who ran the reformed Council. Certainly he was active in the support of new ventures, like the cemetery, the Yarborough Road development, and the Royal Show. He was also active in promoting the Cambridge & York railway in 1844, serving on its provisional committee and as one of its solicitors. Indeed his keenness that the Treasurer and other Governors of Christ's Hospital should join that provisional committee seems to hint at a desire to develop a new career as an officer of a great railway company.[9] Within a couple of months the Cambridge & York scheme had been subsumed within the London & York (later to become the Great Northern Railway)[10] and Carline became just one of many provincial solicitors to that company.

We turn now to the Water Company. Following complaints in 1844 of the inadequacy of the existing conduits,[11] an Act was sought in the 1846 Parliamentary session. That Act would enable the Company to lay its pipes under the streets of the City. It would also (like a railway company) be able to compulsorily purchase land it needed for its major works. In return, it would be limited in the rates it could charge and the dividend it could pay.[12] To protect the rights of private property, the company was required to produce a plan showing the intended works, and the line of the intended main supply pipe with limits of deviation (± 50 yds) together with a Book of Reference listing the owners and occupiers of the affected land. Copies had to be deposited with the Clerks of the Peace for the relevant counties - in this case, Kesteven, Lindsey and the City of Lincoln - by 30 November of the year before, 1845. In that year, 30 November fell on a Sunday, so the plans had to be deposited by 29 November. As was usual, the plans were deposited by the deadline, but only just.[13]

The company had engaged Thomas Hawksley (1807-93) as their engineer. Hawksley was a Nottingham man who had made his name in constructing the Trent waterworks and pumping station there.[14] He was the most prominent proponent of the revolutionary idea that consumers should be provided with a water supply throughout the day and night and that this should be achieved, when there was no convenient water source at a high enough altitude for gravity to serve, by a pumping engine continuously supplying a high-level reservoir. Thus uphill Lincoln would require a reservoir - it was located where the present water tower is[15] - and a pumping engine would be needed somewhere to keep that reservoir continuously topped up.

First, of course, a source of water was needed. The Prial Brook, forming the boundary between Boultham and Skellingthorpe, was selected, not least because the water was fairly soft. To guard against drought, a storage reservoir was needed; one was proposed to be made at the Prial Brook capable of holding enough water to supply 30,000 persons for 87 days. All this was eminently sound. Some of the detailed design would perhaps have benefited from further consideration: the deposited plan *(Figure 2.1)* shows a rectangular storage reservoir, perhaps following the precedent of the Nottingham reservoir at Trent Bridge, but what makes sense on a flat alluvial plain may not be the best solution in a valley with contours. Likewise, placing the filter beds and engine house immediately below the reservoir was, as the company would come to realise, not the best solution either.

The company's Act was passed on 22 June 1846. Conveniently it lists the early shareholders. Most of the prominent Lincoln figures are among them, but one also finds J. W. Drury the printer, W. A. Nicholson the architect, and J. S. Padley the surveyor. The voting arrangements prescribed in the Act gave small shareholders disproportionate voting power in meetings and one wonders whether these gentlemen subscribed in part as a way of getting the company's business. As it happens, the Book of Reference mentioned earlier was indeed printed by Drury, and the company did turn to Padley for some surveying, but the company appointed as its architect Henry Goddard (Nicholson's partner, see page 20). More important for this account, Richard Carline was appointed Secretary.

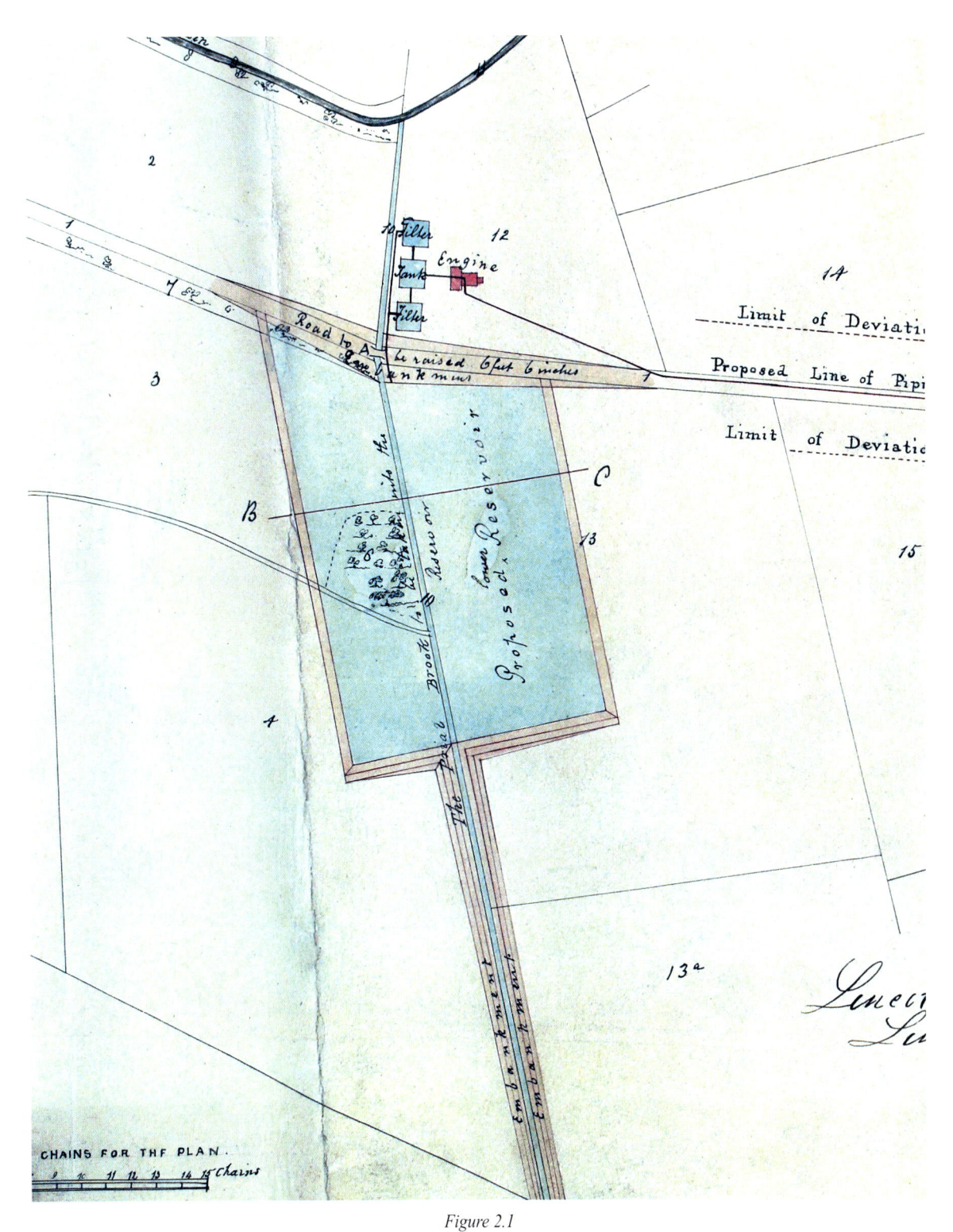

Figure 2.1
The Skellingthorpe Reservoir as shown on the deposited plans
The map is aligned so that 'up' is somewhat East of North. The road running across and forming a dam for the reservoir is that from Skellingthorpe village to Boultham

(LAO Lindsey Deposited Plans 1/41)

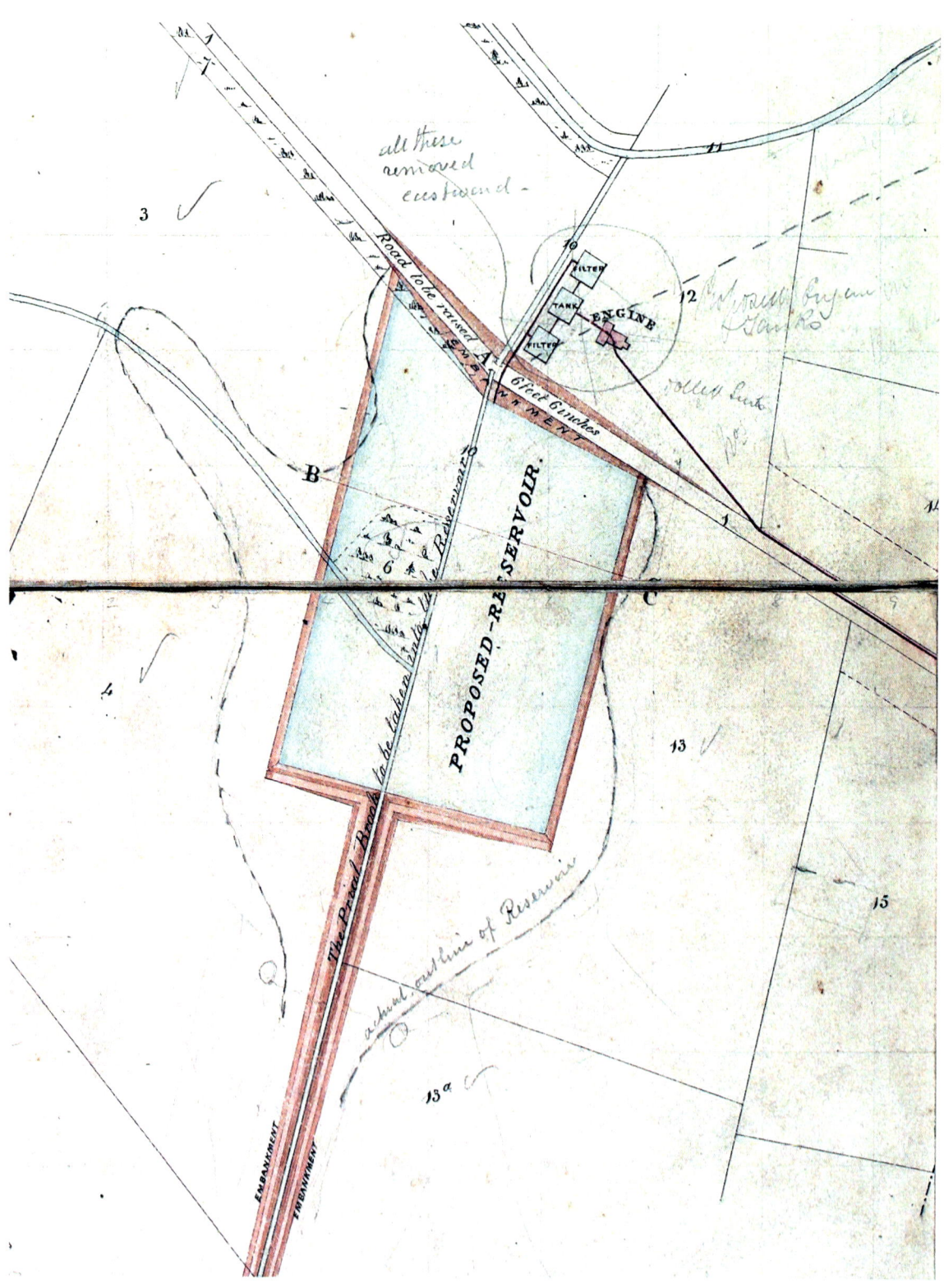

Figure 2.2
The Skellingthorpe Reservoir as amended on the Company's copy of the deposited plans
(LAO Misc Don 1342/4/2)

Exactly what surveying Padley undertook is not recorded, but it was probably a large-scale contoured plan of the area where the reservoir was to be. The original intention recorded in the deposited plans was to excavate earth to the level of the invert of the bridge which carried the Boultham to Skellingthorpe road over the Prial Brook - if the reservoir were dug any deeper than this, the excavations would have no natural drainage. The excavated earth would be used to form a rectangular embankment, allowing the water level to rise above that of the surrounding land. The Prial Brook above the reservoir would also be embanked sufficiently to feed this elevated water level. However, there was a tributary stream joining from the west: was this to be elevated? And how was the land either side of these elevated streams to be drained now that their natural drainage had been separated off by embankments? It must have become apparent that a rectangular reservoir in such terrain made no sense. Simply building a dam and flooding the valley in the modern manner probably would have taken an excessive amount of agricultural land to hold the water required: the valley was a very shallow one. So the solution was a reservoir that followed the contours, but was nevertheless excavated down to the level of the bridge's invert *(Figure 2.2)*. The earth was to be used for a dam along the road, to embank the Prial Brook above the reservoir and the flanks of the reservoir where it entered. The remaining earth was to be used to form an artificial island in the reservoir - of which more anon. The problem of providing drainage for the land flanking the embanked Prial Brook was to be addressed by providing a brick culvert that would run beneath the reservoir and come out below the road. For letting a contract, a detailed plan of the intended works would be needed and it may be that Padley produced this as well.[16] At this date, the ownership of the land was unchanged from November 1845: Major Richard Ellison of Boultham owned the land to the east of the Prial Brook; Christ's Hospital (of London) owned the land to the west.

Specifications were produced along these lines and tenders were invited in September 1846. The company was looking for what would now be called a prime contractor, someone able to contract not only for the earth-moving, but also for the masonry of the weirs and the gate piers, the carpentry of the gate and of a bridge over the Prial Brook, the painting of the latter, and even a padlock to secure the gate. Woodwork was to be painted white and the ironwork (gratings, etc) in black. There was to be a gravel walk around the edge of the reservoir, carried over the Prial Brook by this timber bridge and over the tributary stream by a culvert.[17] The exposed banks were to be covered with topsoil left for the planting of shrubs. It is clear that the reservoir was to serve as an ornamental lake. Whether this was to be for the use of the shareholders, the citizens at large, or only for those who paid for keys to the padlock is unclear. The *Stamford Mercury* did not know either: as late as 19 March 1847 it discovered that the reservoir was to be 'beautifully belted with a gravel path and an outer circle of firs' but failed to inform its readership as to who might enjoy these delights.

Meanwhile, J. S. Padley had submitted a tender. He is not known to have engaged in this sort of activity before but he was well-placed to do so: his work as Surveyor of County Bridges had led to his letting lots of small contracts on behalf of the Parts of Lindsey for earth-moving and masonry. Furthermore, having surveyed the reservoir for the company, he would have had more confidence that there were no problems lurking than might other potential bidders. Padley's tender for £4500 was accepted on 20 October 1846. Padley was required to start work by 1 November (even though the contract was not signed until the following day) and to complete everything by 1 March 1847.

Actually, there was one task that Padley would not have needed to supervise before: the culvert under the reservoir was to be surrounded by well-puddled clay to prevent water from the reservoir from seeping under pressure through joints in the brickwork. Puddling was a task that needed careful supervision. As Sir Joseph Banks had been informed when he sought advice prior to the construction of the Horncastle canal, 'neither puddlers or masons ought to be left to themselves even one Day, in some particular situations ...'.[18] Padley perhaps lacked the necessary knowledge to supervise it properly.

Work progressed more slowly than it should have. Padley subsequently blamed the number of variations the company had made to the specification, and this seems not to have been disputed. Eventually on 5 May 1847, work was sufficiently complete to allow the filling of the reservoir to start: there was concern that sufficient water should be accumulated to supply the city in the event of a dry summer. The Directors made an inspection, the water of the Prial Brook was allowed to flow into the reservoir and, as the *Stamford Mercury* coyly put it, 'the workmen were indulged with a treat'.

Alas, on 22 May, it was observed that rather more water was issuing from the brick culvert than there should have been. The reservoir was ordered to be drained and Hawksley came to inspect. He reported to the Board on 1 June, though for the exact nature of his report we are dependent on his letter of 23 June 1847[19]: the force of the springs uncovered by the digging had brought with them large quantities of quicksand which had so incommoded Padley's workmen that they had failed to envelop the tunnel in clay puddle as prescribed. Whilst the work had not been completed in accordance with the specification, 'I wish it to be understood that the extreme mobility of the sand ... did in my opinion materially interfere with Mr. Padley's operations. ... It is however satisfactory to say that Mr. Padley will at his own cost replace the defective tunnel with other work of a sound and satisfactory character.' That sounds rather tough on Padley: normal practice was for contractors to receive some compensation if a task turned out to be abnormally difficult for reasons they could not have foreseen.[20] According to Padley, the Company's minutes had acknowledged that the problem arose from the nature of the soil and not from any defect of workmanship, but nevertheless ordered that the tunnel should be taken up and relaid around the east edge of the reservoir, the work being done at Padley's expense but any additional materials being provided by the company. However, he claimed that he had not been informed of the terms of this resolution; he was simply ordered to relay the culvert along the east edge. This he regarded as a variation to the contract that had come about from the unsuitability of the original plan; he therefore expected to be paid as for any other variation to the contract.

While Padley might not have been officially informed, he seems not to have been unaware of the Directors' thinking. He carried out his work after 5 May 'slowly and in a bungling manner'[21] and by August was pressing for an interim payment. Goddard, the company architect, inspected the work on the tunnel but declined to authorise any payment: only Hawksley could do that. On 14 August, Goddard promised that Hawksley would inspect within the week; Hawksley failed to appear and on 28 August Padley declared that he could no longer continue without payment. Work stopped that evening.

Padley reckoned that he had undertaken work which, with the variations ordered by the company, amounted in value to £5003 19s 4d. Stage payments totalled £3400. He therefore sued the Company for the difference, first at the assizes, then (it having become apparent to his solicitor[22] that his case would not stand at Common Law but hinged on a matter of equity) in Chancery. He probably had a fairly strong case: even if the problem with the culvert had indeed arisen through his negligence, the company was at liberty to offer him the choice of rectifying the defects or of re-routing the culvert. However, if it *directed* him to re-route the culvert, that would indeed appear to be a variation on the contract, and he was entitled to cost it on that basis. Moreover, his dealings with Goddard suggested that the Company was by no means clear what line it was taking with him.

Meanwhile, Padley was seriously out of pocket, with no very certain prospect of recovering his money. The urgency of his need for cash seems to have forced a sale on 5-6 June 1848 of his antiquarian collection: 100 books, his collection of archaeological finds, 'a large collection of copper tokens', even some items contributed by his son Augustus. All these raised £219 net of expenses.[23]

The Chancery case continued at least until the Spring of 1850. The inconclusive nature of the papers suggest that the parties settled out of court. With the financial uncertainty removed, Padley seems to have been able to send off to the engraver revisions to his large-scale plan of Lincoln, a project which seems to have been on hold since 1847.[24] Nevertheless, a surviving diary and cash book for 1851 suggests that he was monitoring his expenditure carefully.[25] What is more, the new, chastened, Padley had lost his wild ambition. A widower since 1842, he had re-married, and seems to have found his place in society, and been content with it.

The whole dispute raises the question of how a man who is generally recorded as getting on with everyone, and whose position as Lincoln's leading surveyor almost *required* him to get along with everyone, should have got into a position where he was in dispute with many of the leading citizens in their capacity as directors or shareholders, such that his competence was being publicly questioned. The Chancery papers seem to hint at a particular animosity between Padley and Hawksley. Hawksley was one of the two leading water engineers at this date; the other was George Leather, the same George Leather whose plan Padley had so unwisely purloined back in 1829.[26] Had Leather perhaps conveyed his views on Padley to Thomas Hawksley?

There is another aspect of interest here. Richard Carline's brother John's affairs had been a sore trial to him for most of the 1840s. John had continued their father's business as a mason and architect at Shrewsbury and had contracted to carry out restoration work on Hereford cathedral. The architect, L. N. Cottingham, had taken a very harsh view in refusing to authorise payment for work which he considered unsatisfactory; John had been forced to give up business and Richard ended up meeting his debt to the bank of £1358 10s 6d.[27] So it is interesting to find J. S. Padley in a position closely analogous to that of John Carline, and to see Richard doing little or nothing to temper Hawksley's rigour.

But we must return to 1847 and the business of the Lincoln Water Company. Its original intention set out in the deposited plans was to have the pumping engine and filter beds immediately below the Skellingthorpe reservoir. The pumping engine would need coal, and this coal would have to be transported along the lane from Boultham to Skellingthorpe. In contrast, if the pumping station was built next to the Witham, coal could come by barge up the Witham. (In retrospect, a site where the pipeline crossed the newly-constructed railway from Nottingham might have been even better.) There was only one problem: their Act gave the company power to take the land set out in the deposited plans at a fair valuation but gave them no such powers over land not so indicated. Acquiring the new site depended on striking a deal with Major Ellison, and the deal was not cheap. In essence, Ellison sold them one acre of land for £300 - well above its agricultural value. He also gave his consent to any widening of the catchwater drain to take barges and allowed them to have the excess water from the lake in Boultham Park. The water company undertook to lay a water main from the pumping station to Boultham and to supply Boultham Hall and Ellison's tenants in the village.[28] At least Ellison and his tenants agreed that they would pay the normal rates for their water. Other companies in such circumstances found themselves conceding a free water supply in perpetuity.[29]

When the company turned its attention to arranging the purchase of the land where it had built the Skellingthorpe reservoir, it must have received a very disagreeable surprise. The details are somewhat obscure. In fact, one gains the impression that Richard Carline took care that the details should remain obscure.[30] Certainly Christ's Hospital sold the company the land that it needed on the west side of the reservoir.[31] But on 6 April 1847 Carline seems to have purchased the land to the east of the Prial Brook from Major Ellison. The resulting position is shown in *Figure 2.3*, a plan produced for Christ's Hospital by William Hardy in 1847. This shows the Christ's Hospital estate and the farms into which it was divided; it also shows (in a yellow tint) the land of other freeholders. Richard Carline, Esq, is shown as the owner of that part of Skellingthorpe lying east of the Prial Brook and bounded to the north by the catchwater drain and to the south by the Hospital's plantations. He also owned other, smaller, plots in the parish but these need not concern us here.

As the reservoir filled in May 1847, Carline would be in a position to point out to the directors that the water was flooding his land, including land which the company was not empowered by its Act to take compulsorily. And his terms were more demanding than those of Major Ellison. He wanted, not merely the right to water, but the entire reservoir, freehold, which he would then lease back to the water company for 999 years. This lease would allow the company to do everything necessary for the storage of water (and would require the company to maintain its works) but Carline and his tenants were to have exclusive rights of fishing, fowling, and boating on the reservoir, with the right to erect a boathouse and to plant such trees and aquatic plants as he or they saw fit. If the company wished so much as to walk the banks to inspect their works, they had to give a day's notice.

The directors must have been in a difficult position: whatever plans they might have had for the gravel walk they had laid out around the reservoir must now be abandoned. Of course, they could always apply for a supplementary act (at no small expense) or they could reduce the size of the reservoir to stay within the bounds drawn on the deposited plan.

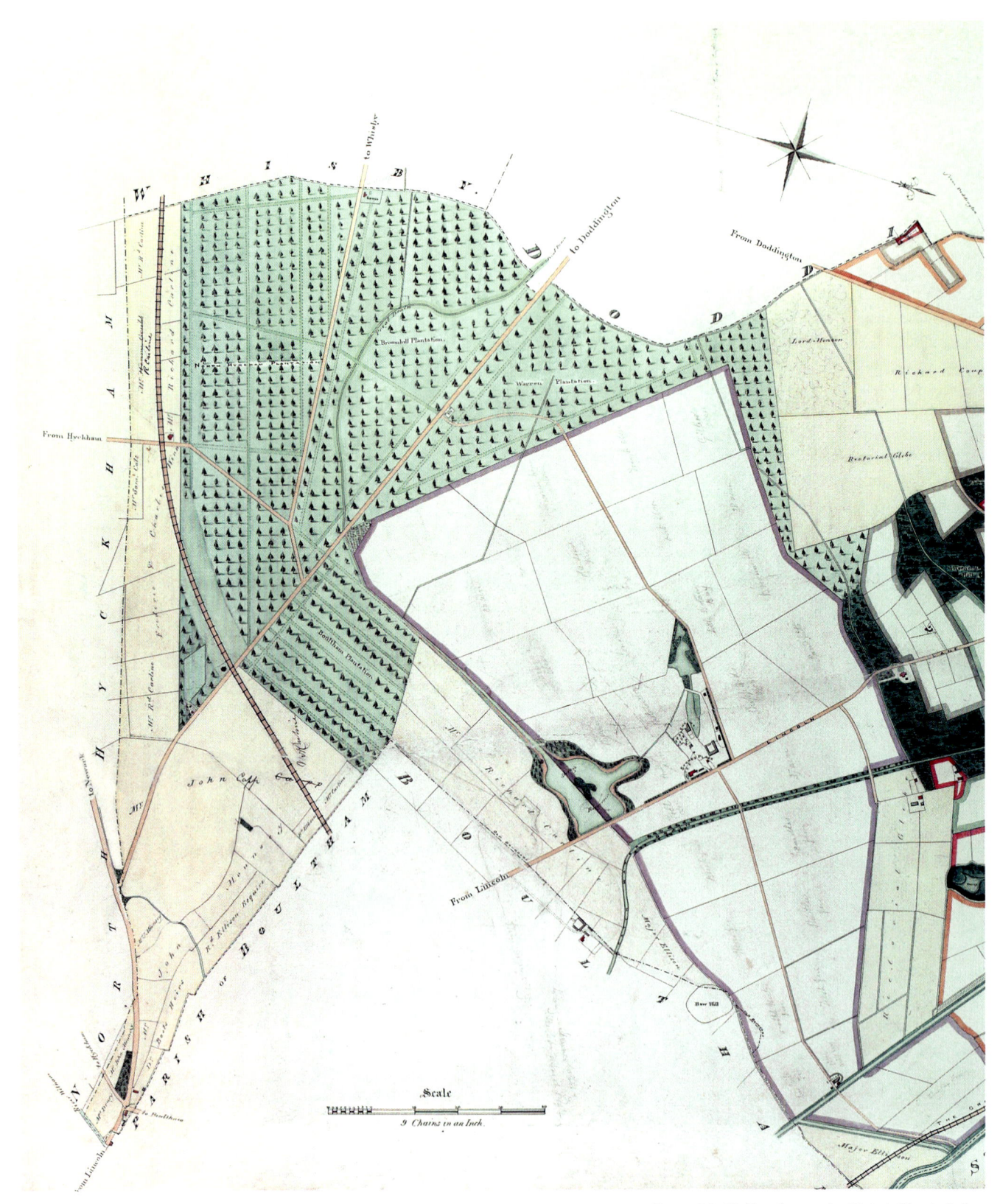

Figure 2.3. Skellingthorpe: the Christ's Hospital plan.

SKELLINGTHORPE RESERVOIR

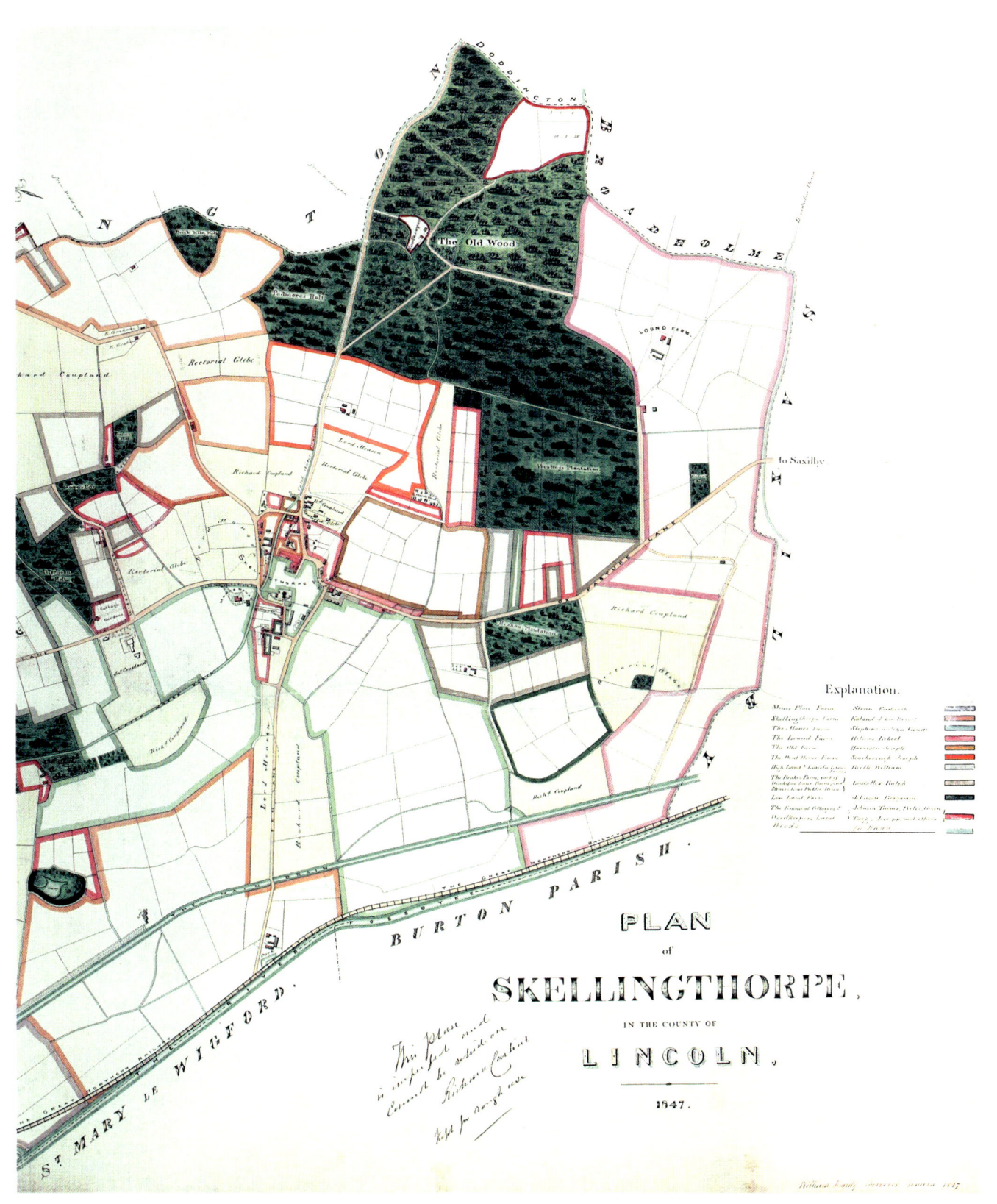

Note that 'up' is a little South of West (LAO TLE 43/4)

But Carline must have persuaded them that his plan was not without its advantages for them. He and his tenants would have every incentive to protect the works from any form of trespass; otherwise they would surely have needed to erect a lodge and provide a keeper of some sort. Moreover, a sale and leaseback (to use the modern term) will have reduced their capital requirements; few companies of this nature found that their costs had been kept within the original estimates. We must suppose Carline to have deployed some such arguments, because there was no breach between him and the company; he remained its Secretary.

The sale to Carline does not survive, but the lease was drawn up in June 1850.[32] The company was to pay a premium of £490 and an annual rent of £50 thereafter. The terms do not appear unfair. Carline had obtained what he wanted and would have had no wish to sour relationships by extracting more than his pound of flesh.

Carline had already been taking steps to improve his property. A bill[33] survives from the architect W. A. Nicholson for work in April 1848 on a 'design for a farmstead proposed to be built upon your estate at Hartsholme'. Subsequent work included superintending and measuring the works, so the farmstead must have been built by the time the bill was presented in July 1849. Although Hartsholme never became Carline's residence, it was more than a commercial farm. The employment of Nicholson suggests polite architecture of some form, and a letter[34] survives of Sunday 23 July 1854 written by Carline to his brother John from Hartsholme. Perhaps he used it to escape from the noise and stench of Lincoln on summer weekends. We even know the name of Carline's establishment: the Register of Electors for 1851 lists him under Skellingthorpe, qualified through ownership of *Hartsholme Manor Farm* and land near the railway. The ancient manor of Hartsholme had lain north of the Lincoln road; this remained part of the Ellison estate. Land east of the Prial Brook and south of the road had been added at enclosure. So Carline's purchase might be considered part of the manor by association.

As a result of Carline's deal with the water company and other changes, the Hospital's plan of 1847 was out of date. Carline seems to have annotated it: 'This plan is imperfect and cannot be relied on. Kept for rough use.' Some of these imperfections appear to be indicated by faint crosses in pencil, such as that marking the boundary of the Christ's Hospital estate as running down the middle of the reservoir. The annotation might also deflect any awkward questions from the Hospital's clerk or treasurer about how the hospital's steward had come to be the owner of what a few years before had been the Hospital's property.

Now Carline's 'rough use' of the 1847 map had included some pencil annotations on his own land. These are centred about 10 chains south of the road and 8 chains east of the reservoir. That would place them on the Hartsholme Hall site, midway between the now-demolished house and the estate offices. But these pencil annotations are only a sketch: the possibility should be considered that the quadrangle of estate offices incorporate some of Carline's farm buildings. It is perhaps relevant that they are aligned with the pre-existing field boundaries (as farm buildings tend to be) rather than with the now demolished Hall. Furthermore, although they are often spoken of now as 'the stables', they are described as late as 1906[35] as the 'Farm Homestead' with Bailiff's House attached, and acted as the home farm for an estate of almost 300 acres. Such an arrangement would have accorded with Carline's needs.

In 1861, all this land (together with the lease on the reservoir) was bought by Joseph Shuttleworth, co-founder of the Clayton and Shuttleworth firm and the son-in-law of Richard Ellison, and Hartsholme Hall was erected. The reservoir became an ornamental lake in the grounds of the Hall, thereafter generally known as Hartsholme Lake. One presumes that Carline got a very good price.

So we have two professional men engaging in commercial activities. J. S. Padley was nearly ruined by his venture as a contractor. Richard Carline used information he had gained as Secretary to the Water Company - albeit information that was publicly accessible - to make a packet. But his enjoyment of the proceeds was brief: he died of a seizure on 16 August 1863, while hurrying to catch a train. In contrast, Padley, more cautious but perhaps more contented, lived almost to the age of 90, noted for *his great natural ability, indomitable perseverance, uprightness of life, and such geniality of manner that everyone with whom he was associated both respected him and valued his friendship. During his long life we believe that he never made an enemy.*[36]

His obituarist must have been unaware of the Skellingthorpe reservoir.

Appendix - Tariffs

The tariffs charged by early utilities seem to be dismissed by most writers as unimportant. The companies actually faced a technical challenge, in that any form of metering tended to be impossibly expensive for small customers. Thus one finds gas companies charging at so much per light, according to the hour when the light was to be extinguished, and specifying the time (which of course varied with the time of year) when such lights might first be lit. Parliament, meanwhile, was concerned that private companies to whom it granted statutory powers (and an effective monopoly) should not misuse those powers to enrich their shareholders, and should offer a fair service to the poorer classes of society.

Charges affected the take-up of services, so it is useful to know what companies actually charged their consumers. This information is often difficult to find, so it seemed worth reporting here even though it is somewhat peripheral to the main theme of the paper.

By the time the Lincoln company received its act, the clauses that Parliament would insist on had generally been established. In the case of the Lincoln act[37] they were as follows:

Profits were limited to 10% (clause 21).

Normal water rates for dwelling houses were limited to 6 to 10% of rental value. This excluded any supply for water closets, baths, horses or cattle, any trade or business purposes, washing carriages, watering gardens, fountains, or other ornamental purposes. The additional rate charged per water closet was limited to 8s to 20s per WC, depending on rental value (clause 52). Charges for the other exotic uses, including baths, were not subject to any statutory limit. For houses worth less than £10, rates were payable by the owner (clause 56).

Fire hydrants were to be provided (together with signs marking their position). They might be used for flushing sewers at terms to be agreed (clauses 64-5).

Provision was made for the company to provide pipes and taps within a house and lease them to the occupiers at a controlled rent (clause 74).

This was to deal with the problem of owners not wishing to incur capital expenditure, even when their tenants were willing to pay water rates. This provision was only to come into force following a future Act establishing the terms.[38]

Remarkably, Carline's own copy of the Company's initial tariff survives[39]. The domestic rates set ranged from 6.7% for a house worth £6, to 3% for a house worth £100 per annum. The rate per WC rose from 4s per annum for the smallest houses to 16s for the very largest. Baths were charged at the same rate as WCs, shower-baths at one quarter the rate. There seems to have been an assumption that such conveniences would be used more frequently in larger houses than in small ones. Carline's annotations indicate that he possessed (or was installing) a bath, but had no WC. Of course, at this date there were only a few short sewers leading straight to the river. Quite possibly it was only the residents with a connection to these who felt it was practicable to install water closets.

The rates for industrial uses imply that water meters were not envisaged even for quite large users. Thus we see, for example, that railways were to be charged 6d per engine 'dispatched'. This presumably means per refill of the water tank in the tender. It is a provision that might make sense while the only railway in Lincoln terminated in St Marks: every train leaving Lincoln would have an engine and every engine would need to refill with water before leaving. How such a provision might apply once the Great Northern was running through trains is a puzzle. Or did the Water Company take the view that a railway company could be trusted, in effect, to calculate its own bill?

It would seem from *White's 1856 Directory* that charges by then had become a little less complex, the rates being quoted as 5% for houses worth between £6 and £20 per annum, and falling to 3% for the largest houses.

Notes

[1] R. C. Wheeler, 'J. S. Padley as an Antiquary', *Lincolnshire History and Archaeology*, 39 (2004), pp.20-23

[2] M. J. T. Lewis, *Dunham Bridge, A Memorial History* (Sleaford 1978).

[3] Lincolnshire Archives (hereafter LAO) Padley 3/422c/19 and 32.

[4] That promise was unfulfilled; both served numerous curacies without gaining serious preferment.

[5] Howard Colvin, *A Biographical Dictionary of British Architects, 1600-1840* (1995), p.215.

[6] LAO LD71/18.

[7] LAO LD71/25

[8] Francis Hill, *Victorian Lincoln* (Cambridge, 1974), p.45.

[9] LAO LD71/25, letter of 2 March 1844.

[10] J. G. Ruddock and R. E. Pearson, *The Railway History of Lincoln* (Lincoln, 1985), p.62.

[11] Francis Hill, *Victorian Lincoln* (Cambridge, 1974), p.160.

[12] 9/10 Vict. c.111. Trevor E. Pacey, *To fetch a Pail of Water* (Lincoln, 1998) gives more details of the Act.

[13] LAO KP 4/6 was deposited at 11.30, seemingly p.m. rather than a.m.

[14] G. M. Binnie, *Early Victorian Water Engineers* (1981).

[15] See D. R. Mills and R. C. Wheeler, *Historic Town Plans of Lincoln, 1610-1920* (Woodbridge, 2004), p.1851:2.

[16] The specification plans do not survive but LAO LDP 1/41 must be closely related. The company's own copy of the deposited plans survives at LAO Misc Don 1342/4 and includes a section missing from KP 4/6. Misc Don 1342/4/2 has the outline of the reservoir as built drawn in pencil over the original rectangle.

[17] The full specification and the claims and counter-claims in the resulting dispute are at The National Archives (hereafter TNA) C14/1037/P31.

[18] Samuel Galton to Sir Joseph Banks, 31 May 1792, quoted in William M. Hunt, 'Some aspects of advice relative to canal management and construction, 1792', *Journal of Regional and Local Studies,* 7.2 (Autumn 1987), pp.55-62.

[19] Quoted in Hawksley's *Further Answer,* 30 March 1850, TNA C14/1037/P31.

[20] For example, when the Hobhole Drain was being cut, the contractor found he had to cut through gravel very much harder than anyone had anticipated and he was allowed to claim the extra cost that had resulted.

[21] TNA C14/1037/P31 - answer of Lincoln Water Company.

[22] The solicitor was William Andrew. Dennis Mills alludes to this case of Andrew in considering his political stance in Ch. 5 of his forthcoming book on the 1849 sewerage scheme for Lincoln devised by George Giles, *Miasma, Contours and Politics: sanitary engineering in early Victorian Lincoln.*

[23] The catalogue, for a sale at his James Street house, is in the possession of the family.

[24] R. C. Wheeler, 'Padley's Large Plan of Lincoln - New Discoveries', *Lincolnshire Past & Present* 70 (Winter 2007/8), pp.3-7.

[25] LAO Misc Don 588/8.

[26] Binnie, 1981. George Leather was about to lose his pre-eminence in 1852 when his Bilberry Dam collapsed.

[27] Colvin, *Biographical Dictionary* Misc Don 551.

[28] LAO Lincoln City / Town Clerk / Boultham Water Supply. Agreement dated 1 April 1847.

[29] For example, the Thirsk Water Company in 1879. See *Boltby ... a history* (Boltby, North Yorkshire, 2002).

[30] An abstract of title for the property, LAO TLE34/4/2, ends with an indenture of August 1846 and a pencil note 'Copy Carline's conveyance'. A later part has become separated (LAO TLE42/13/2) which notes a mortgage of 1850 and refers to the 'last abstracted indenture' of 6 April 1847. This missing portion must be Carline's purchase.

[31] A letter of 31 May 1848 from George Trollope, the clerk to Christ's Hospital, to Carline notes that the Committee will propose to the Court that, rather than grant the Water Company a long lease on such land as was needed for the reservoir, it should convey the same absolutely.

[32] LAO Lincoln City / Town Clerk / Boultham Water Supply. Agreement dated 26 June 1850.

[33] LAO Misc Don 551/2.

[34] LAO Misc Don 551/2.

[35] Northants Record Office, FS 24/114 - Sale catalogue. It seems fairly clear from the description and plan that the 'Stabling Department' with its clock tower lay between the house proper and the surviving quadrangle.

[36] Obituary, quoted in P. B. G. Binnall, 'J. S. Padley', *Lincolnshire Life* (September, 1980), p.29.

[37] 9/10 Vict. c.111.

[38] Parliament never actually brought itself to enact so violent an assault on property rights.

[39] LAO Misc Don 551/1.

CHAPTER 3

THE SIBTHORPS OF CANWICK
The rise and fall of a dynasty

Michael Trott

In 1806, despite declining the honour of a baronetcy, the Sibthorps with estates in excess of 11,000 acres certainly qualified for admission to the ranks of the 'aristocracy' as broadly defined by David Cannadine, the chronicler of their decline.[1] The historiography of the rise and fall of this class of major landowners has been a subject of scholarly debate for many years.[2] Although the following study focuses on the career and dynastic aspirations of one key family member, in drawing upon the, largely unpublished, researches of Dennis and Joan Mills into the history of the Sibthorp estates, it may be of interest in the context of this broader theme: the changing fortunes of the gentry.[3]

The Sibthorps, once one of the premier families of Lincolnshire, are no more and their seat at Canwick Hall presents a sad picture of decay and neglect. If they are remembered at all it is for eccentricity: for Colonel Charles Sibthorp, the long serving member for Lincoln celebrated as parliament's licensed jester and regularly lampooned in the pages of *Punch,* or for his brother Richard, still deplored in ecclesiastical circles as the Anglican minister who in 1841 embraced Roman Catholicism, only to quit her priesthood two years later, announcing that he had escaped the clutches of the harlot of the Apocalypse.

Memories are fainter of their eighteenth-century grandfather, Dr Humphrey Sibthorp, but among his contemporaries he was notorious for the somnolence of his thirty-six years as professor of botany at Oxford University. A recent study singles him out as 'one of the worst examples of the depths to which the university had sunk in those days.'[4] According to another scholar, during his long professorship he 'dozed … stirring only intermittently to put in some gentle work in the University Botanical Garden … he published not a single scientific work … and delivered only a solitary lecture - and that a bad one…'[5] He resigned at the age of seventy-two only when sure that his son would succeed him to the chair, and on the premature death of this son twelve years later his own application to be reappointed was politely declined.

Yet to dismiss the Sibthorps as a race of rather inconsequential eccentrics would be profoundly mistaken. By the time of Dr Sibthorp's death in August 1797 the Lincolnshire family was a force to be reckoned with, owning estates in several counties and exercising political influence both locally and nationally. Moreover, among scholars throughout Europe the Sibthorp name was known and revered. Humphrey, notwithstanding his reputation for somnolence, had been relentless in the pursuit of dynastic ambitions. Yet he was endowed with an energy that his successors could not match, and the century and a half following his death was a period of slow decline to eventual extinction.[6]

A rising family

In the century before Humphrey's birth in 1712, his ancestors had risen from obscurity to the possession of significant land holdings in Lincolnshire, and his father John Sibthorp (1669-1718) was wealthy enough to live on his rents as a Lincoln gentleman and to serve briefly as a city MP. Yet John's own father, Gervase (1626-1704) had been born the son of a Nottinghamshire yeoman. It was trade that laid the foundations of family prosperity. Under the auspices of his merchant stepfather, Gervase 'entered into the commercial life of Lincoln' and acquired a house in St Mark's parish.[7] Another factor was almost equally important to Sibthorp success: prudent alliances. At the age of forty Gervase married a widow who brought with her not only personal wealth but the ownership of estates in the Lincolnshire Marsh. Land was key to the establishment of a county dynasty and throughout the century more was acquired through marriages and associated inheritance. But there were also land purchases and trade was not despised as a route to riches. It is possible that John Sibthorp began his adult life in business: it is certain that his younger brother - another Gervase - left Lincoln to make his fortune as a London mercer. There are extant articles of association dated 1707 between him, Henry Horner and Thomas Ravenscroft.[8] The family's commercial relationship with the former must have been long-standing because the will of Gervase senior (1703) provides for money he had loaned to Henry Horner. By 1725, Gervase was living near Covent Garden and dealing in silk.[9] There were other family members active in London's commercial life: for example this will refers to 'my loving nephew Mr John Medley of the City of London, Merchant Taylor.'[10]

In his own will, Gervase's elder brother, John Sibthorp made provision for funds to be provided should any of his younger sons 'be brought up to any public business or employ'.[11] Although not continuing in trade himself he made a decisive contribution to the rise of the family when he came to choose a wife. Mary, the daughter of Humphrey Browne, a Lincoln banker and merchant, whom John married in 1703, brought significant additions to the Sibthorp estates as well as practical skills and shrewdness which she passed on to her sons: Coningsby born in 1706 and Humphrey six years later. Her husband, who was laid to rest at St Mark's church in Lincoln on 27 April 1718, appointed Mary as his sole executrix. She was a widow for twenty-five years and occupies an honoured place in the history of the dynasty. In the words of Canon Maddison the family's chronicler: 'she seems to have been a person of no common character and to have amply justified the confidence he (her husband) reposed in her…'[12] She made a number of judicious land purchases in the county but the most significant was her acquisition in 1730 of the Canwick estate and the subsequent removal of the family from Lincoln to Canwick Hall, a substantial house overlooking the city. It signalled that the Sibthorps had joined the ranks of the county gentry. This was a status confirmed when in 1764, twenty-one years after his mother's death, Coningsby inherited from the bequest of her brother, Gilbert Browne, lands in Lincolnshire and an estate called Skimpans at North Mimms in Hertfordshire.

Of Mary Sibthorp's five children only Coningsby and Humphrey outlived her. Both were sent to school in London, the former to Westminster two months after his father's death. Canwick was purchased not long after he came of age. It was intended undoubtedly as a suitable residence for him and any family he might have. In fact he never married. As member of parliament for Lincoln, High Sheriff of the county and colonel of the Royal South Lincoln Militia he fulfilled everything that might be expected of the chief representative of a prominent county family except to provide for its future by way of an heir.

Humphrey Sibthorp and his London circle

This responsibility fell to Humphrey whose sense of dynastic responsibility was profound. He added to the estates, fathered a large family, and achieved success, somewhat surprisingly, as a physician and a scientist. In tracing the influences that shaped him, his years at Charterhouse School in Smithfield in the 1720s are central. Here he perhaps encountered the institution's resident physician, Dr Henry Levett (1668-1725), who occupies a distinguished place in the history of scientific medicine.[13] However, Levett died not long after Humphrey arrived. More important in determining his future path were the visits he made to relatives and their friends who were helping to generate the capital's burgeoning commercial prosperity. As a younger son he would have to pursue his own way in the world. Did his uncle Gervase encourage him to consider a mercantile career and introduce him to his connections, city families who had made considerable fortunes thereby?

In 1740 Humphrey married Sarah the daughter of a wealthy city liveryman, Isaac Waldo. Gervase Sibthorp can be linked to her family through his business partner, Thomas Ravenscroft who in 1702 had taken as his wife Sarah's aunt, Elizabeth Waldo.[14] With an eye to pleasing wealthy connections Humphrey and his wife were to be scrupulous in their choice of godparents so it is of interest that in 1749 a Mr Ravenscroft was godfather to their daughter Charlotte.[15] Such diligence in family matters could pay dividends. Thus Humphrey was assiduous in visiting his wife's cousin Mrs. Woolaston who entered widowhood with a considerable fortune and no surviving children. Born before him she outlived him dying at the age of ninety-seven. However his son, also called Humphrey, who was her godson, continued to visit and on her death in 1805 inherited most of her fortune. The Waldos had long-established Lincolnshire connections. Sarah Waldo, who became Mrs Woolaston, was a great-niece of Sir Charles Thorold, who had an estate at Harmston in the county.[16]

When Humphrey was at Charterhouse some branches of the Waldo family had left London and were living in comfortable rural retirement south of the city. His future father-in-law Isaac Waldo was at Streatham and Isaac's brother Peter, described as a 'wealthy supercargo', was living in nearby Mitcham. On quitting the India trade Peter Waldo had turned his hand to theology and was the author of a treatise on the Athanasian Creed. His son, also called Peter, was a scholar, a devoted high churchman, who published a standard treatise on the liturgy of the Church of England. He died in 1804 leaving his Sibthorp relatives a substantial bequest, effective on the death of his widow. The second Humphrey took the additional surname of Waldo in thankful anticipation. The inheritance was long delayed: Mrs Waldo died in 1842 at the age of 101.[17]

The first Peter Waldo married his cousin, Mary Dubois. Her brother the eminent botanist Charles Dubois (1657-1740) also lived in Mitcham. Their mother, Sarah Waldo, had married John Dubois, a considerable figure in the City, a strong Protestant and a Whig, heavily involved in Restoration politics.[18] His son, Charles, began in the silk trade but in 1702 was appointed to the post of Cashier-General of the East India Company in which office he became quite wealthy, although his house in Mitcham and its 15 acres of grounds he inherited from his father.[19] The botanical garden he established there was famed and became an important scientific resource. In the introduction to his *Catalogus Plantarum* (1730) Philip Miller wrote: 'To him ... we are greatly indebted for many valuable Trees and Plants which enrich this catalogue.'[20] In the 1720s Dubois was in regular contact with a number of botanists living in London including Sir Hans Sloane (1660-1753) owner of the Chelsea physic garden and an eminent physician, also William Sherard (1659-1728) and Johann Jakob Dillenius (1687-1747). Sherard and his brother had a botanical garden at Eltham and Dillenius who worked there went on to become - under the terms of his patron's will - the first Sherardian professor of botany at Oxford. In 1729, the year Humphrey was completing his studies at Charterhouse, the Swiss naturalist Johann Amman (1707- 41) was in London advising Sir Hans Sloane. He later became professor of botany at the Russian Academy of Sciences. Sibthorp's subsequent academic career brought him into contact with many of these naturalists and it is reasonable to suppose that his interest in natural history began when he was a boy with visits to Mitcham.[21] When Dubois died at the age of eighty-three he left an herbarium comprising seventy-four folio volumes. These Humphrey purchased and presented to Oxford University where they form an important constituent of its botanical collection.[22] In London as a young man considering his path in life he was presented with a gratifying prospect: wealth in the service of scholarship. His long life would be characterised by the determined pursuit of both.

Humphrey became a demy[23] of Magdalen College, Oxford in 1731. By this time Dillenius, although not yet botany professor (he replaced the existing incumbent three years later), was already working at the University physic garden, the splendid entrance to which was just a few yards away from the College. For centuries the study of plants had been key to the practice of medicine. Thus the appointment of the Sherardian professor was placed in the hands of the Royal College of Physicians, and both Dillenius and the celebrated Swedish botanist Linnaeus (1707-1778), who visited Oxford in 1736, were medical men. It is therefore unsurprising that on graduating in 1734 and being elected a fellow of his College, Sibthorp opted for the study of medicine, becoming, in the words of his son, Dillenius's 'favourite pupil'.[24] In both English universities the teaching of medicine was notoriously poor and Humphrey found time for regular visits to London, paying attendance upon Sarah Waldo, and cultivating her wealthy connections. Their marriage in 1740 necessitated the resignation of his fellowship. This was a sacrifice, but he was already quite wealthy, having inherited £1000 from his father's estate on his twenty-fourth birthday in 1736, and the same sum a year later on the death of his uncle, Gilbert Browne. When he graduated as bachelor of medicine in 1743 it was as a 'grand compounder' implying an annual income of over £300.[25] He was awarded his doctorate two years later. Popular physicians could command a good income and Humphrey did practise, but the extent and nature of his clientele is unknown.[26]

The newly-weds maintained close links with their London connections and their first child, a girl born in July 1741 who lived only two months, was buried at All Hallows Church in Bread Street. The birth of a son in October the following year must have delighted his grandmother, Mary Sibthorp, who did not have long to live.[27] She had lived to see her eldest son become a leading county gentleman and from 1734 to 1741 Member of Parliament for Lincoln. Her passing in 1743 marks the end of an era in the history of the family. With the accretion of land following the death of her brother's widow in 1764 the Sibthorp estates in Lincolnshire were now substantial. Except when sitting in parliament Coningsby resided at Canwick,[28] but with no children of his own he displayed little interest in purchasing additional acres. Family tradition has it that he was engaged to his cousin Mary Caldecott, but that after her death in 1738 he settled into confirmed bachelorhood.[29] Humphrey was thus aware that the future of the family lay with him and his children and his efforts to establish its good standing and prosperity were to become almost obsessional.

The Sherardian Professor

Science was his chosen path for establishing the Sibthorpian reputation. Dillenius as botany professor was charged with implementing Sherard's plan of updating and completing the *Pinax* of Caspar Bauhin (1560-1624), an encyclopaedia of all plants.[30] Sibthorp too worked on the project and with the professor's sudden death from apoplexy in April 1747 seemed well placed to succeed him in the Sherardian chair. At a time when patronage and connections were more important than ability it is to the credit of the Royal College that the chair was offered first to Linnaeus. Only when he declined did the members turn to an election. There were three candidates and Humphrey must have prepared the ground well, receiving twenty-eight out of a possible thirty votes.[31]

This was the peak of his professional career. He applied for several other positions, all without success. He twice attempted to become physician to the Charterhouse. Although the stipend was modest there was the opportunity to build up a medical practice and the perquisites included a fine house built by Levett in Charterhouse Square. In 1752, when the poet Mark Akenside was defeated for the post by one vote, Sibthorp was apparently too late in submitting an application. His assault on the post in 1764 was more determined and he directly solicited the governors and other influential personages as well as asking his M.P. brother to approach the Whig leader, Lord Rockingham, soon to become Prime Minister. In writing for support he quoted an impressive array of academic references, stating for example that Albrecht von Haller (1708-1777) the eminent naturalist had dedicated a book to him.[32] Sibthorp also mentioned that he was one of only ten overseas fellows of the Russian Imperial Academy and that in 1754 the Empress Elizabeth had presented him with a diploma allowing him to practise physic in her dominions.[33] Not least the 'great Linnaeus' had named a plant in his honour which was 'noticed by Borlase in his Natural History of Cornwall'. It was all to no avail. Even the denigration of his main rival as not having been educated in the school and possibly even a Dissenter did not help.[34]

In 1755 he managed to augment his income by becoming deputy to the non-resident and elderly regius professor of physic, William Woodford. Three years later on hearing that he was dying, Sibthorp petitioned the king to be appointed in his place, urging that the medical and botanical professorships should be combined. He also directed letters to Lord Hardwicke, the Duke of Newcastle and others, quoting eminent figures such as the Archbishop of Canterbury 'who has so long been acquainted with my character and several connections of life'[35] who supported his application. He argued that most continental universities had joint chairs and that the two stipends would better 'support the dignity of the office'.[36] To Newcastle he extolled his 'family's long adherence to our happy establishment in church and state' and offered political support in those parts of the country where 'my interests are chiefly vested…'[37] On being rejected he wrote of the mortification of being superseded 'by one so much my junior'.[38]

In all these applications Sibthorp referred to his academic achievements at Oxford and certainly at the start of his long professorship he did not regard the post as a sinecure. He added to the herbarium with plants from the garden and from overseas and worked on its annotation.[39] As well as beginning a new catalogue of the garden he undertook his own researches.[40] He obtained seeds from all over the world, conducting in Latin an extensive academic correspondence,[41] and was particularly interested in botanists working in Russia.[42] Scientifically, he was among the early proponents of the Linnean system of classification, which transformed the intellectual world. At the start of his tenure he engaged G. D. Ehret to supervise the garden *(hortus praefectus)*. This was quite an achievement as the

Figure 3.1
Portrait of Professor Humphrey Sibthorp (1712-1797) holding an illustration of Sibthorpia Linnaei *the plant named by Linnaeus in his honour. Maddison identifies the artist as Jean Baptiste Charpentier.*

(By permission of the Plant Sciences Department, Oxford University.)

German botanical illustrator, who had settled in England, was highly regarded and securing him involved Humphrey in writing a number of 'flattering letters'.[43] Ehret arrived in 1750 but stayed less than a year. Both he and Sibthorp were strong-willed men and following numerous disputes he was asked to take an oath to be 'obedient to the Professor'. He refused, alleging that Humphrey was 'a tyrannising man' who claimed 'an arbitrary power' and was 'not capable of giving me any directions in the garden.'[44] The fault may not have been all on one side; Ehret's successor as gardener, James Benwell, stayed for forty years and although not formally educated was widely regarded as an extremely accomplished botanist.

Despite all this, posterity's view of Sibthorp's academic record has been almost uniformly negative. That he lectured only once is notorious. Yet few professors did lecture: in 1720 a correspondent of *Terrae Filius* observed that at Oxford 'no one had lectured publicly in any faculty except in poetry and music for three years past.'[45] The problem was the absence of an audience.[46]

Yet neither did he publish, which does support the scepticism of some contemporaries. In October 1747 the London naturalist Peter Collinson wrote to Linnaeus that 'Dr. Dellenius was prosecuting … the *Pinax* when he died. What will be its fate I know not, for the present Professor I do not think of skill sufficient to undertake it'. A few years later he wrote again: 'It is certain that the *Pinax* is at an end and as you well observe with concern Botany is in a low way at Oxford and I know not when it will revive.'[47] Perhaps Collinson was too harsh. In its 1824 entry on 'Dillenius' *The Encyclopaedia Britannica* noted that the *Pinax* 'was never finished; for indeed, neither Dillenius, nor anyone else, could even at that time be competent to it: still less, as botanists and botanical works multiplied excessively, was this undertaking practicable.'

Although Sibthorp sought to contribute to his subject, his intellectual gifts did not place him in the first rank of scientists.[48] Additionally, his attention to academic matters was always constrained by a primary concern for the financial well being of his family. Thus part of his dispute with Ehret was over the income arising from sales of garden produce. In canvassing for the chair of physic he argued that with 'my family … very numerous and increasing' the enhanced income would allow 'my withdrawing myself from the practical part to be more at liberty to attend the speculative'.[49] Having purchased and presented to the University Dillenius's library and the Dubois herbarium he became reticent about committing his own funds. In 1758 he complained that 'the interest of the botany (chair) is entirely vested in the stocks which with these last few years has been much reduced.'[50] Ten years later he was still complaining, 'our library is so destitute of modern books having no fund, that there are none since the late benefactor Consul Sherard's demise.'[51]

One significant obstacle to any attempted rehabilitation of Professor Humphrey Sibthorp's scientific reputation is the fact that most of his papers and correspondence were destroyed. They were kept at his house in Oxford and after his death became the property of his widowed daughter Lady Sewell who lived there. With her passing in 1820 they were sold among the household effects and may have been the documents referred to in this letter of Dawson Turner:

> Mr Upcott has mentioned to me, that he found upon a druggists counter at Oxford, sundry letters

written by Sibthorpe, Dillenius, etc, and that the druggist had told him they were a portion of a large quantity he had bought from the Botanic Garden; so large that after keeping what he wanted for himself, sufficient remained to be worth sending to a neighbouring paper mill.[52]

Some insight into Sibthorp's academic seriousness may be obtained from a letter of his included in the published correspondence of the American naturalist John Bartram. In April 1762 Benjamin Franklin was in Oxford to receive an honorary degree and Sibthorp took the opportunity of raising with him the needs of the physic garden. As a result Franklin agreed to forward to his friend Bartram a letter from Sibthorp requesting the seeds of named plants.[53]
It is also significant that Humphrey's youngest son, John Sibthorp, grew up with a deep love of botany. This was surely a testimony to his father's genuine involvement in the subject.

The Sibthorp estates

Humphrey was married to Sarah Waldo for little more than twelve years during which time she bore him eight children. The first and one other died in infancy. His heir Coningsby Isaac, born in 1742, became like his father a fellow of Magdalen and was a promising scholar but died at the age of twenty-four. Humphrey, two years younger than his brother, lived to pass on the family name. Girls were born in 1743 and 1748, the first, Mary Elizabeth married Sir Thomas Sewell, an eminent judge appointed Master of the Rolls; her sister Sarah became the wife of Montague Cholmeley of Easton in Lincolnshire. In 1749 came the last of their children: twins, a boy and a girl, the former lived to age thirteen with no record of what became of the latter. Sarah died in Oxford on 1 August 1753, aged 40, and was interred at Lincoln in the family vault of St Mark's parish church. Four years earlier her

Figure 3.2
Magdalen College and bridge, with Botanic Gardens from the Cherwell, Oxford
(Published by Alden & Co Ltd, Oxford, 1880)

husband's uncle Gervase, the London merchant, had been buried there, to be followed in 1757 by his widow, the last Sibthorp to rest in the city.

The return of Sarah Sibthorp's body to Lincoln was significant. Despite his Oxford home and his London connections, Humphrey's dynastic ambitions were focused on the county of his birth. As heir to his unmarried brother he had a strong interest in ensuring the effective management of the family estates and encouraged his children to cultivate the affection of their uncle. Some light is thrown on family relationships by an extensive series of letters from 1768, reproduced by Maddison. They concern the wish of the professor's second son, Humphrey, to marry a 'Miss F.' whom he had met whilst staying at Canwick two years before. Both his father and uncle Coningsby were of one mind in their disapproval, but it was the response of the latter that compelled obedience. He was outraged at his nephew's duplicity. 'Little could I think that when you went daily to Lincoln to scate *(sic)* it was an artifice only to pay respects to the young lady.' Despite his age - he was sixty-two and a life-long bachelor - he threatens marriage: 'If you are bent to go on with your present Scheme… it will put me upon doing what I never intended to do, and it may possibly deprive you of all you ever expected from me…' To reinforce his point Coningsby brings in another family member, 'Your present condition produces many a tear, and I know my dear Molly shares in my grief.'[54] This was his niece Mary Elizabeth. She and her younger sister, Sarah who was by now engaged to Montague Cholmeley of Easton, were often in Lincolnshire. Their brother did not pursue his planned union and the overall impression is of close family co-operation to rein in an errant member.

With the death of his first wife Sibthorp was left with at least six young children. Many of their godparents were drawn from his Waldo relations who would have rallied round to assist in the management of his Oxford household. In December 1757, he was remarried to Elizabeth Gibbs aged thirty, daughter and co-heir of John Gibbs of Clapham, a merchant whose wife had inherited a share in the estates of Thomas Floyer of Brent Pelham in Hertfordshire.[55] Under the terms of the marriage settlement the couple acquired her father's manor of Instow, comprising land in a number of parishes bordering the confluence of the rivers Taw and Torridge. This estate became Humphrey's home in retirement and final resting-place.[56] Indeed even while he continued as professor he spent increasing time in Devon where he was able to undertake the horticultural projects that interested him: the planting of grape vines for instance, as advocated by Philip Miller in his *Gardeners' Dictionary* of 1735.[57] As a landowner he was assiduous in asserting his rights. At the Devon Quarter Sessions of 1775 a certain John Shaddick was acquitted after trial 'for unlawfully rescuing four horses which had been distrained by Humphrey Sibthorp M.D. for damages faissant and for assaulting him'.[58] Increasingly cantankerous he bickered with his wealthy neighbour Denys Rolle, famous for having established an ill-fated colony in Florida. They lived long enough to become close friends and died within weeks of each other, a circumstance celebrated by the *Gentleman's Magazine*, which reported that they were:

> great botanists, great travellers, great walkers, and great talkers; fond of the open air; and living like the Neapolitans, *au jour, toute la journée.* They were both indefatigable in getting and heaping up: and yes, in some cases, they parted with their best acquisitions without a sigh; as when Dr Sibthorpe lost the plant which Linné had called after his name … out of the physic garden at Oxford … and Denys Rolle gave up his estate in Florida, on which he laid out £40,000.[59]

Humphrey and Elizabeth had only one child who lived, a son John born in 1758.[60] After graduating from Lincoln College in 1777 he followed his father in pursuing a scientific career, studying medicine (including a period at Edinburgh, where the instruction was a good deal more practical than at Oxford) and then botany. He wrote to his half-brother that he traced his 'Botanomania … up to the Loins of my Father.'[61] The latter may have looked for a continuing family connection with Oxford because in old age he embarked on a building project there. The construction of the new Magdalen Bridge required the demolition of the botany professor's residence. So in 1775 Humphrey paid £500 for land adjoining the Physic Garden, including 'the waters and the fishings in the river' and four acres of arable land in Cowley fields, where he built a mansion, Cowley House. This became the residence of John Sibthorp and later home for his widowed half-sisters: Lady Cholmeley

Figure 3.3
Portrait of John Sibthorp (1758-1796).
Portrait inscribed 'J. Smith & Sons 1850' by an unknown artist.
(By permission of the Plant Sciences Department, Oxford University.)

who died in 1818 and Lady Sewell, following whose death in 1820, it was sold, eventually becoming the nucleus of St. Hilda's College.[62]

Humphrey's financial position was secured when in 1779 he succeeded his brother as head of the family. He established himself at Canwick and in the autumn embarked along with John on a tour of the Lincolnshire estates. The latter, anxious to pursue his medical studies, by no means relished this filial responsibility. He did however, admire his father's continuing energy and concern for effective estate management. Two years later, after another joint tour, he wrote to his half-brother, Humphrey: 'My father I believe has almost exhausted the Marsh, from the piteous countenances the poor devils put on I had not believed there had been so much money in the country.'[63] Returning to Canwick he found his father's enthusiasm for the 'Assemblies etc. the Lincoln Races offered' extremely trying. 'You know he has far more of the mercurial composition than myself whom am rather of a saturnine complexion … I found myself … in too solemn a mood to trip it with the light fantastic toe.'[64] However, with the old man's growing eccentricity and preference for Instow, his heir, Humphrey, although living in Hertfordshire, took an increasing responsibility for the Lincolnshire estates and was probably active in the land exchanges associated with the Canwick enclosure awards of 1787. Subsequently the family continued to acquire small parcels of land in the parish, all aimed at ensuring their holdings formed a consolidated area around the hall.

In 1777 the younger Humphrey had married Susannah Ellison. It was another judicious union: her family owned considerable property and her father was a partner in a Lincoln bank. The couple lived at Skimpans, the property at North Mimms inherited from Gilbert Browne. Although trained as a lawyer, as a landowner Humphrey knew the value of agricultural improvement and took a practical interest in the subject, acquiring for example forty-one volumes of the county Reports of the Board of Agriculture.[65] In his correspondence with Lady Sewell, who eventually went to Instow to care for their ageing father, he asked to be informed of local produce prices and made arrangements for the importation of Devon cattle into Lincolnshire.[66] In 1805 Humphrey let the Fullingcott farm at Instow to a Lincolnshire farmer, William Lill, who there pioneered land drainage and the use of improved fertilisers.[67] Twenty years earlier John Sibthorp had written to his brother from Gottingen:

> You are the practical farmer, while I am here learning the theory … I think upon my return we shall talk learnedly upon this subject and perhaps I shall be able to assist you the practical farmer with some useful hints.[68]

Following the death of his mother Elizabeth in 1780, John's inheritance included the estate of Instow, but anxious to pursue his studies he was content that his father should continue to manage it. His commitment was to scholarship and his contribution to botany - in particular two arduous journeys to the Near East which resulted in the *Flora Graeca,* one of the most sumptuous works of botanical illustration ever published - is widely celebrated and the subject of two recent studies.[69] Where the demands of botany on his purse might lead him was a cause of much anxiety to his father. In December 1783 the library and manuscripts of Linnaeus came up for sale. John immediately offered £1000, much to his father's consternation. His son wrote to reassure him:

> Have you any reason to infer either from my conduct at school, or at the university or in my

travels that I was prone to Dissipation why should you then tremble lest I should destroy the Establishment of a future family by the sale of an Estate which you had raised and nurtured with particular care?

He never married and botany remained his first love, 'I will say the calmest and happiest hours I ever have spent and probably ever may spend were passed in the silent contemplation and admiration of the works of nature…'[70]

By the time this letter was written from Spa in June 1784, John had been appointed as the third Sherardian professor. It seems his father had resigned the previous December at his request and the transfer was effected reasonably smoothly.[71] Later in the year he embarked on his first botanical tour of the Levant, not returning until the end of 1787 when he properly took up his professorial duties. As well as working on the material he had brought from the east he was concerned to improve the Botanic Garden, complaining like his predecessors about the parsimony of the university authorities. He prepared and published a *Flora Oxoniensis* and took over lecturing from his deputy George Shaw (originally appointed by his father).[72] He reported good attendances: 'respectable personages … Heads of Houses …' In 1793 at the urging of Lord North the botanical school received a royal grant and its head was designated regius professor.[73] During these years Ferdinand Bauer, the artist who had accompanied him to Greece, worked on the illustrations for the *Flora Graeca*. Perhaps to appease his father, John also invited him to paint a number of views of the Instow Estate.[74]

John Sibthorp was always mindful of the practical aspects of his scholarship: the medical uses of plants, improved farming methods and the search for new cultivars. By 1791 his financial position was such that he was able to implement his desire to emulate his brother as a practical farmer and he began buying land around South Leigh in Oxfordshire. Over the following two years he was absorbed in supervising its enclosure, and gave this as the reason for delaying his departure on a second tour to Greece. Thus on 22 October 1793 he wrote to his friend John Hawkins - waiting for him in Germany - that he had sixty-four men employed: 'carpenters, hedgers, ditchers, roadmen, woodmen … and most of these on day pay'. He added that in the absence of a trusted manager such as his father had at Instow he must remain on site.[75]

He eventually left in March 1794. By the time of his return in July the following year he was extremely ill and died at Bath on 8 February 1796. Under the terms of his will part of his Oxfordshire lands, the estate of Stanton Harcourt, said in 1800 to be worth a gross annual rental of £275, was left to the University of Oxford. He stipulated that the income be used to fund the publication of the *Flora Graeca* and its *Prodomus* and upon completion of these works to establish a chair in Rural Economy to be joined to that of Botany. The trustees appointed to oversee the publications encountered massive obstacles to do with the cost of the undertaking, which was not completed until 1840. But the magnificent volumes and the Sibthorpian chair (now of Plant Sciences) that was then established still honour the family name.

It is not recorded how his father reacted to this alienation of part of the family property but it is known that the Royal College declined the old man's petition to be re-appointed to the chair.[76] He was probably not too disappointed at being rebuffed as Devonshire was now absorbing his full attention. Under the terms of his marriage settlement with Elizabeth Gibbs he had undertaken to invest £1840 in property, but did not make any significant acquisition until 1787 when he made a number of purchases of land adjoining his son's estate, the biggest being the Manor of Bickleton which cost £2,345.[77] He was perhaps anxious to secure his own place among the Devonshire landowners. However, he continued to live at the Instow manor house at Fullingcott, to which he added a half-hexagonal extension. Lady Sewell, widowed in 1784, went to live with him there. Intriguingly, her husband, although Master of the Rolls, had died intestate and she was compelled to leave her home at Ottershaw Park. The following year John Sibthorp had written to his father:

> your plagues seem to multiply with your possessions - I wish rather you had bought Ottershaw as gratification for Lady Sewell - as an improveable estate, and in every respect a (more) suitable mansion for my brother and his dependants than Bell Bar which is attended with much expense.[78]

Bell Bar refers to the mansion of Brookmans Park purchased by Dr Sibthorp in 1785. Perhaps Skimpans was deemed unsuitable for his son Humphrey's growing family? John's caution was heeded and Brookmans sold the following year.[79] Before the turn of the decade Humphrey and his family moved to Canwick and here in 1792 his last child Richard was born. With habits of economy inherited from his father and with five sons and a daughter the future of the dynasty seemed secure with him. In 1794 he acquired an estate of over 2000 acres at Hatton and Langton-by-Wragby not far from Lincoln. He was active in buying and selling probably with the aim of consolidating the family holdings and soon after his father's death began the process of barring the entail of the Hertfordshire property, freeing the way for its sale.[80] He seems to have been a rather astute negotiator. In 1807 W. Franklin wrote to his son regarding a contract for their purchase of land at Beckering, which provided for 'possession of the rents and profits and not the possession of the estate itself'. When he sought to regularise the matter, Colonel Sibthorp told him that 'on account of settlements, annuities, etc, he could not dispose of any estate of his own without applying to the Court of Chancery.'[81]

When Humphrey moved to Canwick his father turned his full attention to Instow where he saw a great deal of commercial potential. With the death of John Sibthorp he became owner of all the family estates there and despite his advanced age welcomed the unhindered authority to pursue his various projects. As Lord of the Manor, and benefiting financially from the sea trade, he initiated maintenance work on the quay and as waywarden was responsible for improving the roads. He saw the French War as a significant business opportunity. The Royal Navy had become a major purchaser of foodstuffs so Humphrey spent money on rehabilitating a tide mill - which operated through damming a small stream running into the Torridge - and building a bake house and oven. In March 1797 this was advertised in the *Exeter Flying Post:*

> To millers: to be lett ... a very good accustomed tide-mill which may be almost constantly employed from a back water or reservoir; lately built for shelling of oats as well as for grinding corn; together with a large oven and baking room for bread and ship biscuits....[82]

Figure 3.4
Watercolour of 'Marino' by Ferdinand Lucas Bauer. The house was built by Professor Humphrey Sibthorp in 1797
(By permission of the Trustees of the British Museum)

On the other hand he also saw scope for the development of the village as a watering place and built new houses on the waterfront, including a residence for himself, called *Marino*. *The Traveller's Guide* of 1805 praises Instow as having 'several advantages for bathing, and has some good lodging-houses erected by the late Dr. Sibthorp ...'[83] All this activity seems to have stemmed from an old man's anxieties for the financial future of his family, and these fears were associated with mood swings and an irritability that must have made Lady Sewell's latter days with him particularly irksome. She often left him at Fullingcott and stayed in the new house; her father demanded to be taken there himself but was prevented by illness. Days before his death in August 1797 she wrote to her brother:

> my father's mind is still too much burthened with worldly cares. Anxiety for the establishment of his family and success to his Instow speculations will remain with him to the latest moments and even extend beyond his expiring health. He gave me his will to read but as written by his own hand I fear it will be difficult to understand. It will not however, I hope give rise to litigation ...[84]

Her wish was disappointed. Colonel Humphrey Sibthorp, his heir, inherited the family estates absolutely with one exception: the will provided that 'the quay at Instow, and several cellars and warehouses and houses adjoining ... together with the pottery'[85] should pass to him conditional on his bringing up a son 'into a mercantile line'. The old man, fearful of the future and perhaps remembering how the family's fortune was built, believed that commerce and entrepreneurial flair held the key to continued prosperity. To reinforce the point there was a sanction: if no son came forward he stipulated that a cash amount should go to Magdalen College. Humphrey apparently assured his father that his son Richard born in 1792 would be brought up as a merchant. However, this undertaking was quietly forgotten and eventually the College instituted legal proceedings. In 1830 Lord Brougham ruled that because of uncertainty of the testator's intentions ('it would perhaps be impossible to find a more senseless and absurd collection of words') the money should remain with the family.[86]

On the face of it the old man's fears were purely imaginary. When he died in August 1797 the Sibthorp lands were at their greatest extent comprising substantial holdings in Lincolnshire, Devonshire and Oxfordshire, and lesser parcels elsewhere, particularly Nottingham, London and Bristol. The inheritance was in good hands. When not occupied in parliament (he represented Lincoln between 1800 and 1806) or on wartime manoeuvres as Colonel of the South Lincolnshire Militia, Humphrey Sibthorp's prime concern was the efficient management of his estates. For example, the 1810 lease he awarded to a tenant on the South Leigh estate in Oxfordshire contains very detailed covenants regarding farm management.[87] His sister, Lady Sewell who lived in Oxford witnessed the document and kept a shrewd eye on the family's interests there and not until 1875 did economic circumstances necessitate the sale of the Oxfordshire property. Instow was more problematical. Colonel Humphrey Sibthorp certainly appreciated his Devonshire estate: he enjoyed spending time at *Marino* and invited Bauer to paint it.[88] There were however, rumours locally that his inheritance was tainted and the property should have returned to the Gibbses. Quite remarkably, in 1847, a group of United States citizens claiming Gibbs ancestry commissioned a representative to journey to England to enquire into the matter. Perhaps not wishing to disappoint his sponsors the agent said that when the estate was sold in 1819 it was reported that 'the Sibthorp title ... was supposed to be defective' and that the buyer required letters of indemnity.[89] He could not have seen the 1757 marriage settlement, which leaves little doubt that the property passed to the rightful heir. Nevertheless, possible problems with tenants seeking excuse to withhold rent[90] and the distance from Canwick led to the decision to sell. After some years as an invalid Colonel Sibthorp died in 1815 and it was left to his

Figure 3.5
The Marine Hotel, Instow. At the end of the Napoleonic War the Sibthorps disposed of 'Marino', with the coming of the railway it became the Marine Hotel and was demolished in 1972

(St Albans Series postcard)

eldest son Coningsby to progress the sale. In 1819 Augustus Saltren Willett, a substantial local landowner, paid £23,000 to become the new owner of Instow, funds he raised by selling-on part of the estate and by borrowing the balance from the vendors on the security of a 1000 year lease. The mortgage was redeemed in ten years.[91] When Coningsby died in 1822 his brother Charles de Laet Waldo Sibthorp, completed the winding-up of the family's interests in Devon with the disposal of the Manor of Bickleton to George Acland Barbor of Fremington.[92]

Colonel Humphrey's only daughter, Mary Esther, inherited her grandfather's botanical interests. In 1801 she married John Hawkins, John Sibthorp's close collaborator and one of three trustees charged with responsibility for publishing the *Flora Graeca*. They carried out botanical investigations together, though Mary was recognised as an authority in her own right.[93] Of her five brothers, Henry, who in 1793 enlisted as a midshipman, had a real curiosity about the natural world and was responsible for securing the return to England of valuable material that Hawkins had left on the island of Zante. He was drowned when his ship caught fire in the Dardanelles in 1807. The youngest child Richard, eschewing the world of commerce, pursued a priestly vocation and lived until 1879. The eldest son, Coningsby, served in parliament but was in poor health and never recovered from a carriage accident in 1821. He died the following year. Charles, his successor, continued the parliamentary tradition, representing Lincoln almost continuously from 1826 until his death in 1855.

Spending most of his time in London, Charles left it to his brother, another Humphrey, the rector of Washingborough, to manage the family's local interests.[94] Although the nineteenth century was largely a period of retrenchment some property was acquired. In 1849 Charles inherited a mansion and land in Hertfordshire, and in 1870 his grandson Coningsby purchased, perhaps for sentimental reasons, the nearby ancestral home of his forbears, North Mymms Park. With the agricultural depression, in 1888 both these properties were sold and the Sibthorp lands were once again confined to Lincolnshire.[95]

Of the five sons of Colonel Humphrey Sibthorp only his successor, Charles had sons and there were but two grandchildren. Of these, the eldest, Coningsby who died in 1932, left no descendants. His brother, Montague, had only daughters, and with the death of his widow in 1937, the Sibthorp name was extinguished. Not long thereafter all the remaining estates were sold. Thus were the fears of Professor Humphrey Sibthorp realised: within four generations the thriving family concern that he had handed down to his son had ceased to exist. Perhaps decline was inevitable. David Cannadine has shown that the trend of history was against the greater gentry.[96] As the agricultural depression of the late nineteenth century was succeeded by the social and political upheavals of the twentieth, the privileges of birth were increasingly less secure. The sorry state of Canwick Hall bears its own testimony to a new world. But maybe there is something more to be said. The early Sibthorps were merchants, scholars and agricultural improvers. These were traits that perhaps reached their zenith in the second Sherardian professor. His descendants, although still acquiring land and income by inheritance, had other interests, or were prepared simply to steward what they already had. When the provisions in the old man's will regarding the development of a mercantile interest were ignored, perhaps the fate of the dynasty was sealed.

Figure 3.6
Recent photograph of the north front of Canwick Hall, the Sibthorp family seat. First occupied in 1730, the hall was substantially rebuilt by Colonel Humphrey Sibthorp in 1811
(Rob Wheeler)

Appendix 3.1

Simplified Sibthorp Family Tree

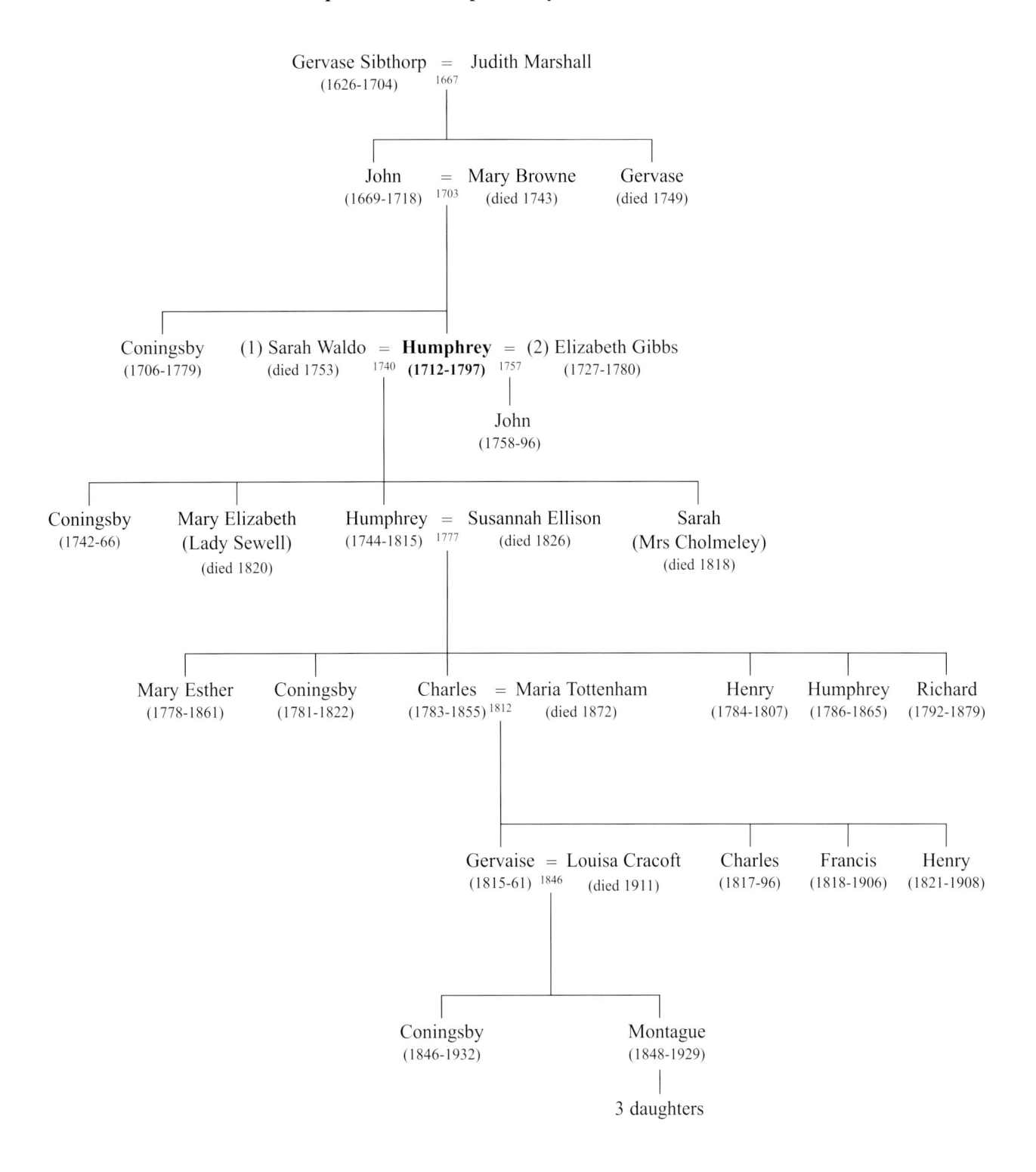

Gervase Sibthorp (1626-1704) = [1667] Judith Marshall

- John (1669-1718) = [1703] Mary Browne (died 1743)
- Gervase (died 1749)

Children of John and Mary Browne:
- Coningsby (1706-1779)
- **Humphrey** (**1712-1797**) = (1) [1740] Sarah Waldo (died 1753); = (2) [1757] Elizabeth Gibbs (1727-1780)
  - John (1758-96) [by Elizabeth Gibbs]

Children of Humphrey and Sarah Waldo:
- Coningsby (1742-66)
- Mary Elizabeth (Lady Sewell) (died 1820)
- Humphrey (1744-1815) = [1777] Susannah Ellison (died 1826)
- Sarah (Mrs Cholmeley) (died 1818)

Children of Humphrey and Susannah Ellison:
- Mary Esther (1778-1861)
- Coningsby (1781-1822)
- Charles (1783-1855) = [1812] Maria Tottenham (died 1872)
- Henry (1784-1807)
- Humphrey (1786-1865)
- Richard (1792-1879)

Children of Charles and Maria Tottenham:
- Gervaise (1815-61) = [1846] Louisa Cracoft (died 1911)
- Charles (1817-96)
- Francis (1818-1906)
- Henry (1821-1908)

Children of Gervaise and Louisa Cracoft:
- Coningsby (1846-1932)
- Montague (1848-1929)
  - 3 daughters

Notes

[1] David Cannadine, *The Decline and Fall of the British Aristocracy,* (Yale, 1990).

[2] See for example, F. M. L. Thompson, *English Landed Society in the Nineteenth Century,* (1963); G. E. Mingay, *The Gentry: The Rise and Fall of a Ruling Class* (1976); J. V. Beckett, *The Aristocracy in England 1600-1914* (1989).

[3] For the impact of the Sibthorps on Canwick see D. Mills, 'Canwick (Lincolnshire) and Melbourn (Cambridgeshire) in Comparative Perspective within the Open-Closed Village Model', *Rural History,* 17.1 (2006) pp.1-22.

[4] M. and J. Gribbin, *Flower Hunters* 2008, p.73.

[5] D. E. Allen, *The Naturalist in Britain* (1976), p.13. Allen is quoting the assessment of the distinguished botanist, James Edward Smith (1759-1828) who in Allen's opinion 'disliked' Sibthorp 'and coveted his position'.

[6] Because the Sibthorp propensity to give successive generations of children the same limited number of names can be confusing, a simplified family tree is included at Appendix 3.1.

[7] A. R. Maddison, *An Account of the Sibthorp Family* (Lincoln, 1896), p.13. Canon Maddison was a family friend and chronicler of the Sibthorps. Much of the biographical information in this study comes from this work.

[8] Chancery document, The National Archives (hereafter TNA) C111/230.

[9] Maddison, *An Account of the Sibthorp Family,* pp.15-16.

[10] In 1638 Gervase's sister Susanna had married Thomas Medley of Belton.

[11] Maddison, *An Account of the Sibthorp Family,* p.25.

[12] *Ibid.,* p.26.

[13] Levett is especially remembered for his pioneering treatment of smallpox.

[14] M. C. Jones, *Notes Respecting the Family of Waldo,* (printed for private circulation), 1863, p.14.

[15] Maddison, *An Account of the Sibthorp Family,* p.42.

[16] I am indebted to Dr Rob Wheeler for this information

[17] Jones, *Notes Respecting the Family of Waldo,* p19.

[18] John Dubois died in 1684. As a prominent political figure in the City and opponent of the Catholic succession his actions incurred the wrath of Charles II. See Jones, *Notes Respecting the Family of Waldo,* pp.19-20.

[19] L. Jessop, 'Notes on Insects, 1692 and 1695 by Charles duBois', *Bulletin of the British Museum, Natural History,* Third Series, 17.1 (May 1989), pp.1-23.

[20] Dubois was not only 'very industrious to procure plants from abroad, but also as generous in communicating whatever his garden would afford, as also many useful observations relating both to their culture and uses.' John Loudon, *Arboretum et Fruticetum Britannicum,* 1 (1838), pp.62-3.

[21] There may have also have been a genetic factor to his love of botany. In 1699 Humphrey's father visited Leyden and recorded in his travel diary, 'a good Physick garden full of medicinall plants….' Maddison, *An Account of the Sibthorp Family,* p.22.

[22] Humphrey and his wife kept in touch with Charlotte Dubois, the unmarried botanist's niece and heir. In 1749 she was godmother to their daughter Charlotte who may have been named in her honour.

[23] A demy is a foundation scholar of Magdalen College (a 'half fellow').

[24] Inscribed on a memorial to Humphrey Sibthorp erected by his son at Instow Parish Church, Devon. Whether he was being ironic or really acknowledging the progress of his brother's medical studies, in writing to his mother in June 1737 Coningsby refers to Humphrey as 'ye Dr.' See Maddison, *An Account of the Sibthorp Family,* p.32.

[25] Maddison, *An Account of the Sibthorp Family,* pp.26 and 30-31. While at Oxford Humphrey was acquiring land in his own right but information is scanty; e.g. in 1744 he conveyed a mortgage for the Talbot Inn, Caistor. (LAO 1 Dixon 1/H/1/5). *A Catalogue of All Graduates in the University of Oxford, 1659-1800* (Oxford, 1801).

[26] In 1768 when he objected to his son's proposed engagement to a girl whose family were 'in trade' the latter responded by accusing his father of hypocrisy, asserting that her family 'with equal reason might call you Dr. Glister Pipe …' Maddison, *An Account of the Sibthorp Family* p.60.

[27] *Ibid.,* p.42. Their first son was named Coningsby in honour of his uncle. His godparents were 'Mr. Waldo, Coningsby Sibthorp, and Mrs. Chase.' Chase was the maiden name of Sarah Sibthorp's mother. Tragically this son died aged twenty-four when a probationary fellow of Magdalen College and is buried in its chapel. He was succeeded as his father's heir by Humphrey, two years his junior.

[28] Coningsby also represented the city in the parliaments of 1747-54 and 1761-68. With the inheritance in 1764 of Skimpans, Gilbert Browne's mansion at North Mimms, the family possessed a seat within convenient travelling distance of London.

[29] Maddison, *An Account of the Sibthorp Family,* p.35.

[30] Bauhin's *Pinax Theatri Botanici* (Illustrated Exposition of Plants) was published in 1623.

[31] Humphrey Sibthorp's letter to the Duke of Newcastle, 14 October 1758, British Library (hereafter BL) Add. MSS. 32884 fol. 370.

[32] Haller taught at the University of Gottingen, Sibthorp carefully noted the Hanoverian association with this recent foundation.

[33] He referred to the celebrated astronomer James Bradley as another fellow of the Academy. Bradley, however, had died in 1762.

[34] Letter to Duke of Newcastle dated 9 February 1765, BL Add MSS. 32965 f. 352. Sibthorp's failure was unexpected. In November 1764 the *London Magazine* announced his appointment to the post (*London Magazine,* 33 (1764) p.599).

[35] Secker, a noted Whig, had only just been elevated to Canterbury, having been since 1737 the Bishop of Oxford and a natural political ally of Sibthorp. There may also have been a family connection. Secker's birthplace was Sibthorpe in Nottinghamshire.

[36] Letter to Lord Hardwick dated 19 October 1758, BL Add MSS. 35595 f. 283.

[37] Letter to the Duke of Newcastle dated 14 October 1758, BL Add MSS. 32884 f. 370.

[38] Letter to Lord Hardwicke dated 14 February 1759, BL Add MSS. 35595 f. 348.

[39] 'The Herbarium of W. Sherard … contains over 14,000 sheets, which are labelled by Sherard and Dillenius: Sibthorp subsequently added the Linnean names in many cases.' S. H. Vines, *An Account of the Herbarium of the University of Oxford* (Oxford, 1897), p.8.

[40] H. W. Lack and D. J. Mabberley, *The Flora Graeca Story, Sibthorp, Bauer and Hawkins in the Levant* (Oxford, 1999), p.16. There is in the Wellcome Library a manuscript in the hand of Humphrey Sibthorp describing fungi found in his brother's copses at Skimpans (MS. 7605/7).

[41] Among Humphrey's scientific correspondents were Carl Linnaeus; John Bartram (1699-1777) an American botanist; Peter Simon Pallas (1741-1811) who worked in Russia; Joseph Banks (1743-1820) whilst he was with Captain Cook; the Swiss naturalist Albrecht von Haller, and the East India Company supercargo John Bradby Blake (1745-1773) who sent him seeds and plants from China. His commonplace book kept at Oxford includes drafts of letters to Guiseppe Monti (Bologna), Angelo Attillio Tilli (Pisa), Adrian van Royen (Leiden) and Johann Gottfried Zinn (Gottingen).

[42] Speaking of the University's general herbarium S. H. Vines a subsequent Sherardian professor specifically mentions Siberian plants sent by Johann Hebenstreit during Sibthorp's professorship. Vine, *An Account of the Herbarium*, p.15. It seems that the Anglican priest Daniel Dumaresq who was chaplain to the Russian factory brought the seeds to him and on returning to Russia he took with him specimens from the Oxford Botanic Garden. See J. H. Appleby, 'Daniel Dumaresq (1712-1805) Promoter of Anglo Russian Science and Culture', *Notes and Records of the Royal Society of London,* 44 (1990), pp.25-50. Correspondents in the Sibthorp's commonplace book include two early travellers in Siberia: Johann Georg Gmelin (he later became director of the Botanical Garden at Tubingen) and Stephan Petrovich Krashennikov.

[43] Lack and Mabberley, *The Flora Graeca Story,* p.16.

[44] G. D. Ehret's letter to J. Ellis, 10 November 1751. See W. T. Stearn and G. D. R. Bridson, *A Bicentenary Guide to the Career and Achievements of Linnaeus and the Collections of the Linnean Society* (1978), pp.93-95.

[45] A. D. Godley, *Oxford in the Eighteenth Century* (1908). *Terrae Filius,* essays satirising Oxford in the early eighteenth century, was the work of Nicholas Amherst.

[46] Sir J. E. Smith relates that Joseph Banks as a student at Christ Church College, finding Sibthorp did not lecture, arranged for the Cambridge Botanist, Israel Lyons, to come to Oxford and in July 1764 some sixty people went to hear him. However, Lyons was a celebrity and there were probably few undergraduates in his audience. It was normal for professors to appoint substitute lecturers and it was Sibthorp not Banks who approached the Cambridge botanists for assistance. See L. B. Glyn, 'Israel Lyons: a short but starry career', *Notes Rec. R. Soc. Lond.,* 56 (2002), pp.275-305. Towards the end of his professorship Sibthorp appointed as deputy the extremely capable George Shaw who did lecture and went on to become curator of natural history at the British Museum. See A. H. T. Robb-Smith, *A Short History of the Radcliffe Infirmary* (Oxford, 1970), p.39.

[47] Letters to Linnaeus, dated October 1747 and John Frederick Gronovius dated 24 March 1753, in *Forget Not Mee and My Garden: Selected Letters of Peter Collinson, 1725-1768* edited by A. Armstrong (Philadelphia, 2002), pp.143 and 166. However, Collinson continued to provide seeds to Sibthorp. See W. Darlington, *Memorials of John Bartram and Humphry Marshall* (Philadelphia, 1849), p.428.

[48] In 1771 Linnaeus wrote to the botanist Anna Blackburne (bap.1726-93) that he knew of her as one of three ladies who 'disputed in 1769 with and triumphed over the botanist in the physic garden at Oxford about the geranium'. A. B. Shteir, Blackburne, Anna, *Oxford Dictionary of National Biography (*Oxford, 2004) [http://www.oxforddnb.com/view/article/2512]. In 1772 Sibthorp wrote to Joseph Banks: '… the Linnean system is the least fallible and most durable but considering the largeness of the field too complex or scientific for such as would read as they run and have not leisure for the most nice enquiry.' Perhaps he was referring to himself? Letter dated 16 February 1772, State Library of New South Wales, Banks Papers Series 72.145. In the judgment of A. H. T. Robb-Smith he 'was probably not much of a scientist, but his reputation for laziness …is not justified.' (*Radcliffe Infirmary,* p.43.)

[49] Letter to Lord Hardwicke dated 19 October 1758; BL Add. MSS 35595 f. 283.

[50] *Ibid.*

[51] Letter to Philip Miller of the Chelsea Physic Garden dated 3 June 1768; LAO HILL 39/7. 'The accounts of the Physic Garden indicate nothing more than unexceptional low-level expenditure particularly after 1757.' Lack and Mabberley, *The Flora Graeca Story,* p.16.

[52] Dawson Turner, *Extracts from the Literary and Scientific Correspondence of Richard Richardson* (Yarmouth, 1835), pp.ix-x. Turner was a wealthy amateur botanist who was seeking to exculpate a later professor (George Williams, appointed in 1796) from accusations of neglecting the archives of his predecessors.

[53] Letter dated 30 April 1762, Darlington, *Memorials of John Bartram and Humphry Marshall,* p.429.

[54] Maddison, *An Account of the Sibthorp Family,* pp.54-55.

[55] *Victoria County History of Hertfordshire,* edited by W. Page, 3 (1912), pp.347-366

[56] According to his memorial in Instow parish church, 'Professor Sibthorp met death … with serenity on the seventeenth day of August 1797, in the 86th year of his age, at Fullincote, the seat of his retirement, in which, among the many others which he in different parts possessed, he most delighted.'

[57] In January 1786 his son John wrote to him from Vienna saying that he would rather be in Instow drinking 'the grape wine made from our own vineyards'. See Lack and Mabberley, *The Flora Graeca Story,* p.33.

[58] Devon Record Office (DRO) QS/1, 1775, No. 367/25. Damages faissant are the right to impound animals entering one's land and spoiling grass or corn.

[59] *Gentleman's Magazine,* 67, (September 1797), p.803. Is there an implied irony? The loss of the *Sibthorpia Europea* (the Cornish moneywort, named by Linnaeus in Humphrey's honour) would not have been grievous; it could easily have been replaced.

[60] According to the *Gentleman's Magazine,* he had 'several children' by his second marriage but only John lived. 67 (September 1797), p.802.

[61] Letter of February 1780 quoted in Lack and Mabberley, *The Flora Graeca Story,* p.18. John Sibthorp had a real interest in medicine and in 1780 was a founder member of the 'Medical Society of Oxford for the promotion of medical knowledge'. Robb-Smith, *Radcliffe Infirmary,* p.39.

[62] Edited by H. E. Salter and M. D. Lobel, *A History of the County of Oxford,* 3 (Oxford, 1954), pp.348-350.

[63] Lincolnshire Archives (hereafter LAO) 2 Sib 4/13, letter dated 23 August 1781.

[64] LAO 2 Sib 4/14, letter dated 23 September 1781.

[65] See catalogue of the Canwick Library, LAO Sib. 1/5-1/11. The Board of Agriculture, established in 1793 to improve agricultural practice, had Arthur Young as its first secretary.

[66] Letter dated 17 June 1797, LAO 2 Sib 4/39. A 1794 report to the Board of Agriculture opines that 'The breed of cattle in the north of Devon is remarkably fine and are perhaps the best in the kingdom.' R. Fraser, *A General View of the Agriculture of the County of Devon With Observations on the Means of its Improvement* (1794), p.66.

[67] A. Grant, *Instow: A History* (Instow, 1999), p.26.

[68] Letter dated 15 July 1785, LAO 2 Sib 4/20; quoted in Lack and Mabberley, *The Flora Graeca Story,* p.31.

[69] The above work and S. Harris, *The Magnificent Flora Graeca* (Oxford, 2007).

[70] Letter from Spa, dated 24 June 1784, LAO 3 Sib 1/5.

[71] Letter from H. Sibthorp to Sir William Pitcairn, president of the Royal College of Physicians, dated 15 December 1783; RCP LEGAC/1001/33. See also Lack and Mabberely *The Flora Graeca Story,* p.20. It is reported that during his interview with the Royal College of Physicians John Sibthorp 'was compelled to divulge the mortifying fact that not one of his few patients had survived his prescriptions.' Robb-Smith, *Radcliffe Infirmary,* p.43.

[72] Keir B. Sterling, John Sibthorp (1758-1796), *Oxford Dictionary of National Biography* (Oxford, 2004). [http://www.oxforddnb.com/view/article/25509]

[73] Lack and Mabberley, *The Flora Graeca Story,* pp.100-104.

[74] They are now at Tapeley Hall the seat of the family that purchased Instow.

[75] Hawkins Papers, Cornwall Record Office (CRO) J3/2/235.

[76] J. R. Bloxam, *A Register of the Presidents, Fellows and Demies of Magdalen College Oxford,* 6 (Oxford, 1853-85) p.229.

[77] I am indebted to the researches of Dennis and Joan Mills set out in their unpublished paper, *Interim Report on the Sibthorp Estates,* 1998.

[78] Letter dated 10 November 1785, LAO 3 Sib 1/9.

[79] *Victoria County History of Hertfordshire,* edited by W. Page, 2 (1908), p.256.

[80] Hertfordshire Record Office (HRO) DEGA/34078 (Bargain and Sale 1 November 1797); the property was acquired by Samuel Gaussen in 1801.

[81] Letter to 'my son Willingham' dated 3 January 1807; LAO 1 Dixon 19/4/1/4. The background to this transaction is unclear. The Caldecott family, to whom the Sibthorps were connected, owned most of the land at Holton-cum-Beckering.

[82] *The Exeter Flying Post,* 35, No.1742 (2 March 1797). In 1808 the Board of Trade survey of Devon agriculture noted that very little oatmeal was manufactured in the county. Charles Vancouver, *A General View of the Agriculture of the County of Devon* (1808), p.179.

[83] W C Oulton, *The Traveller's Guide or English Itinerary,* 2 (1805), p.10.

[84] Letter dated 11 August 1797; LAO 2 Sib 4/42. Although very many of Sibthorp's letters written in old age survive, in the last few years of his life his handwriting became almost illegible.

[85] 'When Instow developed as a watering place, potteries with unsightly piles of clay and smoky kilns were not considered amenities for visitors' and in 1800 the lease for the quayside works was not renewed. See A. Grant, *Instow,* p.128.

[86] J. Russell and J. W. Mylne, *Reports of Cases Argued and Determined in the High Court of Chancery,* 2 (1837), pp.107-116.

[87] Oxford Record Office (ORO) Lease for Six Years, Chap/VII/i/1, 20 October 1810.

[88] A Grant, *Instow,* p.16. Bauer also visited Canwick and painted local scenes, his painting of Lincoln hung in one of the rooms of Canwick Hall (Sibthorp Library Catalogue, LAO 1 Sib. 1/11).

[89] C. Smith, *Report of a Search Made in England for a Property Reported to Belong to the Gibbs's in U.S.A.* (Middlebury, 1848), pp.10-14. Smith also carried out genealogical work but was unable to trace the heirs of John Gibbs. There are intriguing aspects to the disposal of the Instow estate regarding which there is a paucity of documentary record. In Risdon's *Survey of Devon* (1811) appears the confident but incorrect statement that 'the present Colonel Sibthorpe … has lately sold Instow and the adjoining manor of Bickleton, to Richard Preston Esq. an eminent Conveyancer of Lincoln's Inn' (p.424). This might refer to a legal move relating to the entail, Preston represented the Sibthorps in the Chancery case brought by Magdalen College.

[90] C Smith reported that such 'rent strikes' had occurred. The detailed reference to entitlement in the memorial that in 1801 Colonel Humphrey erected for his father at Instow may be significant. The plaque there states that it was by 'the premature death of his son, John Sibthorp' that he 'became chief ward of the extensive royalty, and possessor in fee of considerable estates in the parish of Instow.'

[91] D. and S. Lysons, *Magna Britannia,* 6 (1822), p.292. A. Grant, *Instow,* p.17. In 1821 H. Drake the agent was still writing to Coningsby about the winding-up of Sibthorp interests in the area. Regarding continued requests for funding of the village school Drake told him that he had informed the supplicant that 'as you had disposed of all your property in this part of the county I thought it was rather too much to expect you to continue the school.' LAO 3 Sib 1/14.

[92] North Devon Record Office (NDRO) 1142/T30/11 Assignment of Bickleton Manor, 1823.

[93] She is included in M. B. Ogilvie and J. D. Harvey, *The Biographical Dictionary of Women in Science* (2000).

[94] For Colonel Charles Sibthorp see: Joan and Dennis Mills and Michael Trott, 'New Light on Charles De Laet Waldo-Sibthorp, 1783-1855', *Lincolnshire History and Archaeology,* 36 (2001), pp.25-37.

[95] With the exception of a fishing lodge in Norway.

[96] Cannadine, *Decline and Fall.*

CHAPTER 4

NORTH LINCOLNSHIRE'S COUNTRY CARRIERS

Dan Ellin

But as all sons of Adam must have something or other to say to the rest, and especially to his daughters, this little village carried on some commerce with the outer world; and did it through a carrier.[1]

As Richard Doddridge Blackmore suggested in his novel *Cripps the Carrier: A Woodland Tale*, trade and commerce took place between villages and their surrounding area (both rural and urban) through the medium of the local carrier. Indeed the courtship between the local 'sons of Adam' and the 'daughters' living in the surrounding area may well have been facilitated by the village carrier. This chapter will examine the role of carriers in both rural and urban environments and will examine the importance of carriers in their role as a link between the two communities. It will also attempt to discover whether Lincolnshire's carriers fit the accepted paradigm of the carrier trade in the late nineteenth and early twentieth centuries.

As the county capital, Lincoln was both an important regional urban centre and a rural market town with a busy market held every Friday. Lincoln's manufacturing industry expanded during the latter half of the nineteenth century, and was largely dominated by the production of agricultural machinery and steam engines by firms such as Clayton and Shuttleworth and Ruston, Proctor and Company. The links between the city and rural agriculture are evident. At the Royal Agricultural Society's show held in Lincoln in 1854 it was expected that newly developed agricultural implements would be 'more criticised and less stared at than in Shropshire or Devonshire.'[2] Barry Reay argues that the connections between a village and the town were often stronger than the links between neighbouring villages, and villages may be seen as part of a nucleated urban society.[3] The chapter employs methodologies discussed by Dennis Mills,[4] and cross-sectional quantitative studies of the carrier services drawing upon White's trade directories, from before and after the railway network was established in Lincolnshire. Longitudinal study of villages and businesses is also undertaken. These form the basis of this chapter while the role of the carrier in a wider national context is examined by a study of nineteenth-century literature.

Various transport networks connected Lincoln to other towns and cities as well as the hinterland villages and market towns. In 1850, within living memory, the road from Lincoln was 'extremely bad and heavy'[5], although by 1837 there were over 500 miles of turnpike roads in the county,[6] and carriers and stages frequently came and went from Lincoln. Taking days to reach their destination, long-distance road carriers linked towns, cities and areas nationally through a network of 'carriers' stations', inns and public houses; while short distance county carriers linked market towns with villages in their rural hinterland, usually journeying from their village to the market town on market day and returning the same evening.[7] The River Trent was a barrier to road transport westward from Lincoln between Gainsborough and Newark until Dunham toll bridge was built in 1824.[8] *(Figure 4.1).* However, joined by the Fossdyke navigation at Torksey, the River Trent was part of the wider river, canal and sea transport network linking Lincoln to the rest of the country.[9] This network connected Lincoln with the Humber and Hull in the north, Newark to the south west and Boston via the River Witham to the south east. A branch of the Midland Railway from Nottingham to Lincoln was opened in 1846 and before the end of the century two networks, the Great Northern and the Manchester, Sheffield and Lincolnshire Railway, connected the majority of Lincolnshire's largest towns.[10]

The role of the carrier

During the 1970s, Alan Everitt and his students researched and reconstructed the routes of around 5000 carriers centred on over forty English market

Figure 4.1
Last in Market *by Ralph Hedley*
(Laing Art Gallery, Tyne & Wear Archives & Museums)

towns and urban centres during the nineteenth and early twentieth centuries.[11] However apart from several regional studies, it would appear that this topic has been largely ignored recently.[12] Studying specific locations in the 1880s but also examining carriers' roles in a national context, from the seventeenth to the twentieth century, Everitt's largely quantitative work maintains that the railways led to a decline in long-range carriers, but that local carriers increased in number and prospered until the beginning of the twentieth century.

Everitt maintained that village carriers performed four basic functions,[13] evidence of which can be found in the literature of the period and other primary sources. At least three of these distinct functions can be seen as linking the rural with the urban. Firstly, as agents for people in the villages, carriers bought items from the larger towns as varied as wallpaper, garden plants and tea,[14] which could not be purchased from village tradesmen.

A Lincolnshire carrier was reportedly even entrusted with purchasing a corset for one lady customer,[15] and Thomas Hardy describes how before a carrier was scheduled to leave on his return trip 'errand-boys from the shops beg[an] to arrive with packages, which they fl[ung] into the vehicle'.[16] Born in 1887, Edric, the son of Thomas Hayes a carrier from Ingham, recalled that he and his brothers had to help look after their father's horses and deliver items Thomas had brought from Lincoln to the 'big houses'. He also remembered that the grooms from the 'big houses' would frequently arrive in the morning with parcels to be delivered or with lists of purchases to be made.[17] On one day in May 1889 part of the Glentworth carrier's load consisted of 'a quarter of oats, three or four stones of barley, and a bag of flour on the top of the van.'[18] Unmentioned by Everitt, as well as being rural consumers of items only available from the urban centre, villagers can also be seen to purchase rural produce from other villages via the carriers and urban markets.

Secondly, carriers acted as a link to the railways for their passengers or to deliver bulky goods for further travel. Arranging for her friend to visit, Charlotte Bronte explained in a letter that Wednesday was the only day 'on which there [was] a carrier who c[ould] take charge of [the] luggage from the Keighley Station',[19] and in Hardy's *A Pair of Blue Eyes* Stephen Smith rides with a carrier to the nearest station as 'the carrier's van was so timed as to meet a starting up-train.'[20]

A carrier's third function was as a form of cheap public transport. Carriers were seen as a 'respectable, if somewhat lumbering, class of conveyance, much resorted to by decent travellers not overstocked with money',[21] to both towns and their markets but occasionally also to railway stations for further travel. A Lincolnshire carrier once said he had three fares and explained to a curious passenger; at the bottom of a steep hill on his route 'first class passengers sat tight, second class ones had to get out and walk and the third class had to get out and push!'[22] Although carriers' carts and wagons were distinct from the later omnibuses, it was not unusual for them to provide transport for a great many people. On an ordinary market day Hardy's character 'Burthen, Carrier to Longpuddle' left his stand at the White Hart Inn with a 'burden of fourteen souls all told'.[23] However, at times of fairs, festivals and holidays this number could be more than doubled. A carrier's cart returning to Glentworth from Lincoln on the day of the local May hiring fair overturned near Scampton with 'something like 30 persons being either on top or inside it.'[24] At the inquest into the death of one of the passengers who had been on the roof, the coroner admitted that in 'some instances he ... had heard of as many as 40 persons being in such a van.'[25] Underneath the tilt of Burthen's van Thomas Hardy lists people such as the school master, the parish clerk, the postmistress, a 'world-ignored local landscape-painter' and the village curate,[26] while those named injured in the accident at Scampton were Ann Elison a domestic servant (who later died) and two eighteen year old farm servants, Harry Smith and John Thompson from Glentham.[27]

It seems likely that the carriers' services were used by people from all walks of life who did not have their own transport when they needed (or were able) to go to town. It must be remembered, however, that people also travelled in the opposite direction. During a winter epidemic in Grimsby a local carrier was charged with the carriage of a baby to be cared for by its grandparents in nearby Stallingborough.[28] For many the journey to the nearest market town such as Lincoln was likely to be an anticipated event and, especially on occasions such as the hiring fair, the journey to and from town was as much part of the festivities as the time spent in the town itself. Some of the passengers of the Glentworth carrier which overturned were said to be 'a little elevated in more ways than one',[29] there were eight or nine people on the roof of the van, one 'with a concertina, and another inside with a like instrument',[30] and their 'flow of boisterous fun' was only interrupted by the accident.[31]

The final function of the village carrier discussed by Everitt was to transport rural produce to market in local urban centres. It is likely that this task fell to the wives and daughters of village farmers and smallholders. Thomas Hardy described a carrier's cart that was 'half full of passengers, mostly women',[32] although in some instances the carriers were not always relied on for both legs of the journey. The daughter of a small farmer drove livestock fourteen miles to market in Boston and 'was very thankful of a ride back in the Keal carrier's cart.'[33] Thomas Hardy described a carrier's journey back from market in his novel *The Woodlanders*.

This hour of coming home from market was the happy one, if not the happiest of the week for them. Snugly ensconced under the tilt, they could forget the sorrows of the world, and survey life and recapitulate the incidents of the day with placid smiles.[34]

Although reinforcing the impression of bucolic and 'placid' country-folk, this suggests that the journey to and from market was an important part of rural life and perhaps an anticipated opportunity for social interaction unencumbered by the need for work.

With the exception of providing a link to the railways, the carriers' roles considered by Everitt effectively connected rural and urban communities and both goods and people moved in both directions, but the carrier also performed another function unmentioned by Everitt. Village carriers often acted as a conduit for written and verbal communication. As well as gossip picked up in urban inns and market places and perhaps disseminated in local public houses, the village carrier was also often the local letter carrier. The account book of a North Lincolnshire carrier shows that in 1842 the carrier earned five pounds, fifteen shillings and one penny from the 'letter company' by delivering mail to and from Brigg.[35]

The coming of the railways

As expected, evidence from trade directories shows that the number of village carriers to and from Lincoln increased during the period studied, while long distance carriers were in decline. In 1842, two firms were in competition for long distance trade. J. Slack ran carriers to Birmingham, Leicester, Derby and Hull, and a 'fly van' to London on Mondays, Wednesdays and Fridays, while Hardy, Son and Lawton provided a similar service which also included Nottingham.[36] The multiple routes suggest that unlike the village carriers these were substantial businesses employing several drivers and wagons. However, by 1892, there is no evidence of them in the trade directories, and similarly mid-range carrier services also declined. In 1842 it was possible to send goods from Lincoln by road to Lincolnshire towns within a fifty-mile radius including Boston, Spalding, Spilsby, Louth, Sleaford and Grantham,[37] but by 1892 there were no such services recorded. Lincoln's village carriers flourished, however. White's directory recorded ninety-five carriers stopping at seventy villages in

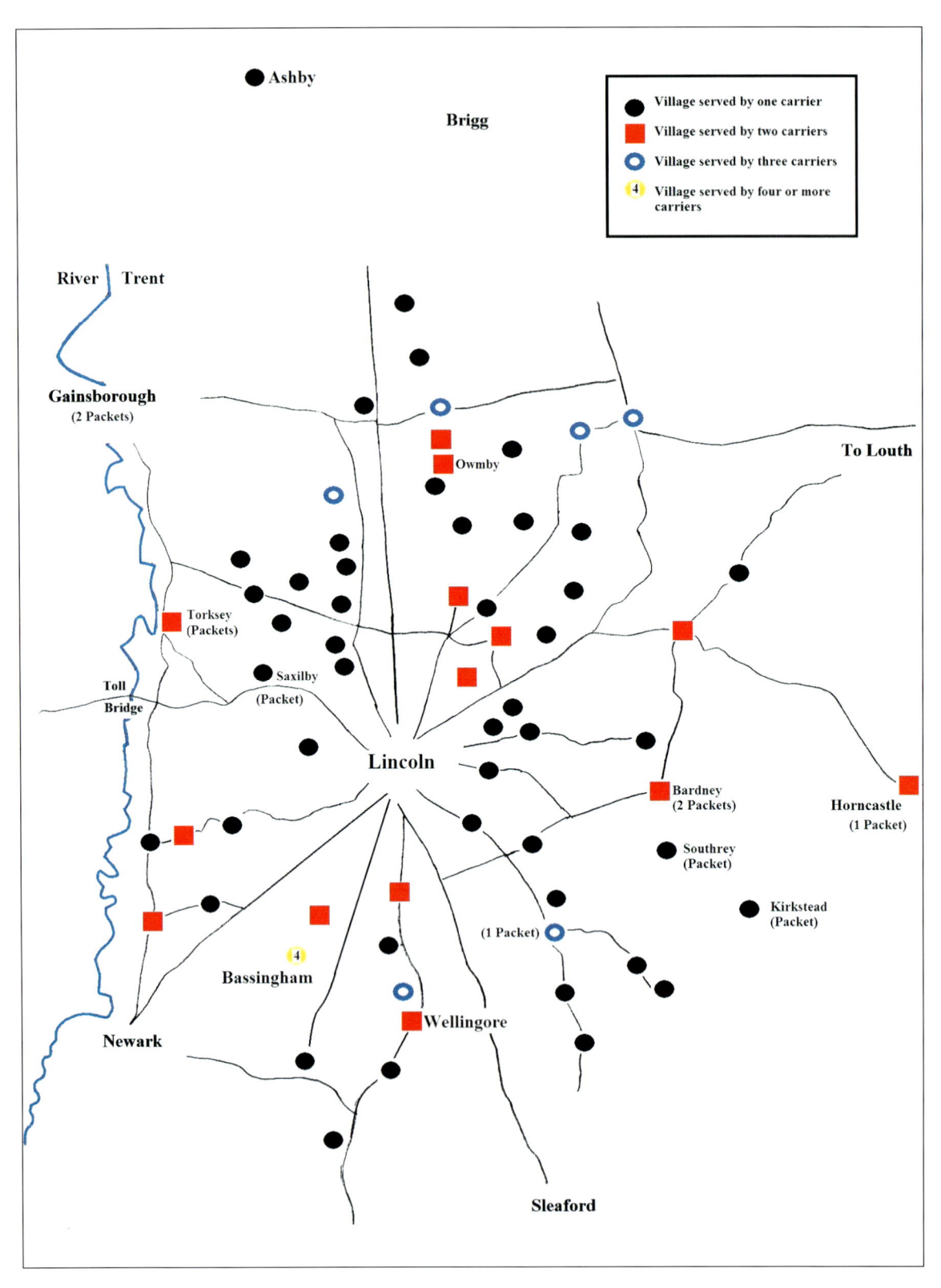

Figure 4.2
Carriers in the Lincoln district, 1842

COUNTRY CARRIERS

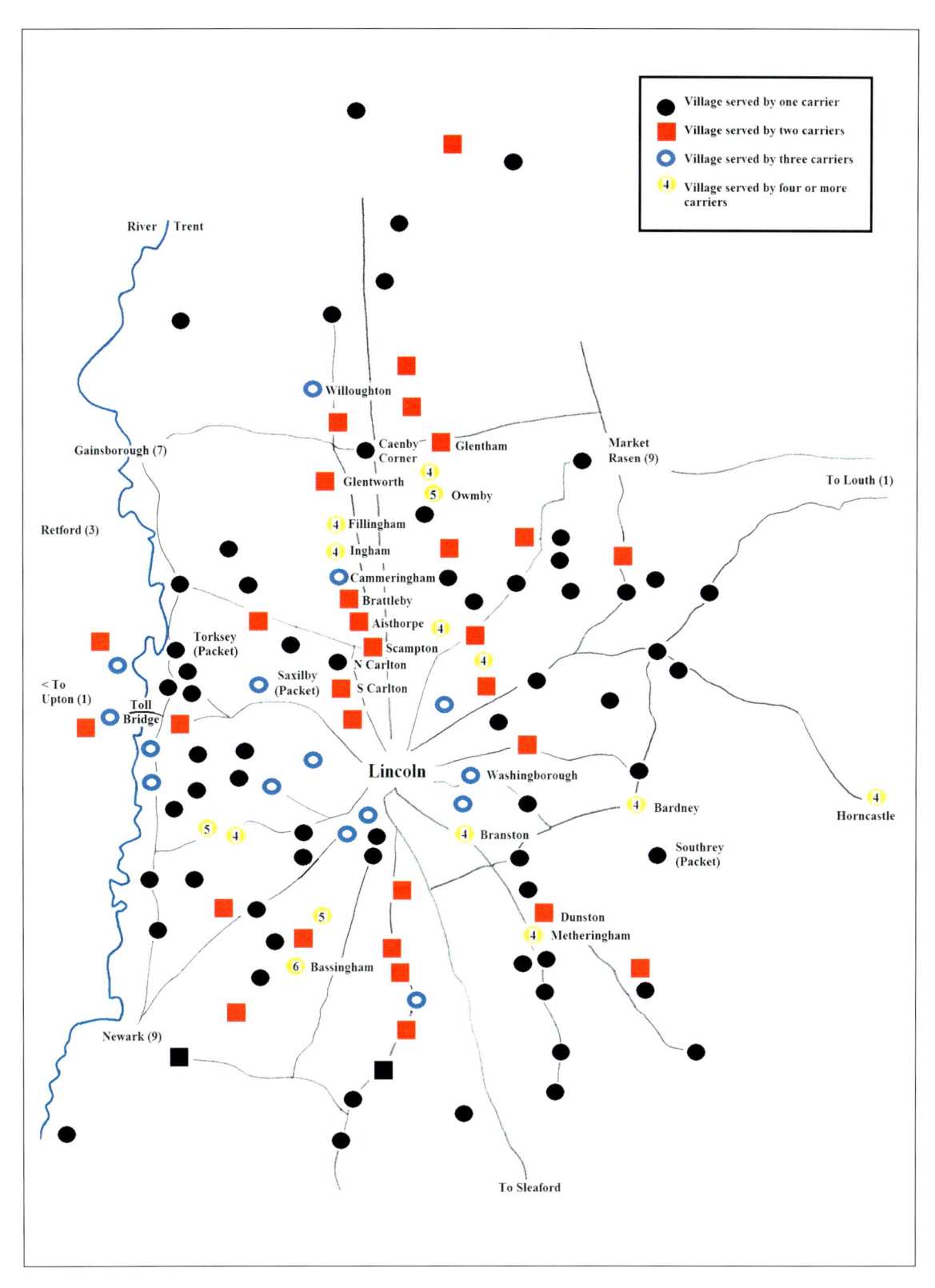

Figure 4.3
Carriers in the Lincoln district, 1892

1842 and this increased to 162 carriers calling at 135 villages in 1892. As plotting the villages visited by the carriers on a map shows, in both the years studied the carriers' journeys extended over a similar sized area *(Figures 4.2 and 4.3)*. However it is clear that in 1892 villagers had much more choice whose service they used. In 1842, the only villages served by three or more carriers were all over five miles from Lincoln, to the north or to the south. In 1892, the increase in the numbers of carriers shows a much more dense spread on the map and several villages within a five-mile radius of Lincoln had a choice of which carrier to use. In 1842, two thirds of the villages were served by only one carrier, but, by 1892, almost half of the villages with a carrier had a choice of two or more. These figures may be misleading, however. It is likely that in both years carriers stopped at villages not listed in the directories.[38] In trade directories, villages without their own service often have the phrase 'carriers pass through.' Increased detail in later directories means that individual carriers' routes can be traced; Thomas Hayes from Ingham ran to The Falcon in Lincoln daily and provided services for those living in Ingham and six other villages, Cammeringham, Brattleby, Aisthorpe, Scampton, North Carlton and South Carlton,[39] but it is likely that the carriers Robert Lee and Samuel May who are listed in 1842 as carriers for Brattleby and Ingham would also have accepted custom from other villages along the way.[40] Passing through villages and hamlets on their way to town, Lincolnshire carriers sounded their approach by 'bugle, whistle or bell', and villagers who required the carriers' services could either place a card in their window or meet them on their arrival.[41]

The evidence shows that carriers' services also became more frequent. In 1842 two carriers offered a daily service, five travelled to Lincoln on Monday, Wednesday and Friday while the majority only came to town on Friday, the market day. By 1892 there were fourteen daily carriers, fifty-five came to Lincoln on three or more days, and forty-four drove to Lincoln on Saturdays including four who travelled on Saturday night.[42] (These were: Barnes to Bassingham, Hunt to Branston, Fowler to Owmby and Woolfit to Washingborough. Although some carriers listed as running daily included the caveat 'if required' in the trade directory descriptions,[43] when the potential number of stops is taken into account, Lincoln's carrier 0service trebled from 120 calls per week to 366 in 1842 and 1892 respectively. Carriers from villages between two towns could increase their trade by visiting them both on alternate days. In the same way as the fictitious carrier John Peerybingle had 'two beats ... one day to the right from [his] house and back again; another day to the left ... and back again',[44] John Redford from Bardney went to Lincoln on Friday and to Horncastle on Saturday.[45]

The distance travelled by the carriers was dictated by the pace of the horse. In nineteenth-century fiction the carrier's horse is frequently described as slow and plodding. Dickens wrote the carrier's horse was 'the laziest horse in the world, I should hope, and shuffled along, with his head down, as if he liked to keep people waiting to whom the packages were directed.'[46] However, the tempo of the horse was the pace of transport before the proliferation of the railways and continued to be so for many afterwards. A carrier's horse or horses may have been thought of as slower than average, but it must be remembered that working twelve or more hours per day perhaps six days a week, the majority of which time was spent between the shafts of the laden cart, would take its toll on the horses.

Often starting early in the morning and arriving home late in the evening, the majority of Lincoln's carriers came from within a fourteen-mile radius, but the furthest distance travelled found in this study was by Mary Richmond the carrier from Ashby, now a suburb of Scunthorpe, who travelled a distance of over twenty-five miles to the Friday market in Lincoln.[47] In order to cover the journey to Lincoln, the carrier from Willoughton set off at 4.30 a.m. to travel the fifteen miles to town.[48] The horses would be rested on arrival in town in one of the inns, while after some refreshment, the carriers themselves would be busy shopping and carrying out their customers' commissions. Carriers could perhaps relax on the homeward leg of their journey because, as Dickens and others have suggested, the horses were so familiar with their routes they could almost have found their way without their drivers.
In Thomas Hardy's *The Woodlanders,* Mrs Dollery's old horse:

> had trodden [the same] road almost daily for twenty years' and 'knew every subtle incline of the seven or eight miles of ground between Hintock and Sherton Abbas - the market-town

to which he journeyed - as accurately as any surveyor could have learned it with a dumpty level.[49]

In 1892, more carriers travelled distances of over ten miles and indeed eleven carriers came from over the Trent; presumably by then it was either economically viable for them to pay the toll, they were exempt, or avoided paying it. In 1914, a carrier from Stallingborough near Grimsby wrote a poem about his fellow carriers and he recorded that 'Bro Dalton... travels from Waltham without paying toll'.[50] Most of Lincoln's carriers 'arrived in Lincoln on Friday morning, market day, and departed from between one to three in the afternoon',[51] while the carrier from Ingham with a journey of eight miles to travel left Lincoln promptly at four o'clock.[52] In this aspect Lincoln's carriers conform to the patterns discovered by Everitt.[53]

However there is evidence of a facet of the carrier trade seemingly ignored in earlier studies. White's 1842 Lincolnshire trade directory lists ten local packets, which presumably performed a similar function to the village carrier with his van, three daily steam packets travelled to Boston, and trading vessels available to be laden with 'goods for all parts' as far afield as Yarmouth and Edinburgh left from wharfs and warehouses on the Brayford weekly.[54] The directory also records that transport to London by water was available from Lincoln, Boston, Grimsby and Gainsborough, and even from the land-locked wolds towns of Louth and Horncastle. Louth was served by a canal,[55] and Horncastle had 'Water Conveyances' via the Horncastle Navigation to 'Hull, Selby' Leeds &c. &c.'[56] However a later edition shows that, by 1892, only the ports of Boston and Grimsby had vessels that regularly sailed to London. This change was rapid. Slater's directory records that in 1851 only Lincoln, Boston and Gainsborough had services by sail or steam to London.[57] The Louth canal had seven locks and there were eleven between Horncastle and the Witham; perhaps as well as the competition from the railways, the number of locks made some of the other journeys uncompetitive. In 1863, William Rainforth was advertising the services of his 'old contract sailing vessels propelled by the steam tugs Hecla and Fury ... to bring goods with extraordinary dispatch ... to and from London Newcastle, Glasgow, Leith, Dundee or any Foreign Port *(Figure 4.4)*.'[58] However, he also advertised his waterproof covers manufacturing business. It could be argued that his transport business fell into decline over the next three decades. By 1872, the company placed more emphasis on sales of agricultural machinery,[59] and, in the 1896 White's Lincolnshire directory, the company was listed as an agricultural machinery manufacturer only.[20] All but three local packets appear to have ceased trading by 1892 and the long-distance trade had gone. Arguably these businesses also suffered from the competition of the railways.

Everitt discovered that the trade directories used for his studies were riddled with inaccuracies and spelling mistakes[61] and this was also evident in Lincolnshire's trade directories.[62] (For example Bardney's John Redford is listed as Retford in the Lincoln entry.) For this project, the information from the pages on Lincoln has been cross-referenced with village entries and a longitudinal analysis conducted using directories by different publishers over

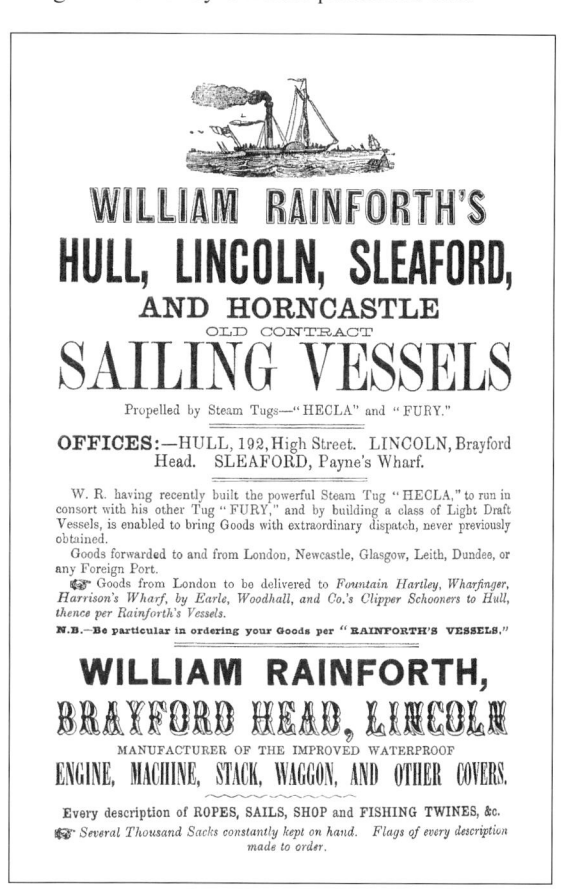

Figure 4.4
Advertisement for Rainforth's Steam Vessels from Morris & Co, Commercial Directory & Gazeteer of Lincolnshire (1863), p.126

**DAVID DICKINSON,
SHRIMPER,**
WHOLESALE AND RETAIL,
FRIESTON SHORE,
And Carrier to the "King's Head" Inn,
BOSTON, every Wednesday and Saturday.

*Figure 4.5
Advertisement for David Dickinson from Morris & Co,
Commercial Directory & Gazeteer of Lincolnshire (1863), p.130*

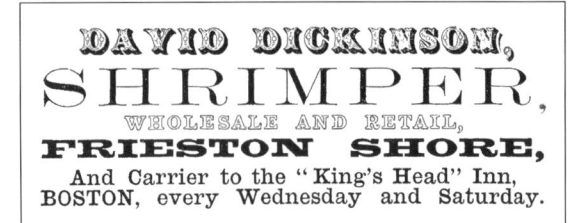

different years. At the start of the period, often only working on market days, many carriers had second occupations, and may not have been recorded as carriers in earlier editions. For example, three of the four carriers serving Bardney listed in the Lincoln entry in 1892 were recorded as having other occupations in the entry for Bardney.[63] John Dawson was a butcher and there were two entries for the surname Knott: James whose business was a beer-house, and Thomas, a boat owner. Thomas Sumner Nelson was a coal dealer and boat owner, and only John Redford was listed as a carrier to Lincoln. These men all performed an important role in their local village community, and arguably having businesses that necessitated them having transport, they may have acted as carrier to augment their income. It should also be borne in mind that this may suggest that there were in fact more carriers than were recorded in earlier trade directories and this may mean that perhaps the increase in the numbers of village carriers was not as large as it at first may seem.

As the period progressed, trade directories became more detailed in some ways. More detailed routes can be deduced, and as has been discussed more stops were recorded in the later directories, but perhaps due to the number of carriers in later editions Christian names were omitted from the Lincoln entry. There were three women carriers travelling to Lincoln in 1842: Mary Jubb, who was also a shopkeeper in Owmby; Alice Thackary from Wellingore and Mary Richmond from Ashby,[64] but a study of the village entries in 1892 highlights only one, Jane Bool, who ran to Lincoln from Metheringham four days a week calling at Dunston and Branston.[65] In Lincolnshire, as in other counties studied, a small proportion of carriers were female. There were between three and five female carriers in Nottinghamshire during the period,[66] and Everitt discovered 'three redoubtable matrons'[67] in Leicestershire. Hardy sketched the character of Mrs Dollery, a carrier in his novel *The Woodlanders* but it is undoubtedly a leap of the imagination to give the women carriers in Leicestershire the epithet 'redoubtable' with as little evidence as a name in a directory.

Flight from the land

While the competition from the railways, as discussed by Alan Everitt, may explain the decline in long range carriers between towns and cities, and the increasing accuracy of trade directories as the nineteenth century progressed may have recorded more carriers than earlier editions, the phenomenon commonly known as the 'flight from the land' may also help to explain the apparent increase in local village carriers.[68] The term describes the changing relationship between urban and rural, characterised by a decline in rural trades and crafts, and a fall in rural population largely due to the depopulating of rural areas and migration to urban centres.[69] This is explained by expanding rural horizons driven by technological advances and education and can be seen in Lincolnshire as Lincoln's population grew from 13,806 recorded in the 1841 census to 37,044 in 1891. Village populations have rarely remained static. Research has shown that rural populations were fluid and family names appear and disappear in census enumerators' returns as people migrate in and out. Village carriers may have helped families and individuals to move their possessions but also may have provided the necessary link to alert people to alternative employment. As has been discussed earlier the carrier's cart that overturned at Scampton had up to thirty people on board, some of whom at least were domestic or farm servants, returning from Lincoln's hiring fair. The novel *Cripps the Carrier: A Woodland Tale* hints that a certain amount of courting and romance may have been facilitated by the village carrier, perhaps on such occasions. Witnesses at the inquiry in to the accident included people from the adjacent villages of Glentworth, Glentham and Caenby Corner.[70] There may be many reasons for this, and while the passengers' motives can not be gleaned from the newspaper, it may be seen as evidence that people sometimes chose to use a carrier other than the carrier local to their village. The carriers from their respective villages might not have been running that day, perhaps a couple from separate villages had chosen to ride together, or

Figure 4.6
Stow, Sturton and Gainsborough carrier's cart
(Copyright Mr Reading)

given that they were returning from a day at the hiring fair, it is possible that individuals had missed the carrier serving their villages and had by necessity settled for a carrier going to the next nearest village rather than be stranded or walk the entire way from Lincoln. Whatever the reason it would seem that as well as being familiar figures in the town, carriers were well known by people of neighbouring villages or of villages through which they passed.

Village shopkeepers relied on carriers to keep their shelves stocked. In 1854 Mathew Hackfath, a carrier from Binbrook, recorded delivering 'christes of soape', 'bags of soder', 'hampers of jugs and potts', 'barills of treakle'... 'half-tones of coles' [and] 'shugar loves' for the local village grocer.[71] However, after the so called golden age of farming in the middle years of the century, an agricultural depression led to a decline in rural production. During the later half of the nineteenth century the countryside gradually changed from being the site of production to one of consumption.[72] In 1851, 18 per cent of the male rural population aged between twenty and sixty-four were employed in the major rural trades and crafts of baker, blacksmith, bricklayer, butcher, carpenter, mason, publican, shoemaker, shopkeeper and tailor rather than in agriculture directly.[73] Whether these traditional trades declined due to a fall in rural population or due to increased competition from industrially mass-produced items available in the urban centres, it is likely that in villages that had lost some or all of these trades by the 1890s, any remaining rural demand for such items was of benefit to the village carrier. Towards the end of the century, as Everitt discussed, 'for anything unusual ... you usually had to visit the country town,'[74] and it is likely that surviving local tradesmen relied on carriers to keep them supplied with their raw materials.[75] The village carrier could be relied on either to take consumers to the urban centre, or by acting as agents, purchase luxuries or items previously available from rural tradespeople for their customers. In Lincolnshire it was also the role of the carrier to deliver fish to inland communities both urban and rural. According to the surviving Lincolnshire carriers' accounts book a large proportion of the business transported by the carrier in the vicinity of Brigg consisted of 'fish parshills'.[76]

If the phenomenon known as the 'flight from the land' is accepted and village communities did indeed become 'mere satellites of the towns, increasingly reliant on urban sources for their goods and services',[77] such dependence largely took place through the village carriers. The carrier played an important role in connecting urban centres such as Lincoln with the hinterland villages and it must be remembered the movement of goods and people flowed in both directions. As businesses, carriers would be more economically viable if they were loaded and being paid on both legs of their journey. During the period studied, the growing population in Lincoln was an expanding market for rural produce grown in smallholdings as well as large scale agriculture, and perhaps because of the decline of rural trades but in spite of their declining numbers, the rural population represented an expanding market as consumers of urban goods. As the go-between connecting the rural and urban spheres village carriers flourished, their numbers increased and they provided more frequent services as it became profitable for them to do so.

The village carrier

Previous studies have lamented the scarcity of evidence of the lives of carriers other than trade directories. Everitt was fortunate to have discovered a carrier's note book in the archives in Leicestershire but then appears to have made little use of it.[78] Of course the lack of surviving notebooks does not mean that carriers did not keep records but may only indicate that few survived or were deemed important enough to be preserved. The survival in the Lincolnshire Archives of the accounts note book of the carrier who travelled to and from Brigg is a rarity, but several impressions about the carrier that filled it in can be inferred. Wages varied widely during the nineteenth century and from region to region, but at a time when on average an agricultural labourer's annual income can be seen to have been between £24 and £40 a year,[79] the Brigg carrier recorded that including the money he earned from the 'letter company', he grossed only £17 18s. 1d. between September 1841 and September 1842. From this it can be deduced that either this carrier had another occupation or that he did not record every transaction in his accounts. Both possibilities are likely. There are no passenger fares recorded among the list of items carried such as 'Barill of Oyl', 'sack of tatos' and even 'carigg of Dogg', and interestingly there does not appear to be a weekly pattern of entries in the notebook. The carrier recorded a small sum of money for the carriage of various 'parshills' on every day of August 1841, but in November of the same year there are no entries against thirteen separate days. This suggests that perhaps the carrier recorded only payments for consignments he delivered on credit. Despite the unorthodox spelling, the author obviously received an education and the book was completed in ink in a careful copper-plate hand. The Brigg carrier should probably be regarded as upper working class or lower middle class.

As until only recently such note books may not have been deemed worthy of preservation, Everitt suggests that despite the rarity of the survival of such records from the nineteenth century, only a small proportion of carriers may have been illiterate and relied on their memory,[80] and the literature of the period corroborates this. Charles Dickens created the character of John Peerybingle the village carrier in his short story *The Cricket on the Hearth.* From the text it can be concluded that the carrier had received an education. Returning home late in the evening Peerybingle is met by his wife, Dot holding their baby, and referring to the practice in arithmetic of carrying the tens (or shillings and pence) over to the next column, he jokes that the pair are 'a dot and carry'.[81] It can also be inferred from the text that Peerybingle is successful and by many definitions may be seen as lower middle class; he employs a boy to assist him in his trade, and a maid to help his wife with the house and the baby.[82] They regularly socialise and 'Pic-Nic' with their friends,[83] and imagining a dynasty of carriers and a new cart with '"Peerybingle Brothers" on the tilt'[84] he dreams of his business expanding. In R. D. Blackmore's *Cripps the Carrier,* Zacchary Cripps hails from a line of carriers,[85] but in Lincolnshire there is little evidence of family businesses continuing over the fifty-year period studied. In the trade directories there are only three carriers' surnames that are consistent for their particular villages in both years examined;[86] Brown from Fillingham, Martin from Bassingham and Jubb from Owmby. Recourse to census enumerators' returns could perhaps confirm these people are related. Again, showing the problems of relying on sometimes inaccurate trade directories, the newspapers revealed that at the time of the crash at Scampton the carrier's cart from Glentworth was being driven by John Sims and that the cart was the property of his father. Over a shorter time frame there is other occasional evidence of the longevity of a family business. William Hayes was a carrier in Ingham in 1876,[87] and in the 1890s Thomas Hayes carried goods between Ingham and Lincoln daily while William Hayes junior travelled to Gainsborough on Tuesdays and Lincoln on Fridays and Saturdays.[88] It could be argued that these few exceptions to a general lack of continuity among carriers is evidence of the rapid changes rural society experienced in the second half of the nineteenth century as part of the flight from the land. However carriers continued to be important and popular people in both rural and urban society. In the 1914 poem by the Stallingborough carrier, Cox recounts that one of his colleagues, 'Bro. Davy', was a 'Methodist preacher' who 'deliver[ed] the message both faithful and true', and that Joe Humberstone who ran from Ashby to Grimsby 'for thirty-three years' was 'highly respected in village and town'.[89] At the inquest into the death of the passenger following the accidental overturning of the carrier's cart at Scampton, the coroner read letters testifying to the 'good character and competence' of the driver, John Sims, from several people including his local vicar.[90]

The village carrier, the town and the railway

On their arrival in Lincoln one of the Hayes' carriers from Ingham stopped at The Falcon while the other waited at The King's Arms. As Alan Everitt noted, 'Inns were the obvious places to furnish the carriers with the facilities they required,'[91] food and drink for the carrier and stabling and feed for the horses, and in the nineteenth century carriers and public houses were irrevocably linked. Carriers transporting some of the Queen's possessions between Buckingham Palace and Windsor were robbed when they 'stopped at a familiar public-house to regale themselves, as carriers are wont to do,'[92] and wagoners' liking for beer was recorded in folk songs, such as 'The Jolly Waggoner':

It's a cold stormy night
We got wet through our clothes;
We'll bear it with contentment
Until we reach the inn,
And then we will get drinking
With the Landlord and his friends.[93]

In 1842 the most popular inns in Lincoln for the carriers were The Queen, The Black Goats and The King's Arms. But with the expansion of the industry by 1892 eleven inns in the centre of Lincoln served as stations for the majority of the carriers listed. On Fridays, Lincoln's market day, forty-three carriers waited at The Black Goats before they began their return journeys, and these would be joined on the High Street by up to seventy-eight other carriers who patronised competing establishments. It would appear that traffic congestion and the struggle to find parking places is not a new phenomenon. On certain days Lincoln's High Street must have resembled Hardy's description of 'Casterbridge':

> [M]ovables occupied the path and roadway to a perplexing extent. First the vans of the carriers in and out of Casterbridge ... and many other towns and villages round. Their owners were numerous enough to be regarded as a tribe, and had almost distinctiveness enough to be regarded as a race. Their vans had just arrived, and were drawn up on each side of the street in close file, so as to form at places a wall between the pavement and the roadway.[94]

The village carriers were familiar figures to the town's errand boys and brought extra business to the

Figure 4.7
Advertisement for the Black Bull from Morris & Co,
Commercial Directory & Gazetteer of Lincolnshire *(1863), p.14*

shops of the urban centres. The canvas tilts of the carriers' carts were even utilised as advertising space for urban businesses where the message could be read by potential customers in both the urban and rural market. The carriers' carts were often 'plastered with soap or tea posters',[95] while Joshua Winn the carrier from North Thoresby was photographed alongside his cart which displayed an advertisement for 'Pure Drugs, Patent Medicines, Wines & Spirits at store prices. FRESHNEY'S Victoria St Grimsby'[96]

However, while the village carriers apparently flourished the coming of the railways must have affected other local businesses to some extent. In 1863 a selling point in the advertisement for The Black Bull was that the inn was 'within a few minutes walk of the Railway Stations' took precedence over the facilities of 'Superior Stabling, Loose Boxes and Lock-up Coach Houses.'[97] In the same year the railway agents Chaplin and Horne offered the services of:

GOODS RECEIVED and FORWARDED
to and from
London, Birmingham, Bristol, Leeds,
Bradford, Leicester, Sheffield, Nottingham,
Newark, Coventry, Leamington, Wolverhampton,
Worcester, &c., &c., and nearly all parts of the
United Kingdom.[98]

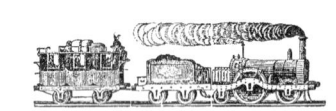

Figure 4.8
Advertisement for Chaplin & Horne from Morris & Co,
Commercial Directory & Gazeteer of Lincolnshire (1863), p.10

By 1892, however, the railway in Lincolnshire had largely replaced the services provided by long-distance carriers, trading vessels and shipping. The railway companies had goods offices and agents at the stations and there were also independent goods agents.[99] But, as Everitt pointed out: 'local traffic on the roads was certainly not brought to an end by the railways. It could not have been, if only because most rural communities had no railway station.'[100] This seems to be true in Lincolnshire in 1892, where only 20 per cent of the villages studied had a railway station, but as these villages also had their own carriers this also suggests that the two forms of transport were not always in direct competition with each other. The road from Lincoln to the villages along the escarpment north of the town remained busy. From the reports of the carrier's cart that overturned at Scampton it can be inferred that on that evening the Glentworth carrier who had the accident was following the carrier from Fillingham while there was another 'horse and cart coming on behind.'[101]

It must be remembered that the village carriers also frequently offered a door to door delivery service for their customers. In Ireland, Elizabeth Smith wrote, 'Tom Quin, the carrier, is almost ruined by having advanced money for the little shopkeepers up and down the country as was his custom, and he cannot get repaid.'[102] Indeed, as was the case in other areas, some Lincolnshire carriers may have offered villagers credit. As has been discussed earlier, it is likely that the carrier serving Brigg did this. His accounts book shows that in some months he received remuneration for his services almost every day but in November 1841 he earned only nine shillings from thirteen daily entries, while in December he recorded being paid only after Christmas.[103] As well as the flexibility of road transport when compared to a rail network limited to a finite number of stations, over short journeys carriers probably offered a cheaper and less complicated alternative to the railways. In the book of the same name, David Copperfield travels to Yarmouth by carrier,[104] and in Lincolnshire there is evidence that by connecting from one carrier to another, village carriers even enabled the rural and urban poor or working classes to travel to other towns or villages. Although the railway line between the two towns opened in 1848,[105] Mrs N. Chappell travelled by carrier from Louth to Cleethorpes to

Figure 4.9
Carriers' carts waiting in the Bull Ring, Grimsby, c.1909
(Copyright Grimsby Telegraph)

enter service aged fourteen and, at the end of the harvest, Mrs H. Wilson travelled for over twelve hours from one village to another via Grimsby and two different carriers.[106] Sometime before the First World War, Dennis Mills's father travelled by carrier's cart the fourteen miles from Lincoln to Willoughton to stay with his grandmother during the school holidays.[107] Even after the turn of the century, the carriers allowed people not only to make journeys connecting places not served by the railways but also, perhaps more importantly, continued to provide a cheaper (if more time consuming) alternative to them. In other cases owing to the economies of scale, carriers acting as agents between their customers and the railway companies could offer cheaper rates than if a customer approached the railway company directly.

A customer wrote to *The Times* complaining that he paid one shilling and ten pence carriage for a parcel but later discovered if he had entrusted it to a carrier it would have been carried on the same train at a cost of only a shilling.[108]

It has been argued that during the earlier period of industrialisation, at the start of the nineteenth century, the transport industry 'was dynamic in structure, ever responsive to the shifts and pressures of the economy, and of specific transport requirements',[109] and it would appear that in this study the village and town carriers were similarly responsive. Arguably over a long distance the railways offered a cheaper and faster service than the carriers' wagons, vans and fly vans, but local village carriers serving their immediate villages and the nearest urban centres thrived. Although he lived frugally Barkis the carrier in Dickens' *David Copperfield* amassed a fortune of nearly £3000 before he died.[110] Carriers can be seen as belonging to the lower middle classes, their routes were businesses and as such they were subject to competition and the market forces of nineteenth-century *laissez-faire* capitalism. Village carriers prospered because they offered a service that the railways could not provide and the two services existed side by side until a newer form of transport offered an alternative in the early twentieth century.

Lincoln's carrier trade did conform to the pattern posited by Everitt after his studies in Leicestershire. There is evidence in the literature of the period supporting the four functions of the village carrier described by Everitt, and in Lincolnshire the long- range carriers did indeed decline during the period immediately after the arrival of the railways. Owing to the unreliability of especially the earlier trade directories, the increase in number of village carriers might not be as large as it at first seems. It can be seen that, during the period studied, the short-distance local carriers serving the villages did indeed flourish and increase in number, and even coexisted with railway stations in some villages. Although ignored by Everitt in Leicestershire, similar changes occurred to the water transport industry in Lincolnshire. The medium- and long-range carriage of goods along the navigable waterways and by sea atrophied and the number of local packets was halved during the period studied. Carriers tended to be individuals from the lower middle classes, business men and women who provided their services to people from all walks of life, providing transport for working-class domestic and farm servants, and acting as agents for the people in the 'big houses.' Many of the functions performed by Lincolnshire carriers have been shown to connect effectively the central market town to the rural hinterland and they were even a link between coastal and inland communities. Carrying passengers, items to market and, while acting as agents, parcels and goods in both directions, carriers effectively connected the two spheres, sometimes even delivering the post and being bearers of news. The journey to and from town was likely to have been an important social event for members of the rural community, but the carrier's cart was an equally familiar sight in an urban high street setting, especially on market day. Photographs show that if not advertising urban businesses on the tilts of their vans, many carts had the carrier's name and village stencilled on the canvas. Such advertisements represent an important link between the two spheres. As well as delivering rural produce to the urban market, as rural populations declined, carriers also enabled villagers to purchase necessities and luxuries, including goods and services perhaps previously available from local village crafts and tradesmen, from the urban centre. The change in the carrier industry was a symptom of the changes occurring in wider society, rural and urban, and carriers were a crucial link between the rural hinterland and the urban centre.

Notes

[1] Richard Doddridge Blackmore, *Cripps the Carrier: A Woodland Tale* (1876), p.1.

[2] *The Lincolnshire, Boston and Spalding Free Press,* 25 July 1854, p.3.

[3] Barry Reay, *Rural Englands* (Basingstoke, 2004), p.17.

[4] Dennis Mills, *Rural Community History from Trade Directories* (Aldenham, 2001) pp.78-82.

[5] John Greenfield Ruddock and R. E. Pearson, *The Railway History of Lincoln* (Lincoln,1974), p.33.

[6] Neil Wright, 'Turnpikes and stage coaches' in *An Historical Atlas of Lincolnshire,* edited by Stewart Bennett and Nicholas Bennett (Chichester, 2001), p.78.

[7] Alan Everitt, 'Country carriers in the nineteenth century', *Journal of Transport History,* 3.3 (1979), p.179.

[8] Ruddock and Pearson, *Railway History,* p.34.

[9] Neil Wright, 'Navigable waterways and canals' in *An Historical Atlas of Lincolnshire,* edited by Stewart Bennett and Nicholas Bennett (Chichester, 2001), p.80.

[10] Neil Wright, 'Railways and docks' in *An Historical Atlas of Lincolnshire,* edited by Bennett and Bennett, p.112.

[11] Everitt, 'Country carriers' *Transport History,* p.188.

[12] See: Susan Cracknell, 'Nottinghamshire county carriers in the late nineteenth century' *Transactions of the Thoroton Society of Nottinghamshire,* 88 (1985 for 1984), pp.76-88; Kathryn Moore, 'Carrier routes in the northeast of Scotland 1803-1914: development and change in a service' *Scottish Geographical Journal,* 119:4 (2003), pp.325-40; and K. Morgan, *County Carriers In The Bristol Region In The Late Nineteenth Century* (Bristol, 1986).

[13] Everitt, 'Country carriers', *Transport History,* pp.181-183.

[14] Alan Everitt, 'Town and country in Victorian Leicestershire: the role of the village carrier' in *Perspectives in English Urban History,* edited by Alan Everitt (1973), p.219.

[15] N. C. Birch, 'Binbrook carriers', *Lincolnshire Industrial Archaeology,* 7.4 (1972), p.61.

[16] Thomas Hardy, *Life's Little Ironies* (1874), p.189.

[17] Edric Hayes quoted in, *Village Life with Particular Reference to Ingham: an Account of Information Gathered During 20 2-hour Classes At Ingham County School, September 1975 to March 1976,* edited by Ivy Ashcroft. Unpublished (1976), p.25.

[18] *Lincolnshire Chronicle* (hereafter *LC*) 28 June 1889, p.7.

[19] Charlotte Bronte., 'Letter from Charlotte Bronte to Ellen Nussey, May14 1847', in *The Letters of Charlotte Bronte: With a Selection of Letters by Family and Friends, Vol.1: 1829-1847,* edited by M Smith (Oxford, 1995), p.627.

[20] Thomas Hardy, *A Pair of Blue Eyes* (1873) (Oxford, 2005 edition), p.96.

[21] Hardy, *Life's Little Ironies,* p.189.

[22] W. E. R. Hallgarth, 'The village carrier', *Lincolnshire Life,* 3.2 (1963), p.29.

[23] Hardy, *Life's Little Ironies*, pp.189-190.

[24] *Lincoln, Rutland and Stamford Mercury* (hereafter *LRSM*) 28 June 1889, p.5.

[25] *LC,* 24 May 1889, p.6.

[26] Hardy, *Life's Little Ironies*, pp.189-190.

[27] *LC,* 24 May 1889, p.6.

[28] Hallgarth, 'The village carrier', p.30.

[29] *LRSM,* 24 May 1889, p.5.

[30] *Ibid.*

[31] *LC,* 24 May 1889, p.6.

[32] Thomas Hardy, *The Woodlanders* (1887) (1972 edition), p.4.

[33] Hallgarth, 'The village carrier' p.30.

[34] Thomas Hardy, *The Woodlanders,* p.4.

[35] Unpublished carrier's accounts book, LAO NEL/10/24/2.

[36] William White, *History, Gazetteer and Directory of Lincolnshire 1842* (Sheffield, 1842), pp.142-143.

[37] White, *Lincolnshire* (1842), pp.142-143.

[38] D. R. Mills, *Rural Community History from Trade Directories,* p.80.

[39] William White, *History, Gazetteer and Directory of Lincolnshire 1892-3* (Sheffield, 1892), pp.580-581.

[40] White, *Lincolnshire* (1842), p.142.

[41] Hallgarth, 'The village carrier', p.29.

[42] White, *Lincolnshire* (1892), pp.580-581.

[43] E. R. Kelly, *The Post Office Directory of Lincolnshire* (1876), p.206.

[44] Charles Dickens, 'The cricket on the hearth' in *The Christmas Books* (1999 edition), p.227.

[45] White, *Lincolnshire* (1892), p.580. and p.123.

[46] Charles Dickens, *David Copperfield* (1850) (1994 edition), p.34.

[47] White, *Lincolnshire* (1842), p.142.

[48] Hallgarth, 'The village carrier', p.28.

[49] Hardy, *The Woodlanders,* p.3. See also Charles Dickens, *David Copperfield,* p.34.

[50] Birch, 'Some of Grimsby's carriers', p.32.

[51] White, *Lincolnshire* (1842), p.141.

[52] *Village Life with Particular Reference to Ingham,* edited by Ivy Ashcroft, p.15.

[53] Everitt, *Perspectives in English Urban History,* p.184.

[54] White, *Lincolnshire* (1842), p.141.

[55] Wright, 'Navigable waterways' p.80.

[56] White, *Lincolnshire* (1842), p.264.

[57] Slater, *Slater's Directory of Lincolnshire 1851* (1851), p.47.

[58] Morris and Co, *Commercial Directory & Gazetteer of Lincolnshire: subscriber's copy 1863* (Nottingham, 1863), p.126.

[59] William White, *History, Gazetteer and Directory of Lincolnshire 1872* (Sheffield, 1872), p.18.

[60] Kelly's Directories Ltd, *Kelly's Directory of Lincolnshire* (1896), p.375.

[61] Everitt, *Perspectives in English Urban History,* p.221.

[62] White, *Lincolnshire* (1892), p.580. and p.123.

[63] *Ibid.*

[64] White, *Lincolnshire* (1842), pp.142-143.

[65] White, *Lincolnshire* (1892), p.686.

[66] Cracknell, *Nottinghamshire County Carriers,* p.80.

[67] Everitt, *Perspectives in English Urban History,* p.229.

[68] See: W. A. Armstrong, 'The flight from the land' in *The Victorian Countryside, Volume One,* edited by G. E. Mingay (1981), pp.118-133.

[69] G. E. Mingay, *Rural Life in Victorian England* (Stroud, 1990), p.193. See also P.A. Graham, *The Rural Exodus: The Problem of the Village and the Town* (1892).

[70] *LRSM,* 28 June 1889, p.5.

[71] Matthew Hackfath's Account book quoted in: Hallgarth, 'The village carrier', pp.28-31

[72] Mingay, *Rural life,* pp.178-179 and 184-185.

[73] Reay, *Rural Englands,* p.26.

[74] Everitt, *Perspectives in English Urban History,* p.223.

[75] Rodney H. R. E. Clapson and Darren M. Stockdale, *The Later History of Barton-on-Humber: Part Nine: Roads, Coaches and Carriers in Barton before 1900* (Barton-on-Humber, 2009), p.63.

[76] Unpublished carrier's accounts book, LAO NEL/10/24/2.

[77] Mingay, *Rural life,* pp.184-185.

[78] Everitt, *Perspectives in English Urban History,* pp.218-219.

[79] See Reay, *Rural Englands,* pp.42-47 and Mingay, *Rural Life,* p.74.

[80] Everitt, 'Country carriers' *Transport History,* p.180.

[81] Dickens, 'The cricket on the hearth', p.192. See also Blackmore, *Cripps the Carrier,* p.3.

[82] Dickens, 'The cricket on the hearth'. p.195.

[83] Dickens, 'The cricket on the hearth', p.226.

[84] Dickens, 'The cricket on the hearth', p.212.

[85] Blackmore, *Cripps the Carrier,* p.3.

[86] See White, *Lincolnshire* (1892), pp.580-581 and White, *Lincolnshire* (1842), pp.142-143.

[87] Kelly, *Post Office Directory,* p.206.

[88] White, *Lincolnshire* (1892), p.500.

[89] N. C. Birch, 'Some of Grimsby's carriers' p.32.

[90] *LRSM,* 28 June 1889, p.5.

[91] Everitt, *Perspectives in English Urban History,* p.227.

[92] Anon. 'The Sublime and the Ridiculous' *The Observer,* 24 March 1856, p.3.

[93] 'The Jolly Waggoner', sung by Edward Dowden (73) at East Huntspill, Somerset, 19 January 1907 in: Cecil Sharp's *Collection of English Folk Songs, Volume Two,* edited by M. Karpeles (Oxford, 1974), p.257.

[94] Thomas Hardy, *The Mayor of Casterbridge* (1886) (1997 edition), pp.59-60.

[95] Hallgarth, 'The village carrier', p.29.

[96] Photograph in Judith Glover, 'The carrier's cart' *Lincolnshire Poacher* 1.3 (Autumn 2000), p.19.

[97] Morris and Co, *Commercial Directory & Gazetteer of Lincolnshire* (1863), p.14.

[98] Morris and Co, *Commercial Directory & Gazetteer of Lincolnshire* (1863), p.10.

[99] White, *Lincolnshire* (1892), p.580.

[100] Everitt, *Perspectives in English Urban History,* p.217.

[101] *LRSM,* 28 June 1889, p.5. See also *LRSM* 24 May 1889. p.5. and *LC* 24 May 1889, p.6.

[102] *The Irish Journals of Elizabeth Smith 1840-1850,* edited by D. Thompson, and M. McGusty (Oxford, 1980), p.220.

[103] Unpublished carrier's accounts book, LAO NEL/10/24/2.

[104] Dickens, *David Copperfield,* p.34.

[105] Wright, 'Railways and docks', p.113.

[106] Birch, 'Some of Grimsby's carriers', p.33.

[107] Mills, *Rural Community History,* p.74.

[108] Letter to the Editor of *The Times, The Times,* 30 April 1844, p.7.

[109] *Transport in the Industrial Revolution,* edited by Michael. J. Freeman, and Derek. H. Aldcroft (Manchester, 1983), p.3.

[110] Dickens, *David Copperfield,* p.368.

CHAPTER 5

THE ALEHOUSES OF KESTEVEN
Control of the trade of licensed victualling 1755-1831[1]

Wendy Atkin

Introduction

The golden age of the public drinking-house in England is considered to be the late nineteenth century, and is inextricably linked to the effects of the so-called industrial and agricultural revolutions, but the Victorian public house had its roots deep in the pre-industrial world - in its predecessor, the alehouse. The social history and the physical development of the English alehouse are fascinating subjects in themselves, but an examination of the regulation and control of this ancient and popular institution during the early stages of the country's shift from a traditional agrarian economy to an increasingly commercial and industrial one throws up a number of wider issues. Dramatic population growth, an increasing demand for food, and the consequent need for industrialisation and agricultural improvement, led to a rise in urban migration and a growth in the consumer economy. This chapter will investigate how the pressures of these complex socio-economic and demographic changes affecting Britain impacted upon the number, density and control of alehouses within the Lincolnshire division of Kesteven, part of a predominantly rural and largely isolated county that was spared the worst ravages of the changes being felt in other parts of the country, particularly the North and Midlands. It will also examine how central government legislation of the licensed trade was implemented at local level by the Kesteven bench over a period of seventy-five years from 1755 to the passing of the Beer Act in 1830, which heralded the demise of the traditional English alehouse and the rise of the Victorian pub.

Typology - inns, taverns and alehouses

Three basic types of drinking house existed in England before the introduction of the beerhouse in 1830. In order of size and status, these were the inn, the tavern and the alehouse. Inns were usually large, fashionable places, whose buildings have survived in relatively large numbers, since their construction was usually of good quality and durability. Compared with other victualling establishments, they formed a select minority. They provided comfortable lodgings and food for the wealthier traveller, particularly in towns and on stage-coaching routes. They offered wine, ale and beer, together with a range of quality food, and boasted large numbers of servants to cater for the many needs of their customers. Other facilities included stabling and a facility for posting and receiving letters and newspapers, as well as large rooms for upper-class social gatherings, such as balls and assemblies. Some even functioned as court rooms.[2]

Taverns were generally found in the larger towns and cities. They tended to sell only wine, and did not normally offer lodgings or food. The tavern had largely disappeared by 1800 or had evolved into the larger alehouse, and there do not appear to have been any in Kesteven.

Alehouses were by far the most prolific and populous type of drinking-house to be found throughout England before the advent of the beerhouse in 1830. They generally occupied smaller premises than inns and taverns and were found in all parts of towns and villages, from the centre to the outskirts. They were of a more 'local' nature than inns, which invariably occupied prime sites next to market places and main thoroughfares, and attracted clientele from greater distances. Alehouses ministered to the needs of the great mass of the populace, serving ale, beer and, later, spirits, and provided basic food and accommodation for the poorer, lower class of customer, including small farmers, craftsmen, artisans, labourers and servants.

By the late-Georgian period, the English alehouse had undergone a lengthy and complex evolution since its emergence from humble and obscure origins in the Middle Ages. From providing basic victualling for the tramping poor and lower classes, the alehouse had generally improved as the living standards of many ordinary people began to rise. In responding to change and adapting to the needs of its customers, alehouses had become larger, less rudimentary and more comfortable. They assumed a more commercial and specialist role in catering for particular groups of customers, such as the skilled artisan and small trader. This was often done by altering the spatial layout by simply separating off taproom from parlour, and generally refurbishing the premises. Alehouses offered a broader range of facilities, and premises were run in a more businesslike manner by landlords of growing respectability.[3] They had also become places for communal gatherings and social interaction, and provided bases for clubs and friendly societies, such as the White Bull Friendly Society in Sleaford, whose articles were approved and enrolled at the Kesteven Quarter Sessions in October 1813.[4]

By the early nineteenth century, the old magisterial licensing system had outgrown its usefulness and was open to abuse. There was the constant problem of enforcement: parish officers took backhanders from publicans as a matter of course and alehousekeepers were still able to serve as constables up to 1823. Occasionally, magistrates tampered corruptly with the licensing laws, and the larger common brewers built up close ties with the local bench and, although prohibited from acting as magistrates themselves after 1752, were able to apply their influence behind the scenes to lessen the chances of their own premises being suppressed.[5] This, together with pressure from all sides to throw open the beer trade and turn it over to a freer market economy (see below), culminated in the passing of the Beer Act of 1830, which virtually removed the alehouse from the retail drink trade and contributed to its eventual demise.[6] Some alehouses succeeded in adapting to change by evolving into the more respectable public house, whilst those that did not fell by the wayside.

Social and moral reform, and the demise of the alehouse

In response to a combination of political and religious forces, fuelled by the social and economic effects of population increase and industrialisation, the late-Georgian period saw a growing tide of moral reform, which had as its main target the traditional English alehouse. This was seen as a place of unlawful assembly and a cause of popular disturbance, heavy drinking, immorality, vagrancy and idleness. This shift in upper- and middle-class attitudes toward popular drinking arose out of the fear that drink was fuelling sedition among the lower classes, leading them to riot and rise out of control (a reality in Kesteven, as mentioned later). This helped to bring about increasingly strict legislation relating to licensees and their premises.

As well as magisterial intervention and a growing involvement of the brewing industry in taking over more and more drinking premises, social and cultural changes were also beginning to make a difference amongst the lower classes, which eventually led to the demise of the English alehouse. There was a growing separation between the skilled artisan and the labouring poor, two groups which had previously been happy to drink together. Skilled artisans, on a better wage than labourers, were beginning to demand more sophisticated services and facilities than the traditional alehouse was able to offer, and consequently began to frequent those premises which had adapted to their needs.

Although the movement for moral reform began in the mid-eighteenth century, when numbers of drinking-houses and the consumption of spirits (especially gin) were already beginning to come under some sort of control through legislation, there remained the fear that the number of alehouses and the undesirable lower-class behaviour associated with them could still spiral out of control.[7] Local authorities were especially alarmed by the proliferation of smaller establishments, which were felt to be less subject to the authorities than larger, more respectable houses. They were held to be dangerous meeting places for political agitators and radicals, posing a threat to political stability at a time of political turbulence following the French Revolution. Ann Allborn (licensee of the Boar's Head in Northgate, Sleaford) complained, and several witnesses deposed, to the Sleaford magistrates that on 3 November 1798 Henry Fox, a weaver from Sleaford, was drinking at her house when she and others saw him take up a tankard and drink success to 'Buonaparte and his crew and the United Irishmen' five times in the presence of several recruits belonging to the First Regiment of Foot Guards. Fox was described by the magistrates as 'a seditious, malicious and ill disposed person'.[8]

Social disorder and rioting were believed to be a result of the influence of the alehouse upon the hordes of poor labourers and unemployed who were casualties of agricultural improvement, industrialisation, urbanisation and demographic growth. Several riots fuelled by drink occurred in Kesteven during the late Georgian period: in 1783, James Elliott was indicted before the Kesteven quarter sessions for 'acting riotously' in the alehouse of John Eminson of Sleaford.[9] There was a large riot in Heckington in 1816, and a bill was found against forty or more people who rioted in Sleaford in 1821, three of whom were named and brought to court.[10]

In urban areas, particularly, the problem of drunkenness and the traditional attractions of the alehouse were proving to be an obstruction to the introduction of more regular, systematic work practices in factories and workshops, which necessitated strict timekeeping and demanded sobriety in operating dangerous machinery. Economic distress was also a problem in rural areas where there were large numbers of landless, poverty-stricken labourers. These were becoming a heavy burden on the poor rate, which doubled or even trebled in almost every parish in the late eighteenth century. The root cause was said by some, as so often in the past, to be heavy drinking, which led to idleness and unemployment.

The attitude of the upper and middle classes towards drinking was strongly influenced by a religious awakening, allied to a general movement to reform society and manners, in which consumption of alcohol was heavily condemned. The temperance movement, led by the Methodists, was involved in public campaigning against alcohol consumption and for the promotion of the work ethic from the early nineteenth century.

Licensing legislation, 1552-1830

The passing of the Beer Act in 1830 was just one more attempt in a long history of government legislation to bring alehouses under stricter control. The first national legislation to impose any sort of regulation on those licensed to sell intoxicating liquor was the Alehouse Act passed in 1552 (5 & 6 Edw. IV c.25), which sought to co-ordinate all local bye-laws and manorial customs, and embody them in statute. The Crown intended the Act to regulate all alehouses as a measure against perceived increases in levels of drunkenness and social disorder. It stipulated that all sellers of ale and beer were to be licensed by local justices of the peace. Licensees were required to enter into bonds, known as recognizances, that they would maintain good order in their houses and not allow the playing of unlawful games, such as quoits, bowls, cards, dice, football and tennis. These recognizances were recorded on file at the sessions court. Penalties were either a fine or loss of licence. Innkeepers were not included in this Act, but much of the subsequent legislation regulating alehouses also applied to inns, as providers of ale and beer.

Under James I, an Act of 1604 (1 Jac. I, c.9) was passed 'to restrain the inordinate haunting and tipling in inns, alehouses and other victualling houses'. Two years later, an act 'for repressing the odious and loathsome Sin of Drunkenness' (4 Jac. I, c.5) made it an offence for alehousekeepers to allow their customers to become drunk.

The 1552 Act had not specified the length for which a licence was valid, but after a few years, some counties and boroughs were renewing licences annually, a practice which was codified in a royal proclamation of 1618. It ordered that licences were to be issued annually at special licensing sessions, and an annual register be kept of licensees and their sureties. It also ordered that alehouses were to be closed on Sundays during the hours of divine service.

An Act of 1729 (2 Geo. II, c.28.11) codified the long-established practice of holding annual licensing at special brewster sessions, and magistrates were ordered to grant licences only to houses within their division. The object of this was to enable local justices with a good knowledge of the area and its requirements to make the grants, instead of those 'who living remote from the places of abode (of the licensees) may not be truly informed as to the occasion of want of such inns or common alehouses.' Legislation required that licences were to be issued in the exact number necessary for the needs of the area, thus formalising the shift of responsibility from county to local level. This Act was, however, repealed four years later.

The 1750s saw another concerted effort to control the drinking business. Legislation of 1751 gave justices summary powers to search premises (24 Geo. II), powers that were bolstered by the Licensing Act of 1753 (26 Geo. II c.31), which brought together and tidied up all the hitherto piecemeal modifications relating to the sale of ale and beer. It became a statutory requirement that full registers be kept of licensees and their recognizances by the clerk of the peace at quarter sessions, and it was only at quarter sessions that licences could be granted, and not at any other time. This prevented individual justices from handing out licences at will without the collective consideration of the whole bench. Each prospective licensee had to produce a certificate of good character signed by the minister and churchwardens of his parish, or other substantial parishioners. As well as the more strict administration of the licensing laws, the 1753 Act and further legislation in 1755 (28 Geo. II c. 19) simplified the power of the justices to proceed against defaulting licensees. The 1753 Act and further legislation in 1756 (29 Geo. II c.12) also tightened up the transfer of licences. The legislation of the 1750s was backed by a stiff range of penalties and it appears to have been successful in bringing down the levels of excessive spirit consumption, especially gin, from over seven million gallons in 1751 to under two million by 1758.[11]

The 1780s marked a turning point in the attitude of justices to one of stricter regulation of alehouses and drinking in general. It was prompted by a fear that the number of drinking premises was still rising out of control, particularly the proliferation of smaller and less visible establishments, which were seen to be less respectable and law-abiding than larger, more prominent houses. In response to a growing tide of protest against the prevailing immorality (attributed mainly to the alehouse), and encouraged by upper and middle class agitation for moral reform, the MP William Wilberforce succeeded in putting enough pressure upon the government to secure a royal proclamation against vice, including Sunday drinking.[12] It was circulated in 1787 to all magistrates, together with an official demand for the strict regulation of the victualling trade. This seems to have propelled magistrates into making fuller use of the powers they already possessed, and over the next few years licensed premises were closed by the hundreds. The minutes of the Kesteven quarter sessions include a transcript of the 1787 circular. It was sent out to all acting justices in the Kesteven division, 'directing the strict execution of the Laws which have been made against the Prophanation of the Lords Day Drunkenness Swearing and Cursing.'[13] It must have been a fairly common occurrence for people to drink on a Sunday during the hours of divine service, but there is not a single prosecution in Kesteven until 1826.

Figure 5.1
Map of the wapentakes of Kesteven, showing the extent of the jurisdiction of the Kesteven magistrates in the eighteenth and nineteenth centuries

No further major legislation was passed until 1828, which largely reversed the hitherto mainly restrictive licensing policy by effectively liberalising the drink trade. Whilst the government recognised the threat that drinking-houses posed to public order, they were also fully aware that they represented a substantial and constant source of public revenue in excise duty. The Alehouse Act of 1828 (9 Geo. IV c.61) repealed almost all earlier legislation relating to alehouses and provided a new framework for granting full publicans' licences to sell beer, wine, spirits and other excisable liquors. Its aim was to eliminate the worst abuses of magisterial licensing, without the structural reforms of the old regime. One of its shortcomings, however, was that it did not provide for the keeping of registers, surely a retrograde step in retaining control of numbers, if only through recorded information. It is fortunate for historians, therefore, that the clerk of the peace continued to maintain the registers for Kesteven. After the 1828 Act, many counties set up new petty sessional divisions, which dealt with the licensing of victuallers, and indeed in Kesteven by 1831 the responsibility for administering brewster sessions had been transferred from the quarter to the petty sessions.

The 1828 Act was too little too late, and was virtually unworkable. Within two years, the Beerhouse Act of 1830 (1 Wm. IV, c. 64) was passed to continue the process of liberalising the popular drink trade by encouraging the sale of beer by retail. Under the Act it was permissible for any householder (assessed to the poor rate) to sell beer, ale and cider by obtaining an excise licence on demand from the local excise office at a cost of just under £2.[14] The Act succeeded in fulfilling its aim of selling more beer, with numerous beerhouses springing up around the country, many operating from a room in the licensee's own home.

Number of alehouses in Kesteven

In order to ascertain the number and density of alehouses in Kesteven during the study period, a number of documents held at Lincolnshire Archives were consulted. These are held in the quarter sessions deposit (catalogued under 'KQS D/1') and include a series of alehouse licence registers, which start in 1678 and run up to 1865 (with gaps). There are also bundles of original recognizances for 1755 and 1756 (KQS D/1), and the quarter sessions minutes for the period 1775 to 1834 (KQS A/1/10-17, 36-7) were trawled for evidence of any directives from central government relating to the licensing of alehouses, and for any comments made by the magistrates regarding implementation.

On a practical point, local trade directories can provide a valuable additional resource for tracking the number of licensed victuallers operating in any given place, particularly where there are gaps in the licensing registers, as is the case with Kesteven for 1813 to 1824. Directories also have added value in that they usually give the sign of the premises, a detail absent from the Kesteven registers until 1825. Dennis Mills has demonstrated how useful trade directories are in this respect.[15]

The jurisdiction of the Kesteven magistrates extended across nine wapentakes *(Figure 5.1)*, but excluded the city of Lincoln and the boroughs of Grantham and Stamford, which held their own sessions.

The annual number of licences issued for each parish within the jurisdiction of the Kesteven bench was counted at five-year intervals (where data is available) from 1755 to 1831. A summary of the totals is given in *Figure 5.2*.

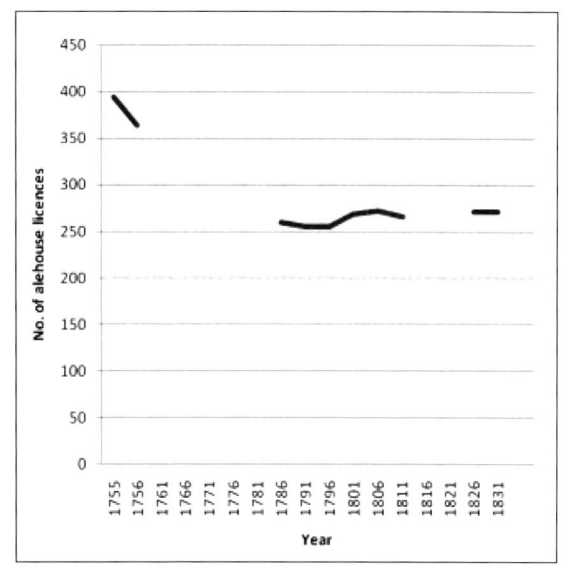

Figure 5.2
The total number of alehouse licences issued annually at Kesteven quarter sessions, 1755-1831

Sources: Alehouse Recognizances, 1755-6 (LAO KQS/D/1); Kesteven Quarter Sessions Alehouse Licence Registers 1784-1812 and 1825-43 (LAO KQS/D/1)

It is immediately obvious that the number of licences issued at the end of the period was considerably lower than in the mid-1750s. Numbers fell dramatically between 1755 and 1756, then further again by 1781. Over the next fifty years, they fluctuated slightly above and below this point, ending on a modest rise by the late 1820s. It is not clear how the economy of the last few years of the Napoleonic wars and the post-war depression might have affected the number of premises, as there are no registers for 1813 to 1824, but for those years where data is available it follows closely the general pattern discernible in other provincial towns, such as Cambridge, Gloucester and Maidstone, and the agricultural counties of Kent, Leicestershire and Oxfordshire.[16] Peter Clark attributes the general upward trend in England in the 1820s to a combination of a period of relaxation in licensing controls and the impact of free-trade ideas on magistrates.[17] The latter presumably involved allowing the market to dictate the supply and demand, resulting in a shake-out on economic grounds of any superfluous or lesser premises that failed to adapt to the changing needs of its customers. *Appendix 5.1* gives a breakdown of the number of licences issued parish by parish in Kesteven.

The data in *Appendix 5.1* points up the high numbers of premises in the market towns of Sleaford, Bourne and Market Deeping. If the numbers in the parishes of New Sleaford, Old Sleaford and Quarrington are added together, we get a total for the town of Sleaford *(Table 5.1)*.

These figures show a decline in Sleaford from thirty-one alehouses in 1755 to twenty-five the following year. This decreases further, reaching a plateau of twenty-one throughout the 1790s to the end of the period, representing an overall reduction of one third. Market Deeping shows a similar pattern, with a net decrease of a third, starting at nineteen in 1755, dipping dramatically to eight in the 1780s and 1790s, before rising to thirteen in 1831. Bourne, on the other hand, shows an initial decrease of one third from fifteen in 1755 to ten by 1786, but by 1831 it has recovered its 1755 level and even surpassed it by one.

Market towns could support a much higher density of inns and alehouses than villages because they did not rely wholly on their residential population. In their role as local and regional meeting places, market towns functioned briefly as larger places when, on market days or during annual hiring fairs, elections or quarter sessions, the population temporarily swelled with an influx of people from the surrounding countryside. Market towns were consequently well supplied with meeting and refreshment places, typically inns and alehouses. These were places where residents and visitors could also read the latest national and provincial newspapers, socialise, pay rent, conduct business and sign contracts. Market Deeping, Bourne and Sleaford are all located along what was a branch of the Great North Road leading up to the Humber. Daily and weekly coaching services brought in waves of passengers, who made use of the amenities offered by inns and alehouses along the way.

Like many market towns, from the late eighteenth century Sleaford underwent a number of improvements to its agriculture, infrastructure and fabric. These began with the construction of the Slea Navigation in 1792 to link the town into the existing national network of canals via the Witham and the Trent, an enterprise supported by the Peacock, Handley and Kirton Bank founded in the same year. The Navigation enabled Sleaford to import and export heavy bulk goods more cheaply. In 1796 the open-field system was enclosed, leading to improved yields and a rise in the value of land. All these improvements helped to boost the town's economy.[18]

Sleaford had long been a centre of local government. The quarter sessions and petty sessions for the northern half of Kesteven were held in Sleaford, along with county elections. The prestigious offices of clerk of the peace for Kesteven and county treasurer for north and south Kesteven were held by Sleaford lawyers from the 1770s until 1866.[19] In 1829, the old town hall was demolished and replaced with a new sessions house, as befitted the town's administrative status. At the same time, the whole town was paved and drained, and one of its bridges and other thoroughfares were widened, all paid for by subscription.[20]

Bourne underwent similar improvements. Its open fields were enclosed in the 1760s, and its fenland was later drained and brought into cultivation. The Bourne Eau was improved in 1781 to link Bourne to the Glen, and so to the Welland. Bourne's old sessions house was replaced in 1821 with newly-built premises, to where the quarter sessions and petty sessions were adjourned for south

Parish	1755	1756	1786	1791	1796	1801	1806	1811	1826	1831
New Sleaford (incl. Holdingham)	28	22	22	20	19	20	20	19	19	19
Old Sleaford	2	2						1	1	1
Quarrington	1	1	2	1	1	1	1	1	1	1
Total	31	25	24	21	20	21	21	21	21	21

Table 5.1
Number of alehouse licences issued for the market town of Sleaford, 1755-1831

Sources: Alehouse Recognizances, 1755-6 (LAO KQS/D/1); Kesteven Quarter Sessions Alehouse Licence Registers 1784-1812 and 1825-43 (LAO KQS/D/1)

Kesteven business. Like Sleaford, Bourne lay at the hub of several turnpike roads, most notably the coaching route from London to the Humber.[21]

The smaller town of Market Deeping, whose hinterland was curtailed to an extent by the proximity of Stamford seven miles away, was in the process of declining as an urban centre during the late eighteenth and early nineteenth centuries, and its market became obsolete between 1830 and 1856.[22] It nevertheless supported a good number of alehouses throughout the preceding century.

A rise in the economic fortunes and populations of these market towns must have led to a rise in alehouse profits, although progress must have been temporarily affected by the economic depression after the end of the Napoleonic Wars in 1815. Unfortunately, this period occurs where there is a gap in the licensing records, but one would expect there to be some degree of fluctuation in numbers around this time. For instance, the failure of Barnard's brewery of Boston in 1814, which owned several alehouses in Sleaford and Bourne, must have affected the ability of its licensees to function properly during a period when their premises were being sold and their future was uncertain. The diminishing purchasing power of the wages of the labouring poor, particularly the many agricultural workers who lived in towns, must also have adversely affected alehouse profits in Kesteven during the post-war depression.[23]

Other factors must also be fed into the equation. The Methodist movement and the rise of teetotalism had a large part to play in changing people's attitudes to public drinking, especially in the towns. It was no coincidence that the Fawcett family, early leading Methodists and champions of the temperance movement in Sleaford from the late eighteenth century, chose to reside in Westgate - an area inhabited by the labouring poor, where there was a concentration of alehouses. The Fawcetts later built a Temperance Hall there.

In contrast to the towns, the licensing data for villages show only small fluctuations in totals between 1755 and 1831. Some drop slightly, such as Threekingham (from two to one) and Langtoft (from five to four). Some rise modestly, as at Baston (from four to six), but in villages such as Anwick (one licence), Folkingham (four) and Horbling (two), numbers remained the same throughout the period. Several villages, including Stainfield and Braceborough, lost their single alehouse altogether. The very small numbers involved in the net changes in village totals are probably more likely to be the result of natural wastage through bankruptcy, illness, retirement and death, rather than the intervention of magistrates. Although the vicissitudes of the lives of individual alehousekeepers and their families was undoubtedly a factor in the number of those applying for a licence in the towns, the greater proportionate reductions involved in town numbers must surely be attributed largely to the success of the licensing legislation - to reduce and control the number of premises.

This greater reduction in the density of urban alehouses between the 1750s and 1831 might be considered even more of a legislative success, when the number of licences is set against the rise in urban populations. *Table 5.2* shows the ratio of the number of inhabitants of Sleaford, Bourne and Market Deeping per alehouse licence from 1801 to 1831, using population data taken from the decennial censuses. Figures for the whole of Kesteven are also given as an average for comparison, plus ratios calculated from the village data.

The number of licences issued within Kesteven as a whole between the period 1801 to 1831 remained at an almost constant level, between 266 and 273 a year, but the population of Kesteven rose by 49%, thus causing the ratio of the number of inhabitants to each alehouse to rise by a similar 48%, from 143 to 212 people per alehouse. Because the number of licences issued in Sleaford and Bourne remained at a constant level, the percentages for these two towns follow the same proportions as the Kesteven average. Sleaford's population rose by 70%, whilst the number of licences remained at twenty-one, resulting in a corresponding rise of 70% in the number of people per alehouse. In Bourne, the population rose by 54%, but the number of licences fluctuated only slightly, causing the ratio of people per alehouse to rise by slightly less, at 50%. The data for Market Deeping shows a different pattern. Its population rose by only 36%, whilst a rise in the number of licences from nine to thirteen (44%) resulted in a slight fall in the ratio from eighty-nine people per alehouse to eighty-four. This difference must surely correlate with its decline as a town and the relatively more vigorous urban development of Sleaford and Bourne.

	Whole of Kesteven			Sleaford			Bourne			Market Deeping		
Year	Pop.(a)	Lics	Ratio	Pop.	Lics	Ratio	Pop.	Lics	Ratio	Pop.	Lics	Ratio
1801	38,455	269	143	1710	21	81	1664	15	111	803	9	89
1811	43,715	266	164	2066	21	98	1784	14	127	899	10	90
1821/25(b)	51,361	273	188	2441	21	116	2242	15	149	1016	12	84
1831	57,569	271	212	2906	21	138	2569	16	161	1091	13	84

	Kesteven Villages		
Year	Pop.	Lics	Ratio
1801	34,278	224	153
1811	38,966	221	176
1821/25(b)	45,662	225	203
1831	51,003	221	231

Notes:

(a) The population of Kesteven excludes that of the boroughs of Stamford and Grantham, which kept their own alehouse licensing records.

(b) Although there is no licence data for 1821, the number of alehouses for Sleaford is known from trade directories to be twenty-one. Numbers for Bourne and Market Deeping in 1821 are taken from the licensing data for 1825.

Table 5.2
Ratio of the number of inhabitants to the number of alehouse licences issued in Kesteven and the market towns of Sleaford, Bourne and Market Deeping, 1801-31

Sources: Kesteven Quarter Sessions Alehouse Licence Registers, 1784-1812 and 1825-43 (LAO KQS/D/1); Decennial Census Returns 1801-1831 (W. Page (ed.) Victoria County History of Lincolnshire, 2, pp.358-78).

By contrast the village ratios are far higher than those of the three towns. The average village population rose by 49% in the period 1801 to 1831, but the net decrease in the number of licences from 224 to 221 was just three. This resulted in a ratio which increased by 50%, from 153 people per alehouse in 1801 to 231 in 1831, suggesting that some premises might have been larger in rural settlements than in the towns.

Although this is a somewhat rudimentary method of analysing the data (it fails to take into account, for instance, any changes over the thirty-year period in the age-composition of the population, and thus the numbers of those of drinking age), it serves to provide a form of comparison between the three towns. Fundamental to the upheavals affecting England from the late eighteenth century onwards was demographic growth, which took off from the 1740s when the birth rate began to exceed the mortality rate. The population of England and Wales was around 9.2 million in 1801, having increased by almost half since the mid-eighteenth century. It had reached 13.9 million by 1831. Towns and cities generally showed the greatest rises, chiefly owing to widespread migration from rural to urban areas.[24]

Convictions under the licensing laws

So, what evidence is there in surviving records of the efforts of the Kesteven magistrates to translate central government regulation of the licensed trade into effective administration at local level? Were their hands tied or were they allowed a degree of discretion and flexibility, and did the number of convictions go up or down relative to the number of premises?

Kesteven's alehouse registers do not give any concrete evidence as to the attitude of the Bench to the licensed trade, but a piece of text regarding a seemingly trivial aspect of licensing law was copied into a volume of Sleaford petty sessions minutes from the *Globe* newspaper of 15 November 1834. It suggests that magistrates previously had a more flexible attitude to the application of the regulations (author's emphasis in italics):

The Beer Act - The case of William JOHNSON adjourned from Saturday [place not specified] ... He had been charged with having the words "Licensed to sell Beer by Retail" and the words "To be drunk on the premises" on two different boards, instead of being on the same one as the Act directs. The magistrates now said *the act was imperative and they had not the power of using any discretion in the matter.* They must therefore fine the Defendant in the full penalty of £10.[25]

An examination of convictions for flouting the licensing laws might provide an index as to how rigorous or otherwise the magistrates were in bringing about successful prosecutions. However, they were somewhat reliant upon the parish constables, who were responsible for bringing offenders to the attentions of the Bench. A trawl through the minute books of the Kesteven quarter sessions from 1779 to 1832 produced a number of memorials of convictions, as did the brewster register of the Sleaford petty sessions, begun in 1831.[26] The latter contained a list of convictions against both alehousekeepers and beerhousekeepers, following the Alehouse Act of 1828 and the Beerhouse Act of 1830. *Table 5.3* gives the number and type of convictions recorded over the period 1779 to 1832.

Year	Selling beer & ale without a licence	Sunday drinking	Drinking after hours	Drunkenness and disorderly conduct	Gaming	Alehouse (unspecified)	Beerhouse (all types)	Total number of convictions
1779	1							1
1780	2							2
1781-1782								
1783	1							1
1784-1792								
1793	3							3
1794-1809								
1810				1				1
1811-1814								
1815		1						1
1816-1819								
1820					1			1
1821				1				1
1822								
1823						1		1
1824						1		1
1825				1				1
1826		1	1					2
1827		3	1	2		1		7
1828			1			4		5
1829		2						2
1830					3			3
1831		8	2	6			1	17
1832				1		7	12	20

Table 5.3
Number of convictions of Kesteven alehousekeepers, 1779-1832 and beerhousekeepers, 1830-2

Sources: Kesteven Quarter Sessions Minutes 1775-1823 (LAO KQS/A/1/10-17); Kesteven Quarter Sessions Draft Minutes, 1824-34 (LAO KQS/A/1/36-7); Kesteven Quarter Sessions Alehouse Licence Register, 1825-43 (LAO KQS/D/1); Sleaford Petty Sessions Offences Book, 1831-40 (LAO SLPS/3/32).

Despite the passing of the 1787 Act, which was supposed to provide a cornerstone in the strict control of the licensed trade, there was only the occasional prosecution in Kesteven until the late 1820s, and then convictions began to rise, jumping dramatically following the passing of the Beerhouse Act in 1830. It would seem that the Act had finally succeeded in focusing the attentions of the Bench, who clamped down particularly upon Sunday drinking and drunkenness in general. When compared to the fairly constant number of premises licensed in Kesteven from 1801 to 1831, the rise in the ratio of the number of convictions is even more remarkable.

The presence of unlicensed premises seems not to have been a problem after 1794, when there were no further prosecutions for this particular breach of the licensing laws. This might suggest that either the constables were turning a blind eye, or had been so effective in conjunction with the Bench in the past in bringing illegal houses to book, that no one dared serve alcohol without a licence. The former is more likely to be the case. In 1829, the Mason's Arms at Rippingale was refused a licence, the only mention to be found so far in the official records of a refusal.[27]

From time to time, central government at Whitehall requested statistics in the form of parliamentary returns, one of which asked for the number of convictions from 1 April 1831 to 1 April 1833 under the Alehouse and Beerhouse Acts. Presumably the government was anxious to see how effective the recent legislation had been in keeping drinking establishments under control. The answer returned by William Forbes, the clerk of the peace for Kesteven, was sixteen publicans and twelve keepers of beerhouses. His return was accompanied by a note, which clearly shows his (and very possibly the Bench's) attitude to the effect of the Beerhouse Act on liberalising public drinking:

> In reference to the above convictions of keepers of beerhouses (which have proved productive of the most baneful effects in this Division) I would beg leave to notice that an atrocious murder was committed at Heckington in these Parts in the month of March last, originating in the disorderly conduct of a set of abandoned characters suffered to associate in a Beer house there.[28]

Conclusion

It is difficult to attribute any one cause to the bringing down and holding in check the number of licensed premises in Kesteven between the mid-eighteenth century and the 1820s. Undoubtedly, the dramatic fall in the number of licences issued in 1755 compared with that of following year shows that the legislation of the early 1750s was beginning to bite. To what degree the provisions for stricter application of the powers granted to magistrates continued to bring about the further decrease evident in numbers up to the 1780s is not certain, but it is likely to have been a combination of existing legislation and the pressures resulting from the demographic, social and economic changes occurring from the 1760s onwards.

The slight clawing back of the number of premises in the 1790s, following a period of relative stability in the 1780s, reached a level which remained more or less constant through to 1831. Clearly, the liberalisation of the trade following the Act of 1828 did not have an immediate effect on the number of alehouses in Kesteven, which remained more or less the same, though we have no data for the number of beerhouse excise licences taken out. Was it the case that the number of alehouses had attained the optimum, commercially viable level to suit the prevailing socio-economic conditions, or were the magistrates applying their more stringent powers more often and more robustly? Mills observes that, in the case of beerhouses, these seem to have been more common in some districts than in others, possibly as a result of differing policies on the part of the licensing magistrates.[29]

When the stability in the number of alehouse licences is viewed in terms of the rise in the ratio of people to premises following the upsurge in population, the density of alehouses could be considered in real terms as being held in check, or even decreasing, especially in urban areas where the rate of population rise was greatest. Individual premises must have increased in size and facilities to accommodate a growing number of drinkers trying to fit into the same or a diminishing number of premises. Beerhouses must have taken up some of the extra demand, as the poorer sections of society left the alehouse for this cheaper, plainer type of establishment.

The marked rise in the conviction rate of alehousekeepers from the late 1820s might imply that the Kesteven magistrates had previously either been lax in applying the law and/or had retained a degree of discretion, which they were now no longer at liberty to exercise.

Appendix 5.1
Number of annual alehouse licences issued in Kesteven by wapentake and parish, 1755-1831

Sources: Alehouse Recognizances, 1755-6 (LAO KQS/D/1); Kesteven Quarter Sessions Alehouse Licence Registers, 1784-1812 and 1825-43 (LAO KQS/D/1).

ASWARDHURN	1755	1756	1786	1791	1796	1801	1806	1811	1826	1831
Aswarby	1	1								
Aunsby			1	1	1	1	1	1	1	2
Ewerby	2	2	1	1	1	1	1	1	1	
Great Hale	2	3	3	3	3	3	3	3	3	3
Little Hale	3	3	2	2	2	2	2	1	2	2
Heckington	5	4	6	5	5	5	5	5	5	5
Helpringham	4	4	3	3	3	3	3	3	3	3
Ingoldsby	2	2	2	2	2	2	2	2	2	1
Kirkby La Thorpe	2	3	1	1	1	1	1	1	1	1
Old Sleaford	2	2						1	1	1
Quarrington	1	1	2	1	1	1	1	1	1	1
Swarby	1	1	1	1	1	1	1	1	1	1
Scredington	1	1	1	1	1	1	1	1	1	1
South Kyme	3	3	1	1	2	2	2	2	2	2
Silk Willoughby	1	1	1	1	1	1	1	1	1	1
Subtotal	**30**	**31**	**25**	**23**	**24**	**24**	**24**	**24**	**25**	**24**

FLAXWELL	1755	1756	1786	1791	1796	1801	1806	1811	1826	1831
Anwick	1	1	1	1	1	1	1	1	1	1
Digby	2	2	1	1	1	1	1	1	1	1
Dorrington	1	1	1	1	1	1	1	1	1	1
Leasingham	2	2	1	2	2	2	2	2	2	2
New Sleaford (incl. Holdingham)	28	22	22	20	19	20	20	19	19	19
North Rauceby	1	1	1	1	1	1	1	1	1	1
South Rauceby	2	1	1	1			1	1	1	1
Ruskington	3	2	2	1	2	2	2	2	2	2
Subtotal	**40**	**32**	**30**	**28**	**27**	**28**	**29**	**28**	**28**	**28**

Continued on page 86

Appendix 5.1
Number of annual alehouse licences issued in Kesteven by wapentake and parish, 1755-1831

AVELAND	1755	1756	1786	1791	1796	1801	1806	1811	1826	1831
Aslackby	2	2	2	2	2	2	2	2	2	2
Bourne	15	15	10	12	12	15	15	14	15	16
Billingborough	5	5	2	2	2	2	3	3	3	3
Dembleby	1	1								
Dowby		1								
Dunsby	2	2								
Dyke			1			1	1	1	1	1
Folkingham	4	4	4	4	4	4	4	4	4	4
Horbling	2	2	2	2	2	2	2	2	2	2
Hacconby	4	2	1	1	1	1	1	1	1	1
Kirkby Underwood	2	2	1	1	1	1	1	1	1	1
Morton by Bourne (incl. Hanthorpe)	8	7	3	3	3	4	2	2	3	3
Newton	2	2	1	1	1	1	1	1	1	1
Osbournby	3	2	2	2	2	2	2	2	2	2
Pickworth	1	2					1	1	1	1
Pointon	2	2	2	2	2	3	3	3	3	3
Rippingale	4	3	3	2	2	3	3	3	3	3
Stainfield	1	1								
Swaton	2	2	1	1	1	1	1	1	1	1
Threekingham	2	2	2	2	2	2	2	1	1	1
Walcott	1	1								
Subtotal	**63**	**60**	**37**	**37**	**37**	**44**	**44**	**42**	**44**	**45**

NESS	1755	1756	1786	1791	1796	1801	1806	1811	1826	1831
Barholm	2	2	1	1	1	1	1	1	1	1
Baston	4	2	4	3	4	4	5	5	6	6
Braceborough	1	2								
Carlby	1	1					1	1	1	1
Deeping Fen	1				1	1			1	1
Deeping St James	12	11	9	8	7	7	10	11	11	11
Greatford			1	1	1	1	1	1	1	1
Langtoft	5	5	3	3	3	3	4	4	4	4
Market Deeping	19	18	8	8	8	9	12	10	12	13
Tallington	3	3	2	1	2	2	2	2	2	2
Thurlby	6	6	2	3	3	3	3	3	4	4
Uffington	3	3	3	3	3	3	3	3	2	2
West Deeping	3	3	2	2	2	2	3	2	2	2
Subtotal	**60**	**56**	**35**	**33**	**35**	**36**	**45**	**43**	**47**	**48**

Continued on page 87

Appendix 5.1
Number of annual alehouse licences issued in Kesteven by wapentake and parish, 1755-1831

LOVEDEN	1755	1756	1786	1791	1796	1801	1806	1811	1826	1831
Ancaster	4	3	3	2	2	2	2	2	2	2
Bennington, Long	6	8	6	6	5	5	4	5	5	5
Beckingham	5	5	3	3	3	3	2	2	2	2
Brant Broughton	3	2	2	1	2	2	2	2	2	2
Carlton Scroop	1									
Caythorpe	5	4	3	3	3	3	3	3	3	3
Claypole	3	3	1	1	2	2	2	2	2	2
Doddington	2	2	2	2	2	1	2	1	1	1
Foston	4	3	3	3	3	3	3	3	3	3
Fulbeck	3	3	2	2	2	2	2	2	2	2
Hough on the Hill	3	3	1	1	1	1	1	1	1	1
Brandon (par. Hough on the Hill)	2	1								
Gelston (par. Hough on the Hill)	1									
Hougham	3	3	1	1	1	1	1	1	1	1
Leadenham	3	2	3	3	3	3	2	2	2	2
Marston	3	3	2	2	2	2	2	2	1	1
Normanton	1	1	1	1	1	1	1	1	1	1
Stragglethorpe	2	1								
Stubton	1	1	1	1	1	1				
Westborough	3	4	1	1	1	1	1	1	1	1
Subtotal	**58**	**52**	**35**	**33**	**34**	**33**	**30**	**30**	**29**	**29**

BOOTHBY GRAFFOE	1755	1756	1786	1791	1796	1801	1806	1811	1826	1831
Aubourn	1				1	1	1	1	1	1
Bassingham	4	4	2	2	2	2	2	2	2	2
Boothby	1	1								
Haddington (par. Aubourn)	1	1								
Boultham	1	1	2	1	1	1	1	1	1	1
Carlton le Morland	2	3	2	2	1	1	1	1	1	1
Coleby	2	3	1	1	1	1	1	1		
Doddington	2					1		1		
Eagle	2	2	1	1	1	1				
Harmston	2	3	2	2	2	2	2	1	1	1
Norton Disney	1		1	1	1	1	1	1	1	1
North Scarle	2	2	2	1	1	1	1	1	1	1
Navenby	4	4	3	2	2	2	2	2	2	2
North Hykeham	1	1	1	1	1	1	1	1	1	1
Swinderby	3	3	3	3	3	3	3	3	3	3
Skellingthorpe	3	2	2	2	2	2	2	2	2	2
Thorpe on the Hill	1	1	1	1	1	1	1	1	1	1
Welbourn	2	2	2	2	1	1	1	1	1	1
Wellingore	4	4	3	3	3	3	3	3	3	2
Subtotal	**39**	**37**	**28**	**25**	**24**	**25**	**23**	**23**	**21**	**20**

Continued on page 88

Appendix 5.1
Number of annual alehouse licences issued in Kesteven by wapentake and parish, 1755-1831

LANGOE	1755	1756	1786	1791	1796	1801	1806	1811	1826	1831
Billinghay	1	1	1	2	2	2	2	2	2	2
Blankney	3	2	3	3	3	3	3	3	2	2
Dunston	3	3	2	3	4	3	3	3	3	3
Heighington	3	3	2	1	2	2	2	2	2	2
Metheringham	3	3	2	3	3	3	3	3	3	3
Martin	2	2	1	2	2	2	2	2	2	2
Nocton				1		1	1	1	1	1
North Kyme	1		1	1	2	2	2	2	2	2
Potterhanworth	4	3	3	4	4	4	4	4	4	4
Scopwick	2	2	2	2	2	1	1	1	1	1
Timberland	1	1	1	1	1	1	1	1	2	2
Washingborough	4	3	2	3	2	2	2	2	2	2
Walcott	2	2	1	1	1	2	2	2	2	2
Subtotal	**29**	**25**	**21**	**27**	**28**	**28**	**28**	**28**	**28**	**28**

WINIBRIGGS & THREO	1755	1756	1786	1791	1796	1801	1806	1811	1826	1831
Allington	3	2	2	2	2	2	2	2	1	1
Boothby	1	2	1	1	1					
Barrowby	4	2	2	2	2	2	2	2	2	2
Boothby [Pagnel]	1									
Cold Harbour (par. Somerby)									1	1
Haydor	2	2	1	1	1	1	1	1	1	1
Honington	1	1								
Humby	1	2								
Little Pointon		1								
North Stoke	1	1								
Ropsley	4	3	3	3	3	2	2	2	2	2
Somerby	2	2	2	2	2	2	1	2	1	1
Spittlegate	5	5	2	3	4	4	4	4	4	4
Sedgebrook	1	1	1	1	1	1	1	1	1	1
Syston	1	1	1	1	1	1	1	1	1	2
Welby			1	1	1	1	1	1	2	1
Wilsford	2	1	3	3	3	3	3	3	3	3
Woolsthorpe	4	4	2	2	2	3	3	3	3	3
Wyville	1	1								
Subtotal	**34**	**31**	**21**	**22**	**23**	**22**	**21**	**22**	**22**	**22**

Continued on page 89

Appendix 5.1
Number of annual alehouse licences issued in Kesteven by wapentake and parish, 1755-1831

BELTISLOE	1755	1756	1786	1791	1796	1801	1806	1811	1826	1831
Bassingthorpe	2	2	1	1	1	1	1			
Bitchfield		1	1		1	1	1	1	1	1
Burton Coggles	1	1	1	1	1	1	1	1	1	1
Bulby		1								
Corby	7	5	6	5	1	4	4	4	5	5
Careby	1	1	1	1	1	1	1	1	1	1
Castle Bytham	3	2	2	2	1	2	2	2	2	2
Edenham	4	3	2	2	3	2	2	2	1	1
Grimsthorpe	2	2	1	1		1	1	1	1	1
Gunby	1	1	1	1	1	1	1			
Irnham		2	2	2	2	2	2	2	1	1
Lavington						1				
Little Bytham	2	1	1	1	1	1	1	1	1	1
Osgodby	1	1								
Swayfield	1	2	1	1	1	2	2	2	2	2
Skillington	2	2	2	2	2	2	1	1	1	1
Stainby	2	1								
Swinstead	5	5	2	2	2	2	2	2	2	2
North Witham		1	2	2	2	2	2	2	3	3
South Witham	3	2	1	2	2	2	3	3	3	3
Toft	1	2	1	1	1	1	1	1	1	1
Witham on the Hill	3	2							1	1
Subtotal	**41**	**40**	**28**	**27**	**23**	**29**	**28**	**26**	**27**	**27**

| **TOTAL** | **394** | **364** | **260** | **255** | **255** | **269** | **272** | **266** | **271** | **271** |

Notes

[1] The germ of this paper came from the author's dissertation: 'Aspects of the trade of licensed victualling in late-Georgian Sleaford, 1784-1831' (Certificate in Local and Regional History, University of Nottingham, 1990).

[2] The general background to the history of alehouses and licensed victualling is taken from Peter Clark, *The English Alehouse* (1983); 'The English Urban Inn 1560-1760' in A. Everitt, *Landscape and Community in England* (1985), pp.155-208; H. A. Monckton, *A History of the English Public House* (1969); J. Gibson and J. Hunter, *Victualler's Licences: Records for family and local historians* (3rd edn, 2009).

[3] Clark, *English Alehouse*, pp.309-10.

[4] 'Articles of a Friendly Society at the White Bull in Sleaford' (LAO KQS A/1/15, Minutes of Kesteven Quarter Sessions, Mids 1810 - Epiph 1815, 7 Oct 1813, p.473).

[5] Clark, *English Alehouse*, pp.259, 264.

[6] Clark, *English Alehouse*, pp.55, 335.

[7] Monckton, *English Public House*, p.66.

[8] Despite a number of witness statements to the contrary from the landlady, customers and Footguards, Fox pleaded not guilty and the jury acquitted him (Kesteven Quarter Sessions Minutes, 1796-1802 (LAO KQS A/1/12, pp.309-10), KQS Sessions Bundle, Epiphany, 1799 (LAO KQS A/2/341/39, 54-61)).

[9] Kesteven Quarter Sessions Minutes (LAO KQS A/1/10, p.275).

[10] Kesteven Quarter Sessions Minutes (LAO KQS A/1/16, p. 280; LAO KQS A/1/17, p.250).

[11] Monckton, *English Public House*, p.66.

[12] William Wilberforce (1759-1833), Yorkshire MP, newly converted to evangelicalism.

[13] LAO KQS A/1/10, p.528, Sleaford, midsummer, 12 July 1787. The letter, dated 2 June 1787, was sent from the Home Secretary, Lord Sydney, to the Duke of Ancaster (Lord Lieutenant of Lincolnshire).

[14] The public house, with its full publican's licence, could sell wines and spirits in addition to beer, ale and cider.

[15] Dennis R. Mills, *Rural Community History from Trade Directories*, Local Population Studies Supplement (Hertfordshire, 2001), pp.24-5.

[16] Clark, *English Alehouse*, fig. 3.5, p.56; fig. 3.6, p.57.

[17] Clark, *English Alehouse*, pp.55, 335.

[18] Arthur Young, *A General View of the Agriculture of the County of Lincoln* (1813, repr. David & Charles, 1970), p.108.

[19] The office of clerk of the peace moved out of Sleaford in 1866 with the death of the solicitor Maurice Peter Moore, and the administrative offices of Kesteven were moved from Sleaford to Grantham in 1888, following the creation of Kesteven County Council.

[20] Sleaford Vestry Book (LAO Sleaford parish 10/2), pp.478 ff. & 491; White, *Directory of Lincolnshire* (1842), p.639.

[21] White, *Directory of Lincolnshire* (1856), p.707; N. Wright, *Lincolnshire Towns and Industry, 1700-1914*, History of Lincolnshire, 11 (Lincoln, 1982), p.42.

[22] Pigot & Co, *National Commercial Directory - Lincolnshire* (1830), p.110; White, *Directory of Lincolnshire* (1856), p.872.

[23] The wages of agricultural workers were stagnating by 1790 and fell back steadily thereafter, becoming badly depressed from 1815 (See Clark, *English Alehouse*, p.252).

[24] E. A. Wrigley and R. S. Schofield, *The Population History of England, 1541-1871* (1981), fig. 8.5, p.315.

[25] Kesteven Quarter Sessions Minutes 1775-1823 (LAO KQS/A/1/10-17); Kesteven Quarter Sessions Draft Minutes, 1824-34 (LAO KQS/A/1/36-37); Sleaford Petty Sessions Minutes, 1831-41, preliminary pages (LAO SLPS/3/32).

[26] Sleaford Petty Sessions Minutes, 1831-41 (LAO SLPS/3/32).

[27] Kesteven Quarter Sessions Alehouse Licence Register, 1825-43 (LAO KQS/D/1).

[28] LAO KQS F/4, Clerk of the Peace papers: 'Convictions under the Alehouse & Beer Acts, sent to Mr Secretary Phillips, 20 May 1833, by William Forbes, Clerk of the Peace for Kesteven, in pursuance of an order made by the House of Commons, 10 May 1833.'

[29] Mills, *Rural Community History*, pp.24-5.

[30] Excluding the city of Lincoln and the borough towns of Stamford and Grantham (except Spittlegate, which was included in the wapentake of Winibriggs and Threo).

CHAPTER 6

'THE DEVELOPMENT OF RURAL SETTLEMENT AROUND LINCOLN' REVISITED
with special reference to farm buildings and loans for improvement

Shirley Brook

In 1959 an article by Dennis Mills was published in *The East Midland Geographer* entitled 'The development of rural settlement around Lincoln, with special reference to the 18th and 19th centuries'. This was based on his recent M.A. thesis 'Population and Settlement in Kesteven, c.1775-c.1885'.[1] In this article Mills considered the factors influencing dispersal of settlement from c.1750. His sources were the 1801 and 1851 censuses, the enumerators' schedules 1851 and the Ordnance Survey Third Edition One-Inch Maps. At a time when enclosure was generally regarded as the principal factor influencing dispersal[2] Mills was questioning and probing more deeply. He concluded that 'the enclosure of land was not the only factor responsible for the large scale dispersal of settlement'[3] and went on to identify a number of other aspects of agricultural change which he considered to be significant elements in the process. These were reclamation, changes in agricultural operations, convenience, efficiency, the availability of capital and a substantial increase in population.[4] This chapter will present a brief outline of the factors Mills identified before revisiting his study to focus more closely on the impact of agricultural improvements, funded by loan capital, on dispersal of settlement.

Mills considered reclamation to be important. Drainage of the fens allowed wetlands to be converted to arable and made it possible for farmhouses and cottages to be built on the fenland. On the uplands, the Norfolk four-course rotation was applied to bring light soils into profitable arable cultivation. Mills observed that wetland and upland usually lay at the extremities of parishes and their conversion to arable brought with it the need for new farmhouses and cottages for those who would work the freshly cultivated acres. He noted that, on the reclaimed wetlands, a favourite location for new roads and buildings was along the banks of drainage dykes.

Not only did the agricultural revolution bring about an extension of the area of land under cultivation, it also involved an intensification of farming processes. Mills considered the keeping of increased numbers of cattle and sheep through the winter months and convenience for the carting of dung to the land to be important factors in the relocation of farmsteads away from the original village to a more accessible site, central to the holding. He pointed out that a conveniently situated farmstead would also facilitate threshing of the corn crop. Efficiency was an important consideration and, as well as being spacious enough to accommodate the increased numbers of stock, new farm buildings on open sites away from the crowded village centre could be laid out in a manner that would promote the smooth flow of farming operations.

Intensive regimes demanded an increase in the labour force. Between 1801 and 1851 there were marked increases in the population of all but one of the twenty-two townships selected by Mills as his sample.[5] He concluded that a significant element in this was an increase in the number of those occupied on the land and that they, along with their families, were frequently accommodated in new 'tied cottages' in dispersed areas of townships. All these agricultural changes required substantial investment on the part of landowners. In his remarkably comprehensive short essay Mills also considered the part played in dispersal by the availability of capital for improvements in farming, noting that costs of other improvements such as enclosure, drainage and fencing would draw heavily upon the landowner's capital resources.

At the time of writing his article the sources used by Mills did not include the records of land improvement companies. Even half a century later they are not widely exploited by historians. A notable exception to this is A. D. M. Phillips's work on land improvement loans and his examination of the correspondence of Andrew Thompson, one of the surveyors engaged to inspect improvement works undertaken with loan capital.[6] The records of land improvement borrowing are held in the National Archives at Kew, in TNA MAF 66. This documentation is the result of a series of land improvement acts, from 1846 to 1864,[7] which allowed landowners to borrow money for a range of specified types of agricultural improvement. The loans were available to owners of settled estates who held their land in trust for future generations under a so-called 'strict family settlement'.[8]

Owners of settled estates were not outright owners but 'limited owners', or 'tenants for life', of their estates and it was required that they would pass on intact, to the next generation, all that lay within the settlement. This meant that they could not sell off parts of their estate to fund improvements but, under land improvement legislation, they could borrow against the security of the estate. The ensuing loan had to be paid off by means of a rent charge on the estate over a period of as much as fifty years. According to J. Bailey Denton, a leading agricultural engineer, provision for the loans was put in place to offset the disadvantage to owners of settled estates arising from the repeal of the Corn Laws which had guaranteed minimum prices for grain.[9] Two leading proponents of the idea of enabling owners of settled estates to borrow for agricultural improvements were Henry Handley and Philip Pusey. Handley, of Sleaford, was MP for South Lincolnshire. He and Pusey were also active in the founding of the English Agricultural Society in 1838. This was incorporated as the Royal Agricultural Society of England (hereafter RASE) in 1840. Pusey became editor of its journal and author of many influential articles including one, in 1843, extolling the quality of agricultural improvements in Lincolnshire.[10]

Applications for loans were subjected to a rigorous process of assessment. A proposed scheme would be inspected by a surveyor appointed by the Inclosure Commissioners, with whom the responsibility for supervising the process rested. The surveyor would report on the suitability of the intended improvements. If the scheme met the standards required by the commissioners a 'provisional order' would be granted. This allowed the landowner to obtain credit and commence the work. The surveyor would make a second visit when the improvements were half finished to make sure they were being executed in a manner that complied with the commissioners' standards of durability. A third visit was made when the work was completed and it was only then, if the surveyor reported that the work met the required standards, that an 'absolute order' was granted and the money released.[11] Some of the money borrowed for agricultural improvement was government money made available under the Private Money Act of 1849 and the Public Money Act of 1850. However, most of the money came from land improvement companies who made large sums of money, which they in turn had borrowed from insurance companies, available to finance improvements sanctioned by the government under a succession of improvement acts. It is the documentation arising from the process of administering land improvement loans that forms the basis for this study.[12]

The documentation produced by the process of borrowing gives the name and place of residence of landowners who borrowed money for improvements together with the acreage and annual rental of the estate to be improved. The parish in which the loan capital was to be spent is identified and the purpose of the loan, the amount borrowed, the rate of interest and the term for repayment of the loan are all set out. An important piece of information also recorded is the date by which the work was completed. Schemes for improvement set out in agricultural writings and estate records may, or may not, have been executed but those in land improvement records are certified as having been effected. The records are, therefore, secure evidence of the timing and exact nature of some, but not all, of the agricultural improvements undertaken in the second half of the nineteenth century.

As with virtually all sources available to historians there are limits to the information we can extract from land improvement loan records. After all, they were produced to administer a process not to satisfy the curiosity of future generations. One of the principal shortcomings of land improvement loan records as a source for historians is that, whilst they identify on whose estate and in which parish the improvements were effected, most of them do not identify the exact holding to which the loan capital was applied. This makes it difficult for those endeavouring to reconstruct the agricultural history of specific farms to use the material unless there is corroborating evidence to help identify the exact location of the improvement works. Even when a holding is referred to individually it is frequently named as 'farm in the occupation of Mr X' or 'Mr Y' and so the record remains hard to penetrate. It is also difficult to quantify the proportion of improvement activity that was funded by loan capital. What can be said is that of the 721 parishes in nineteenth-century Lincolnshire, 373 (52%) had loan capital invested in them between 1855 and 1910.

Land improvement records reveal that considerable sums of money were applied to agricultural improvements in Lincolnshire. A total of 675 loans were taken out for improvements in the county between 15 March, 1855, when the first Lincolnshire loan was granted, and 31 December, 1909.[13] In these fifty-five years the total amount borrowed for all types of agricultural improvement in Lincolnshire was £523,311. The purposes for which money might be borrowed were laid down in legislation applied by the Inclosure Commissioners (later the Land Commissioners) who were responsible for overseeing the loans. The principal objects of loan capital expenditure in Lincolnshire were enclosure, drainage, fencing, roads and water supply, but by far the most frequent improvement for which loans were taken out in the county was farm buildings. Two thirds (66.5%) of all Lincolnshire loans granted between 1855 and 1910 were for schemes that included farm buildings. An estimated £316,832 (60.5%) of the total amount of loan capital spent on improvements in Lincolnshire was invested in farm buildings i.e. farmhouses, cottages and agricultural buildings.

The reason figures for farm buildings' investment must often be given as an estimated amount is that many loans are recorded as having been taken out for more than one purpose. Where this is the case the proportion of the loan allocated to farm buildings' improvements can only be estimated. Of the 675 loans taken out for Lincolnshire up to 1910, twenty-one loans for a variety of purposes, including farm buildings, gave details of the amount spent on each of the categories of improvement. From these figures it was observed that 40% of the total amount borrowed was expended on farm buildings. The figure used to calculate the estimated amount of money invested in farm buildings, when they are included in loans which were taken out for more than one purpose, is therefore 40%.[14]

It is useful to revisit Mills's observations about the impact of agricultural change on dispersal of settlement in the late eighteenth and early nineteenth centuries in the light of understandings gained from the study of land improvement loan records. The sources available to him, at the time of his study, enabled him to measure population growth up to 1851 and to speculate that there was continued growth thereafter which led to further dispersal of settlement. He observed that dispersal was a slow process and inferred from map evidence that it was not complete by 1851. The land improvement records relate to the second half of the nineteenth century, beginning just after the point at which Mills was obliged, by the availability of census material at the time, to halt his analysis. Re-examination of the agricultural changes he identified, with the benefit of evidence contained in land improvement loan records, furthers our understanding of the extent to which the process of dispersal continued after 1851 and the impact of loan capital on its progress.

As we have seen, Mills considered reclamation to be a significant factor. Draining was often the first improvement undertaken by landowners taking out loans. There was then investment in watercourses, sluices and embanking before the laying out of a network of roads and bridges. On the uplands the laying out of farm roads was followed by the planting of hedges and shelterbelts accompanied by the erection of fences. These were all necessary precursors to the institution of new arable regimes. The uplands benefited greatly from the application of manure produced by animals confined in sheltered yards, known as 'crewyards' in Lincolnshire. Stock would be kept over the winter in sheltered yards and fed on rich food such as oil cake. This ensured that, by the spring, these 'machines for converting the straw into dung', as Pusey called them,[15] would have provided the farmer with a plentiful supply of organic fertilizer. As we have seen, Mills noted that attending to the increased numbers of stock kept over the winter, along with convenience for the carting of dung to the fields, were prime reasons for the relocation of farmsteads.

Scopwick, a village on the spring-line some ten miles south east of Lincoln, is a parish in which Mills has taken a particular interest.[16] Here standing buildings afford clear evidence for the relocation of a farmstead in the 1870s, from within the curtilage (area) of the village, to a site that was more convenient for the heath where large quantities of manure were needed. The abandoned farm buildings were altered to provide cottage accommodation, a reminder that conversion of farm buildings for residential use is not exclusively a modern practice. Until recent property improvements and tree planting, evidence for the original use of the buildings was clearly visible in the stonework of the cottages. A photograph taken in the early 1990s *(Figure 6.1)* shows vestiges of former openings, especially in the gable end. Heavy wooden lintels, extending beyond the width of nineteenth-century windows, present evidence of openings of a different nature, and changes in the roof height suggest an assortment of buildings. Behind the row of cottages, away from the main street of the village, an estate of twentieth-century bungalows occupies what was once the stackyard of this village farmstead.

The new farmstead, Scopwick House (formerly known as The Firs), is a large and imposing set of buildings beside the road from Lincoln to Sleaford. Landowners wishing to advertise their status and display their progressive farming ideas to their neighbours would often choose such a site. The owner was Henry Chaplin M.P. of Blankney Hall. Chaplin was a prominent advocate of the agricultural interest in Parliament and, in 1889, was appointed first President of the reconstituted Board of Agriculture. The responsibilities of the Land Commissioners, who by this date were the body supervising land improvement loans, were subsumed into the Land Department of the Board of Agriculture at this point. Chaplin took out twelve land improvement loans between 1871 and 1895, three of which (from 1878 to 1880) were for Scopwick.[17] Although the lack of specific detail in the loan records means it cannot be certain, nevertheless the appearance of the buildings at Scopwick House strongly suggests that it was one of those built with loan capital.

Loan capital was not available to landowners for repairing old buildings. It could only be applied to fresh construction. This gave additional impetus to the relocation of farmsteads on sites where spacious new layouts of buildings could be accommodated. The mid-nineteenth century saw an explosion of literature regarding 'approved' designs for farm buildings which incorporated all the latest scientific understandings about housing stock, managing manure and processing feed and grain. The *Journal of the Royal Agricultural Society of England* (hereafter *JRASE*) provided a forum in which landowners, their agents and leading tenant farmers

Figure 6.1
Converted buildings of old village farmstead, Church Row, Scopwick
(A. S. Brook 1994)

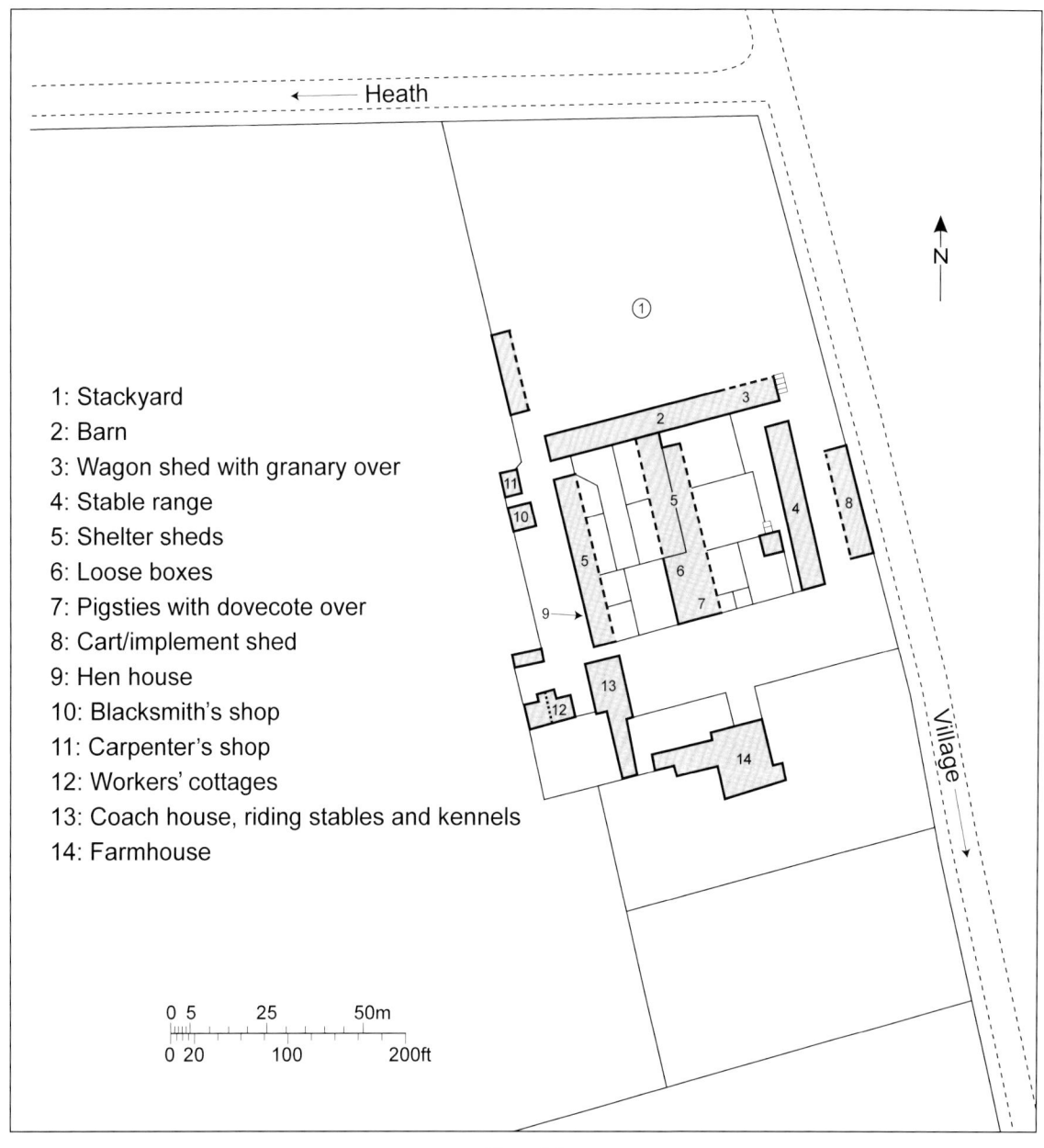

1: Stackyard
2: Barn
3: Wagon shed with granary over
4: Stable range
5: Shelter sheds
6: Loose boxes
7: Pigsties with dovecote over
8: Cart/implement shed
9: Hen house
10: Blacksmith's shop
11: Carpenter's shop
12: Workers' cottages
13: Coach house, riding stables and kennels
14: Farmhouse

Figure 6.2
Plan of the farmstead at Scopwick House, Scopwick
(Dave Watt)

discussed the latest advances in agricultural theory and practice. Nicholas Goddard, historian of RASE, considered that, although membership of the society was by no means large, its journal was a significant element in the information environment of nineteenth-century agriculture. Ideas contained in the journal filtered down to a much wider audience through readings to farmers' clubs and abstracts in the popular farming press.[18] Through this means, and via the shows of the national society and the many county and local agricultural societies that sprang up in this period, information about improvements in farming methods and buildings' provision to serve the industry was disseminated.

In 1846 the repeal of the Corn Laws, which had protected the price of grain, meant that British agriculture was faced with the challenge of

Figure 6.3
Barn range, Scopwick House, Scopwick
(A. S. Brook 2010)

competing in a free market. This new economic situation affected agricultural practices and the design of farm buildings. Agriculture came now to be regarded as a form of manufacturing industry, 'husbandry being in effect the fabrication of meat and bread from raw inedible materials by the toil and ingenuity of man'.[19] To this end, farms were designed to enable a natural flow of activity with raw materials entering at one end and the finished product emerging at the other. Emphasis was laid on 'economy of labour and manure'[20], economy in this sense being efficient management. Mills identified a spirit of efficiency, which promoted the construction of new ranges of farm buildings, as a factor influencing dispersal of settlement between 1760 and 1850.

Although there is evidence of previous farming activity at Scopwick House[21] the former buildings appear to have been demolished to make way for Chaplin's new model farmstead. It is of a single construction and exemplifies the latest ideas, in the third quarter of the nineteenth century, regarding efficient farmstead design. The layout of the buildings is shown in *Figure 6.2* with the structures whose purpose can be securely identified listed in the key. The open-fronted building to the west of the stackyard is no longer present. Its footprint suggests it was probably a second cart and implement shed. The purpose of the small structure in the centre of the eastern set of yards is unclear. This, too, has been removed. The farmstead, serving a 480 acre holding, is large, having a barn range *(Figure 6.3)* of nearly 200 feet long. In the shelter of the barn, standing at right angles to it, were two series of yards each divided into smaller enclosures in which groups of cattle of different ages could be separated from each other. This provided for a throughput of stock and produced a steady stream of beasts which were 'finished' and ready for market. *Figure 6.4* shows how the farmstead operated as a 'manufactory' receiving corn and fodder at one end and producing fatstock for market and manure for the fields at the other.

The flow of activity at Scopwick House began with the corn crop arriving in the stackyard to the north of the complex where it was stored until threshing. Following steam threshing in the yard, using portable threshing equipment (a steam engine and threshing machine), grain and straw were conveyed to the barn range. The barn itself was not used for threshing but for storage of straw and foodstuffs.

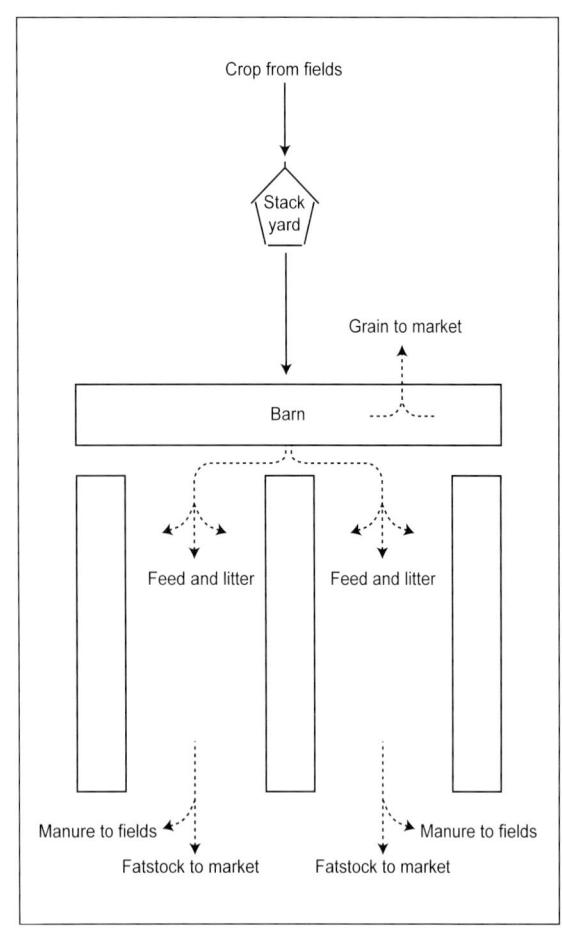

Figure 6.4
Diagram of the industrial process at Scopwick House, Scopwick
(Dave Watt)

It also functioned as a processing house accommodating milling, chopping and crushing machines for converting the threshed crop into feed and litter. Efficient use of time and labour was served by having the granary, where the grain was stored, in the barn range also. It was at the end of the range, at first floor level, over the wagon sheds. A trap door in the floor of the granary allowed grain to be loaded efficiently into wagons waiting below. There was then ready access to the roadway because the open front of the wagon sheds faced away from the farmyard and towards the road.

From the barn, fodder and litter could readily be distributed to the horse and livestock ranges. The stable range housed the heavy workhorses. Ventilators along the ridge of the roof, and 'hit and miss' sliding windows allowed the passage of air through each stable without admitting too much light, which was thought to be bad for the horses' eyes. 'The keeping of cart-horses is a very important item in the economy of the farm; they require at all times to be in good condition and ready to do a good day's work', stated one of the entrants in the *JRASE* Prize Essay competition for an economical and efficient plan for farm buildings.[22] Each of the three stables in the range was fitted with four stalls and eight harness pegs. The horses were stabled in pairs and the stalls had stout timber partitions and solid end posts.[23] The floors of the stalls were of stone cobbles to resist wear and tear from the horses' hooves. They were angled for drainage at exactly the required gradient to avoid the motive power for the farm being compromised by the horses going lame. Each stall had a stone feeding trough, wooden manger, cast iron ventilator and tethering rings.

After the repeal of the Corn Laws, falling income from grain and greater demand for meat to feed an increasing urban population led to intensification of livestock husbandry. Emphasis was laid upon cake feeding in sheltered yards such as those at Scopwick House. Plans for animal accommodation were based on scientific principles: 'The theorists, headed by Liebig and Johnston, tell us that if the external state of the bullock be cold, damp and cheerless, a large proportion of the food consumed is required for the production of animal heat', readers of the *JRASE* were informed in another of the farm buildings' prize essays.[24] The layout of Scopwick House acknowledged the animals' need for warmth with its two groups of south facing crewyards warmed by the sun and sheltered by the huge barn range to the north. Open-fronted sheds provided shelter for stock and for the troughs of expensive purchased feedstuffs. The ranges also contained other animal housing such as bull pens and loose boxes.

In addition to grain and fatstock the other main product of a nineteenth century farmstead was manure. The winner of the *JRASE* Prize Essay on farm buildings compared the practice of allowing the valuable ingredients of yard manure to wash away in the rain water flowing off the roofs to that of placing a tea-pot under an urn and leaving the water to run through the tea leaves before using the contents.[25] The well-trodden manure in the yards at Scopwick House was carefully protected by the provision of guttering on all the buildings. The 'tile water' from the roofs was collected in a 1000 gallon, lead tank which fed all the water troughs in the buildings. This is an example of the type of integrated system which so pleased the Victorian engineers who, rather than architects, were frequently the people engaged to design farm buildings in the second half of the nineteenth century.

Subsidiary activities such as the keeping of pigeons, hens and pigs were provided for around the edges of the main complex. The dovecote had boxes for 1000 birds and the hen house was fully equipped with built-in nesting boxes and a roosting bar *(Figure 6.5)*. The siting of such buildings was as carefully planned as the rest of the farmstead. 'There ought not to be the slightest convenience on the farm, down to a pigsty, that is not so precisely in the right spot, that to place it anywhere else would be a loss of labour and manure', wrote one agricultural commentator in 1851.[26] Women's work, tending hens and feeding pigs, was not allowed to interfere with the main thrust of production. Accordingly, the

Figure 6.5
Interior of hen house, Scopwick House, Scopwick
(A. S. Brook 1994)

entrance to the hen house is away from the principal flow of activity, on an outer wall, and the troughs in the vaulted pigsties under the dovecote were filled through chutes from the lane which separated the house yard from the main farm yard. It was also more convenient not to have to cross a dirty yard when dressed for domestic chores. The Victorian landowner's perceived responsibility for the moral welfare of the lower orders was also accommodated in this arrangement which separated male and female workers.

Outlying buildings accommodated peripheral activities that served the farming operations. The smithy and carpenter's shop lay to the west and a cart and implement shed to the east where there was unhindered access to the nearby road. There was also a pair of labourers' cottages set slightly away from the farmyard but close enough for convenient supervision and care of the livestock within the buildings. In the house yard there were riding stables, kennels for gun dogs and a coach house. These provided for the accoutrements of the affluent lifestyle adopted by wealthy tenant farmers. A popular nineteenth-century ballad, 'The new-fashioned farmer', comments bitterly on their rise in status:

> A good old-fashioned, long grey coat
> the farmers used to wear, sir,
>
> And old Dobbin they would ride to market
> or to fair, sir;
>
> But now fine geldings they must mount
> to join in all the chase, sir,
>
> Dressed up like any lord or squire
> before their landlord's face, sir.[27]

Figure 6.6
Chaplin estate cottages, Temple Bruer
(A. S. Brook 2010)

The farmhouse at Scopwick House was a commodious gentleman's residence, facing away from the agricultural buildings. Accepted thinking amongst agricultural writers was that 'intelligence and capital are ever found associated with a comfortable home'.[28] Accordingly many landowners equipped their holdings with farmhouses which, it was thought, would attract and retain tenants with the necessary enterprise and capital to farm a large holding efficiently and productively. At nearby Temple High Grange land improvement money was invested in major repairs and alterations to the farmhouse. Correspondence between the Chaplin estate and the commissioners who regulated improvement loans reveals that upgrading the farmhouse to attract the right sort of tenant was accepted as a justifiable object for agricultural loan capital: the commissioners queried the irregular shape of the dining room at Temple High Grange but the architect responded that the intention was to 'afford space for a large sideboard and greater facility for waiting at table',[29] and the loan was duly sanctioned.

Another aspect of the rising social status of the mid-Victorian tenant farmer was the distancing of himself and his family from his workforce. This, too, was the subject of rustic comment in popular song:

> The farmer and the servant together used to dine,
> But now they're in the parlour with their pudding, beef and wine,
> The master and the mistress, their family all alone,
> And they will eat the beef, my boys, while we may pick the bone.[30]

Up until the 1840s it had been common practice in eastern England for unmarried agricultural labourers to be accommodated in the farmhouse.[31] When farmhouses were remodelled by landowners seeking to attract suitable tenants the opportunity was taken to discontinue this arrangement. Landowners engaging in improvements to farmhouses and agricultural buildings frequently improved the cottage accommodation on their estate as part of the same process, consequently loans for farm buildings were often expended on three purposes: cottages, farmhouses and working buildings.

The landscape of the Chaplin estate at Temple Bruer and Thompson's Bottom, on the heath land south west of Scopwick, is dotted with pairs of estate cottages. These are well-built dwellings providing a standard of accommodation which was considered suitable for farm labourers by those who wrote treatises on the subject in *JRASE* and other farming publications.[32] Some of the cottages are dated and those at Temple Bruer *(Figure 6.6)*, dated 1871, were almost certainly built with some of the £2938 borrowed by Chaplin, between 1871 and 1873, for farm buildings at Temple Bruer and Metheringham.[33] If this is so, it is clear evidence of the impact of loan capital on dispersal of settlement.

As has been noted, the latest detailed census data available to Mills as he undertook his research were the 1851 figures and this meant that his observations about the impact of agricultural change on the development of rural settlement related principally to the period from around 1765 to 1850. However, the other source for his study, the One-Inch Ordnance Survey maps based on a survey of 1883-8, led him to conclude that the dispersal of settlement was not complete by 1850. He considered this to be the case particularly in the spring zone parishes of his census sample, situated on the limestone cuesta at its junction with lower-lying clays on both the dip and the scarp slope, rather than in the clay vale townships. It was in the spring zone that his map study suggested dispersal of settlement continued to a later date. Building improvements on the Chaplin estate, funded by loan capital, are an example of just such continued dispersal of settlement in the spring zone, in the second half of the nineteenth century. Furthermore, they demonstrate that the agricultural changes identified by Mills as promoting dispersal in an earlier period, continued to have an influence on dispersal in the second half of the nineteenth century.

For just one of his spring zone parishes, Nocton, Mills had population figures for 1891 and 1901 which demonstrated that the percentage of the population living in dispersed dwellings continued to rise until the end of the nineteenth century.[34] Nocton is a parish for which there is land improvement loan evidence. Records of land improvement borrowing for Nocton show that, between 1857 and 1879, £4442 was borrowed for the construction of farm buildings.[35] Therefore, there is evidence to suggest that, in Nocton, land improvement borrowing was an element in the dispersal of settlement that continued beyond mid-century. The availability of capital to fund improvements which led to dispersal was an important factor noted by Mills. In the land improvement records for Nocton we have an example in which the source of capital for some, if not all, of the dispersal of settlement in the parish, in the second half of the nineteenth century, is clearly identified as being land improvement loan money.

To explore the possible connection between land improvement borrowing and continued dispersal in the second half of the nineteenth century, the incidence of loan activity in Mills's other spring zone parishes was compared with that in his parishes in the clay vale. This was in order to test whether there was a greater incidence of borrowing in the spring zone where Mills considered dispersal went on longer. Revisiting his sample of twenty-two parishes, and using land improvement loan records to identify those parishes in which loan capital was invested, it was found that sixteen (73%) of them experienced improvement funded by land improvement loans. The purposes of these loans were: draining, roads, bridges, enclosure, watercourses, sluices, embanking, farm buildings and water supply.

Eight out of eleven parishes in each of Mills's two zones, the clay vale and the spring zone, had loan capital applied in them between 1857 and 1909.[36] *Table 6.1* shows the number of loans taken out for improvements in each parish together with the first and last year in which money was borrowed. The estimated total amount expended in each parish, on all types of improvement, is given as well as the estimated total amount expended on farm buildings' improvements. The need for an estimation of the amount expended on farm buildings has been explained above, along with details of how the estimated amount was calculated. Frequent borrowing for more than one parish, under a single loan, is the reason why the total amount borrowed for each parish is also an estimated amount. In such circumstances the amount of the loan was divided by the number of parishes to which the loan applied in order to estimate the total amount invested in improvements for each individual parish.

It was immediately apparent that there was greater loan activity in the spring zone parishes. Loan activity started here slightly earlier, and finished slightly later, than in the clay vale parishes.

Spring Zone	First loan	Last loan	Number of loans	Farm Bdgs only	Fm Bdgs and other purposes	Other purposes only	Total all improvements £	Total Fm Bdgs £
Coleby	1865	1876	9	2	3	4	8904	3231
Hackthorn	1861	1896	13	4	9	0	2395	1437
Harmston	1888	1890	3	0	2	1	1557	573
Ingham	1873	1873	1	0	1	0	2812	1125
Nocton	1857	1879	5	5	0	0	4442	4442
Saxby	1874	1880	16	13	3	0	4093	3654
Spridlington	1882	1903	2	0	0	2	459	0
Welton	1861	1909	12	3	8	1	2188	1324
All	**1857**	**1909**	**61**	**27**	**26**	**8**	**26,850**	**15,786**
Clay Vale								
Aubourn	1875	1890	5	2	2	1	1740	756
Doddington	1879	1906	3*	1	0	1	1005	255
Dunholme	1861	1861	1	0	0	1	79	0
Reepham	1884	1884	1	0	0	1	287	0
Saxilby	1876	1876	1	0	0	1	215	0
Skellingthorpe	1873	1873	1	1	0	0	190	190
Thorpe on the Hill	1875	1891	4	2	0	2	409	183
Wickenby	1861	1879	25	14	11	0	3876	2831
All	**1861**	**1906**	**41***	**20**	**13**	**7**	**7801**	**4215**

*For one of the three Doddington loans the purpose was not specified

Table 6.1
Land improvement loan borrowing in Mills's sample parishes 1855-1910
Sources: D. R. Mills, 'The development of rural settlement around Lincoln, with special reference to the 18th and 19th centuries', *The East Midland Geographer*, 11 (June, 1959), p.7; all records of land improvement borrowing for the listed parishes in TNA MAF 66.

An estimated £26,850 of loan capital was invested in improvements in the spring zone parishes, almost 3.5 times the estimated £7801 invested in the clay vale. For farm buildings an estimated £15,786 was invested in the spring zone and £4215 in the clay vale. Therefore the estimated amount of improvement loan capital invested in farm buildings in the spring zone was 3.75 times that invested in the clay vale. The coincidence of higher spring zone borrowing activity, especially for farm buildings, and Mills's observation of greater dispersal of settlement in spring zone parishes on the 1883-8 Ordnance Survey maps, strongly suggests that the higher incidence of land improvement loan investment in the spring zone was a factor influencing the continued dispersal of settlement in this area in the second half of the nineteenth century.

It might be questioned whether some of the new buildings funded by land improvement loans were erected in village centres. That this was not generally the case, except in estate villages where cottage building was part of what Mills identified as the 'pre-conceived plan' undertaken by the 'landed family who resided there',[37] can be confirmed by observation of standing buildings. Cottages, farmhouses and agricultural buildings erected with loan capital exhibit a certain uniformity of appearance which is the result of regulations governing their construction. Because of the protracted period over which loans were repaid (typically twenty-five or forty years) it was often the current owners' heirs who inherited the debt and the responsibility for paying off the loan. The interests of these so called 'tenants in tail' or 'remaindermen' were protected by legislation requiring that the improvements, for which they would bear the burden of debt, would be durable enough to outlive the term of the loan and benefit future generations.

Amongst Chaplin's papers deposited at Lincolnshire Archives is a printed list of requirements regarding construction standards for buildings erected with land improvement loan capital. In this, particulars such as the required depth for the foundations, the weight of lead to be used for the gutters and the size of timbers for different parts of the roof, are stipulated.[38] In general, stone was preferred to brick for the construction of farmhouses, cottages and agricultural buildings, and slate was preferred for roofs rather than pantiles. These regulations resulted in the uniformity which enables buildings erected with loan capital to be identified upon observation, as does the existence of pattern books containing 'approved designs' for farm buildings. The best known of these is J. Bailey Denton's *The Farm Homesteads of England.* The subtitle of the work sums up its contents: *A collection of plans of English homesteads existing in different parts of the country, carefully selected from the most approved specimens of farm architecture to illustrate the accommodation required under various modes of husbandry, with a list of the leading principles recognised in the construction and arrangement of the buildings.*[39]

Denton, a founding member of the Institute of Surveyors, was one of the new breed of professionals who emerged in the mid-nineteenth century. As a witness before Parliament for various bills connected with railways, water supply, drainage, sewerage works and public health he was described variously as surveyor, land valuer, land agent, civil engineer and as Principal Drainage Engineer to the General Land Drainage and Improvement Company.[40] The General Land Drainage and Improvement Company was one of the companies which lent money for agricultural improvements, including farm buildings. It was in his capacity as engineer to the company that Denton published *Farm Homesteads of England.* The volume was, almost certainly, a reference book for those seeking designs for farm buildings that would be approved by the Inclosure Commissioners.

Landowners whose ownership of their estates was limited by strict settlement were not the only category of owner to whom land improvement loans were available. The clergy were also able to benefit from this legislation because they too were not the outright owners of the land they occupied but held it in trust for those who came after them. As a result a number of them took out loans to improve their glebe. In the spring zone sample thirteen loans (21%) were taken out by the vicar of the parish. In the clay vale, clergy were the applicants for five loans (12%). For Lincolnshire as a whole the proportion was greater; clergy took out 30% of the 675 loans for the county between 1855 and 1910.[41] There was considerable clergy borrowing activity in Nocton: in November 1857 the Rev. Edward Wilson borrowed £860 for farm buildings on his glebe from the Lands Improvement Company[42], one of the companies from which owners of settled estates, or 'limited owners' as they were sometimes known, could borrow. There was, however, another source of loan capital from which clergy could borrow for a number of purposes, including improvements to their glebe, and this was under the provisions for Mortgages Under Gilbert's Acts.

These mortgages made money from Queen Anne's Bounty available to clergy for improvements to their livings. The purpose of this was to encourage clergy residence and combat the perceived evils of pluralism and non-residence of clergy in their benefices. Between 1840 and 1910, 470 loans were taken out under the terms of Mortgages Under Gilbert's Acts for improvements to benefices in Lincolnshire. The vast majority of these were for improvements to the parsonage house designed by leading local architects such as E. J. Willson and F. H. Goddard of Lincoln, Charles Kirk of Sleaford and James Fowler of Louth. W. A. Nicholson, who designed Chaplin's estate village of Blankney, was also engaged in such works. In some cases architects of national repute, such as S. S. Teulon, Anthony Salvin and Arthur William Blomfield, were engaged. For the rebuilding of the Deanery in Eastgate, Lincoln, in 1847, which was funded from this source, William Burn was the architect. Although principally involving improvements to the parsonage house, many of these schemes included 'other offices' or 'out offices'. Where specifications and plans survive it is apparent that some of these included a range of buildings which, if they were attached to a farmhouse, would be regarded as farm buildings.[43]

Clergy operated like other landowners in that they let out their glebe land as farm holdings. The records

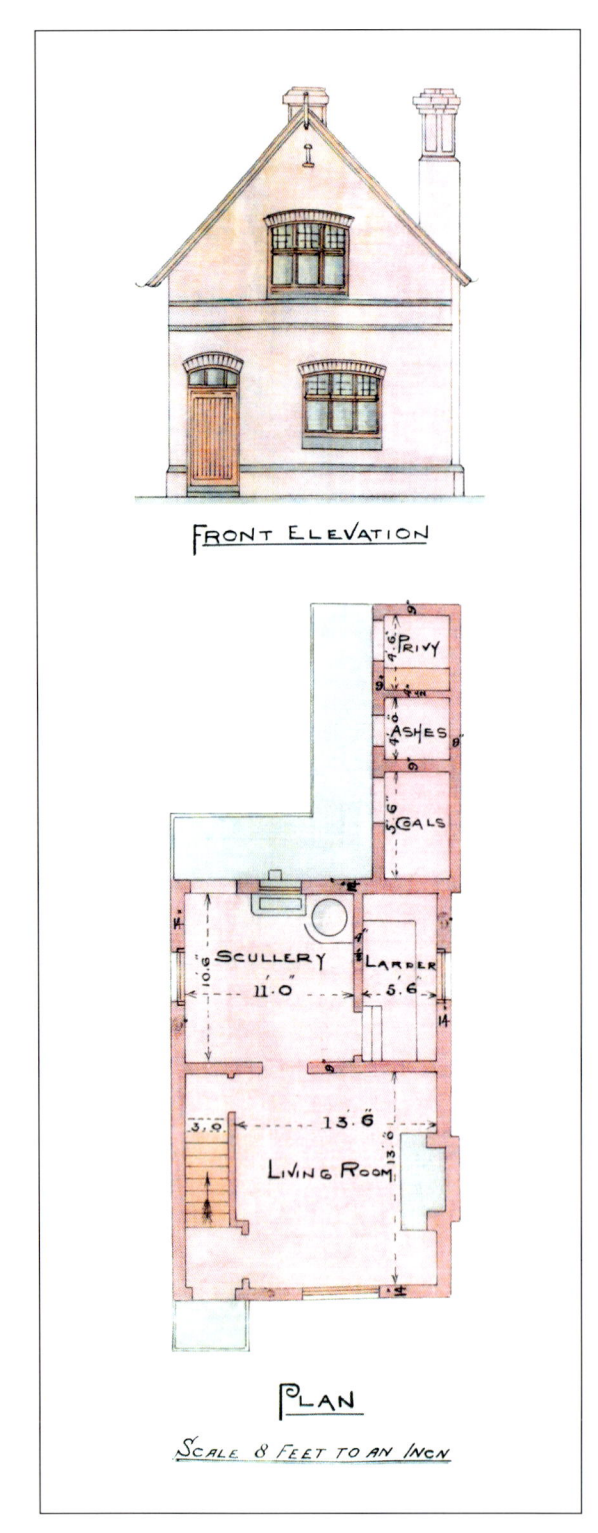

Figure 6.7
Front elevation and ground plan of proposed cottages, Nocton glebe (LAO MGA 716)

(With the permission of the Diocese of Lincoln and Lincolnshire Archives)

show that Mortgages Under Gilbert's Acts' capital was used to equip farms on glebe land just as land improvement loan money was. Vicars of Nocton borrowed a total of £1365 under the provisions for Mortgages Under Gilbert's Acts. In January 1873 the Rev. Edward Wilson borrowed £300 for an unspecified purpose. The Rev. Arthur Charles Wilson borrowed £665 in December 1876 for alterations to the farmhouse, stables and outbuildings on his glebe and in July 1886 the Rev. Henry Footman borrowed £400 for two single cottages on his glebe which were to replace an old pair of cottages which were 'past repair'.[44] It was money invested in this manner, in farmhouses and cottages rather than in the parsonage house, which is further evidence of loan capital stimulating building activity that promoted the dispersal of settlement in the second half of the nineteenth century.

The plans for improvements at Glebe Farm on Nocton Heath, in 1876, were drawn up by the architect William Watkins. They involved enlarging the farmhouse which, his report stated, was erected within the last 20 years and 'is now too small as it only contains two sitting rooms on the ground floor'.[45] New stables were proposed at Glebe Farm because of the distance of the present accommodation from the farmhouse and the unsuitability of the lean-to shed in which the farmer's nag was housed. These are further examples of the rise in status of tenant farmers and increasing expectations regarding their living standards. It is probable that the farmhouse and buildings erected twenty years previously were those built with the £860 borrowed by the Rev. Edward Wilson from the Lands Improvement Company in 1857.

John Wigram of Collingham, Surveyor, drew up the plans for the two new cottages to be built on the glebe at Nocton in 1886 *(Figure 6.7)*. This suggests the involvement of a member of a profession, other than that of architect, in the planning of farm buildings and cottages in the nineteenth century. The new cottages were to have three bedrooms and two ground floor rooms plus a larder and out offices (coal house, ash house and privy).[46] The location of one of the cottages has not been identified but it is possible that the other was the dwelling erected on glebe land at the top of Nocton Fen, at the junction of the Car Dyke and the parish boundary with Potterhanworth, beside Bottom Barff plantation.[47]

This appears on the 1905 25" Ordnance Survey map but is no longer extant.[48] Of the farmhouse and buildings at Glebe Farm on Nocton Heath, only a barn remains standing. The money borrowed in the case of Glebe Farm and the two new cottages at Nocton was for the enlargement or replacement of existing buildings so was not automatically responsible for an increase in the number of residents, which would constitute dispersal of the population in areas beyond the village nucleus. However, it may be argued that the improved accommodation would have encouraged an increase in the number of occupants. Therefore loan capital could be said to have promoted improvement resulting in the ongoing dispersal of settlement in the parish which was identified by Mills.

It has been demonstrated that money borrowed under the provisions of land improvement loans and Mortgages Under Gilbert's Acts formed part of the capital applied to the improvements believed by Mills to be a major factor in the dispersal of settlement in nineteenth-century Lincolnshire. Mills considered the availability of capital to be an important issue. There remain two questions: what proportion of improvement activity was funded by loan capital and what was the source of the rest of the money invested in improvements in Lincolnshire? The proportion of improvement capital that is represented by land improvement loan capital and Mortgages Under Gilbert's Acts is difficult to calculate. At national level we have an insight afforded by the evidence of James Caird to the Select Committee on Improvement of Land in 1873 in which he estimated that, in the case of drainage, loan capital had funded 20% of what needed to be done. However, other witnesses were not as sanguine about the extent of its impact.[49] For Lincolnshire we have seen that 373 parishes (52%) were subject to investment of loan capital. What we do not yet have are exact figures, at parish level, for the proportion of the capital expended on improvements which came from the two sources identified in this study. A possible way forward in answering this question will be for the amount of capital borrowed from land improvement companies and under the provisions of Mortgages Under Gilbert's Acts to be compared with the total amount invested in improvements, in individual parishes.

This leads us to the question of where the rest of the capital for improvements came from. There is firm evidence for a combination of owner's money and loan capital being invested in improvements on at least one estate in Lincolnshire: that of Christopher Turnor. Evidence of the source of capital invested in improvements on his lands, in both north and south Lincolnshire, is to be found in the correspondence of Andrew Thompson, agent of the Sneyd estate in Staffordshire. Thompson was the surveyor appointed by the Inclosure Commissioners to report on Turnor's loan applications. In correspondence held at the University of Keele, Thompson states that:

> The applicant for many years past has been improving his extensive Estates by drainage and buildings under the Public and Private Money Drainage Acts, & the Act of the Lands Improvement Co. The greater portion of the land has been drained, and new Buildings and Labourers Cottages have been provided for many of the Farms partly at the cost of the owner.[50]

At Stoke Park Farm, South Stoke, £800 of loan capital from the Lands Improvement Company was invested in a new farmhouse in 1865. At the same time Turnor himself funded the conversion of the former farmhouse into cottages and additions to the working buildings on the holding. Under the same loan new agricultural buildings were to be erected at Lissington whilst the repair of the existing buildings and alteration of the stables were to be at the owner's cost.[51]

In the case of Grange Farm, Little Ponton, on Turnor's South Lincolnshire estate, a similar process to that at Scopwick took place with the old village farm buildings being replaced by a more conveniently positioned new farmstead. Thompson reported that the original farmstead at Little Ponton consisted of 'four very old Stone & thatched barns, stables and some very dilapidated sheds, all worn out and very inconvenient' and that the farmhouse was 'a long and narrow inconveniently arranged dwelling'. He went on to explain the proposed re-siting of the farmstead: 'The nearest tillage field to this old steading is half a mile distant. It is proposed to erect a new steading on a convenient site near the centre of the farm.'[52] We are told that Turnor again laid out capital of his own (£400) on this and a concurrent improvement scheme at Manor Farm, Kirmond le Mire.[53] This combination of loan capital and the owner's personal finance reflects the fact that land improvement loan capital was only available for new works whilst the owner was responsible for funding works which involved repairs and alterations to existing buildings. Owner's capital invested in agricultural improvements may have been personal wealth, perhaps from mining or other types of mineral extraction, as on the Scarbrough estate,[54] or from marriage, as on the Sledmere estate in East Yorkshire.[55] Alternatively, the money may have been raised by borrowing which was not secured against the value of his settled estate.

There is a danger that the historian's interpretation of the past can be distorted by the windows through which it is possible to view bygone events and activities. The evidence available to us can lead to a fragmented view of past events as a result of its incomplete and disparate nature. It is necessary to attempt to regard the raising of capital for agricultural improvements from the perspective of those 'on the ground' at the time. Taking this view we begin to see a pattern emerging wherein a comprehensive scheme for improvements across a parish would be drawn up. Sources of funding would then be explored and a 'funding package' including land improvement loan money, Mortgages Under Gilbert's Acts and owner's own capital from various sources, would be put together.

There is evidence of related borrowing for an integrated improvement campaign at North Coates, on the Salt Marsh south of Cleethorpes. Here, Gervaise Tottenham Waldo Sibthorp Esq. borrowed £3927 for 'embanking etc.' from the Lands Improvement Company on 27 February, 1857, and, on the very same date, the Rev. Charles Pilkington borrowed £1523 from the same company for the same purpose.[56] The programme of improvement continued the following year. On 6 May, 1858, Pilkington borrowed £1251 and Sibthorp £2124 for enclosing and roads.[57] In June Sibthorp borrowed a further £1062 for the same purpose.[58] The next year, on 11 April, 1861, Sibthorp borrowed yet again; this time he took out a loan of £649 for farm buildings.

At North Coates the priest, the Rev. Charles Pilkington, who borrowed money for agricultural improvements was not the incumbent. The Pilkington family, along with the Sibthorp family, were major landowners in the parish.[59] However, a high proportion of those who took out loans for the same parish at the same time were squire and incumbent. It was common, in the nineteenth century, for presentation to a living to be in the gift of the landowner. Therefore the individual chosen as parson was frequently one of his younger sons, a nephew or some other person enjoying his support and sponsorship. This could account for the close co-operation of parson and landowner in improvement activity in a parish. Even if there was no consanguinity or similar close ties there are other possible reasons for concerted action. One is that once some of the holdings in a parish had been improved it would be necessary for other owners of land, including clergy with their glebe, to bring the provision on their farms up to an equivalent standard in order to compete for the best tenants. Another is that, in an age when it was seen as the duty of major landowners to set an example of 'best practice' in agriculture, it was common for their neighbours to follow their lead in such matters.

Examples of connected borrowing activity by landowner and incumbent can be identified. In August, 1857, the Rev. Benjamin Jesse Wood borrowed £188 from the Lands Improvement Company for farm buildings and roads on his glebe at Ruckland, Farforth and Maidenwell and in October of the same year the Lord of the Manor, William Oslear Esq., also borrowed for farm buildings.[60] This loan, for £810, was from the Lands Improvement Company also. Under two loans, in 1875 and 1876, Ralph Henry Christopher Nevile Esq. borrowed £1463 from the Lands Improvement Company for farm buildings in eight parishes including Thorpe on the Hill. The following year the Rev. Henry Bickersteth Otley, vicar of nearby Newton upon Trent, borrowed £154 under the provisions for Mortgages Under Gilbert's Acts for new farm buildings on his glebe at Thorpe on the Hill.[61] The £1463 borrowed by Nevile was not a large sum of money to equip farms in eight parishes with new buildings. Therefore it is reasonable to suppose that, as on the Turnor estate, Nevile was combining his own capital with improvement borrowing, in order to improve his farm buildings. If this is so, at Thorpe on the Hill we have an example of an improvement package that included loan capital from a land improvement company, funding from a Mortgage Under Gilbert's Acts and landowner's own capital.

In the opinion of Stephen Daniels and Susanne Seymour, '"Improvement" is arguably the key word in the literature culture of the eighteenth and nineteenth centuries and certainly of that culture's designs on the landscape'.[62] Mills identified agricultural improvement as being the impetus behind dispersal of settlement in the late eighteenth and early nineteenth centuries. Enclosure, which was thought by some to be the principal element in this process, was one aspect of such improvement. Records of borrowing for agricultural improvement, and the farmhouses, working buildings and cottages which were part of the ongoing development of rural settlement in Lincolnshire in the second half of the nineteenth century, are important sources of evidence which increase our understanding of how the process of dispersal continued after 1851.

Throughout his long academic career Dennis Mills has enthusiastically opened up new areas of historical research and generously shared his knowledge and expertise with other researchers, among them myself. It is hoped that this introduction to two under-exploited sources, land improvement loans and Mortgages Under Gilbert's Acts, will inform readers and inspire them to look more closely at the evidence for nineteenth-century agricultural improvement these records contain. Perhaps they will also look with a more discerning eye at the farm buildings of Lincolnshire.[63]

Notes

[1] D. R. Mills, 'The development of rural settlement around Lincoln, with special reference to the 18th and 19th centuries', *The East Midland Geographer,* 11 (June, 1959), pp.3-15. This article was reproduced in, *English Rural Communities: the Impact of a Specialised Economy,* edited by D. R. Mills (1973), pp.83-97.

[2] W. G. Hoskins, *The Making of the English Landscape* (1955), pp.157-160; M. B. Gleave, 'Dispersed and nucleated settlement in the Yorkshire Wolds, 1770-1850', *Transactions and Papers (Institute of British Geographers),* 30 (1962), pp.105-118. This article was also reproduced in *English Rural Communities,* edited by Mills, pp.98-115.

[3] Mills, *East Midland Geographer,* p.9.

[4] *Ibid.,* pp.9-11.

[5] Mills selected parishes for which the enumerators gave sufficiently accurate address details to enable the location of the property in which each household resided to be identified. He compared two groups of eleven townships, one in the spring zone and one in the clay vale. The spring zone townships were: Cammeringham, Canwick, Coleby, Hackthorn, Harmston, Ingham, Nettleham, Nocton, Saxby, Spridlington and Welton. The clay vale townships were: Aubourn, Cherry Willingham, Doddington, Dunholme, Fiskerton, North Hykeham, Reepham, Saxilby, Skellingthorpe, Thorpe-on-the-Hill and Wickenby. All except Canwick saw an increase in population between 1801 and 1851. Mills, *East Midland Geographer,* pp. 6-7.

[6] A. D. M. Phillips, 'Landlord investment in farm buildings in the English midlands in the mid nineteenth century', in *Land, Labour and Agriculture, 1700-1920: Essays for Gordon Mingay,* edited by B. A. Holderness and Michael Turner (1991), pp.191-210; A. D. M. Phillips, *The Staffordshire Reports of Andrew Thompson to the Enclosure Commissioners, 1858-68: Landlord Investment in Staffordshire Agriculture in the Mid-Nineteenth Century* (Stafford, 1996); A. D. M. Phillips, 'Rebuilding rural England: farm building provision, 1850-1900' in *Home and Colonial: Essays in Celebration of Robin Butlin's Contribution to Historical Geography,* edited by Alan Lester, Historical Geography Research Series, 39 (2005); A. D. M. Phillips, *Land Improvement in Mid-Nineteenth-Century England and Wales: Andrew Thompson's Reports to the Inclosure Commissioners* (forthcoming).

[7] Phillips, *Staffordshire Reports,* pp.6-12, provides a useful introduction to land improvement acts.

[8] Barbara English and John Saville, *Strict Settlement: a guide for historians* (Hull, 1983).

[9] J. Bailey Denton, 'On land drainage and improvement by loans from government or public companies', *Journal of the Royal Agricultural Society of England* (hereafter *JRASE*), 2nd ser. 4 (1868), p.125.

[10] P. Pusey, 'On the agricultural improvements of Lincolnshire', *JRASE,* 4 (1843), pp.287-316.

[11] Registers of Loans Sanctioned, Absolute Orders, Assignments and Rent Charges, Works Executed and Minutes of Lands Improvement Company Directors' Meetings 1860-3 are all held in The National Archives (hereafter TNA) MAF 66.

[12] For a detailed discussion of the legislative process which enabled the setting up and operating of the system of land improvement loans see David Spring, *The English Landed Estate in the Nineteenth Century: its Administration* (Baltimore, 1963), (hereafter Spring, *Landed Estate*) pp.135-177.

[13] The author's post-graduate research project, funded by the University of Hull, included an examination of records for over 15,000 loans (1855-1910) and transcription of all information regarding the 675 that were for Lincolnshire improvements.

[14] A. S. Brook, 'The Buildings of High Farming: Lincolnshire Farm Buildings 1840-1910', PhD thesis, University of Hull (2005), p.208.

[15] Pusey, 'Agricultural improvements of Lincolnshire', *JRASE,* 4 (1843), pp.300-1.

[16] *Kirkby Green and Scopwick: Historical Sketches of two Lincolnshire Parishes,* edited by P. Baumber and D. Mills (Scopwick, Lincolnshire, 1993).

[17] TNA MAF 66/35/597; TNA MAF 66/35/743; TNA MAF 66/36/223.

[18] Nicholas Goddard, 'Information and innovation in early-Victorian farming systems', in *Land, Labour and Agriculture,* edited by Holderness and Turner (1991), p.167. See also Susanna Wade Martins, *Farmers, Landlords and Landscapes: Rural Britain, 1720 to 1870* (Macclesfield, 2004), pp.13-15.

[19] J. A. Clarke, 'On the farming of Lincolnshire' *JRASE,* 12 (1851), p.328.

[20] G. H. Andrews, *Agricultural Engineering,* 1 (1852), p.52, quoted in R. Brigden, *Victorian Farms* (Marlborough, 1986), p.28.

[21] Jo Garner, 'Scopwick House (The Firs)', in *Kirkby Green and Scopwick,* edited by Baumber and Mills, p.37.

[22] J. Hudson, 'A plan for farm buildings', *JRASE,* 11 (1850), p.283.

[23] Scopwick House was therefore a 24 horse farm. It was reckoned that on the light land of the Lincolnshire heath one horse was needed for every 20 acres. This tallies with the farm's extent of 480 acres.

[24] C. P. Tebbut, 'On the construction of farm buildings', *JRASE,* 11 (1850), p.308.

[25] Sir Thomas Tancred, Bart., 'Essay on the construction of farm buildings', *JRASE,* 11 (1850), p.193.

[26] G. A. Dean, *The Land Steward* (1851) quoted in S. Wade Martins, *Journal of the Norfolk Archaeology Society,* Special Conference edn. (1981), p.10.

[27] 'The new-fashioned farmer,' in *The Painful Plough,* edited by Roy Palmer (Cambridge, 1973), p.14.

[28] J. Bailey Denton, *The Farm Homesteads of England* (1864), p.102.

[29] Lincolnshire Archives (hereafter LAO) BS 13/1/5/12. See also Baumber and Mills, *Kirkby Green and Scopwick,* pp.8-10.

[30] 'Country hirings', in *The Painful Plough,* edited by Palmer, p.15.

[31] C. Hayfield, 'Farm servants' accommodation on the Yorkshire Wolds', *Folk Life,* 33 (1994-5), pp.7-28.

[32] J. Young Macvicar, 'Labourers' cottages', *JRASE,* 10 (1849), pp.401-421; Henry Goddard, 'On the construction of a pair of cottages for agricultural labourers', *JRASE,* 10 (1849), pp.230-246; H. J. Little, 'The agricultural labourer', *JRASE,* 2nd ser. 14 (1878), pp.780-3.

[33] TNA MAF 66/33/279; TNA MAF 66/34/79; TNA MAF 66/34/99.

[34] Mills, *East Midland Geographer,* p.7.

[35] TNA MAF 66/2/9; TNA MAF 66/35/504; TNA MAF 66/35/574; TNA MAF 66/35/703; TNA MAF 66/36/46.

[36] There was no land improvement borrowing between 1855 and 1910 for three of Mills's spring zone parishes: Cammeringham, Canwick and Nettleham, and for three of his clay vale parishes: Cherry Willingham, Fiskerton and North Hykeham.

[37] Mills, *East Midland Geographer,* p.13.

[38] 'Minute of the Inclosure Commissioners for England and Wales with reference to the Erection of Farm Buildings and Labourers' Cottages in England under the Several Acts for the Improvement of Land', November 1864, LAO BS/13/1/5/3.

[39] Denton, *The Farm Homesteads of England* (1864).

[40] Database of Witnesses in Committees on Opposed Private Bills 1771-1917, keyword search 'Denton', 7.7.98; billcode search of all bills identified in the 'Denton' keyword search, 10.7.98. The Parliamentary Archives expect this database to be available on line in March 2011.

[41] Brook, 'Buildings of High Farming', p.232.

[42] TNA MAF 66/26/9.

[43] Brook, 'Buildings of High Farming', pp.233-4.

[44] LAO MGA 577; LAO MGA 617; LAO MGA 716.

[45] LAO MGA 617.

[46] LAO MGA 716.

[47] Plan of Nocton Glebe, LAO 10-Nott/2/72. I am grateful to Sue Morris for her assistance in attempts to locate these cottages.

[48] OS 1:2500 County Series, Lincolnshire Sheet 79.9, Second Edition (1905). The buildings shown here are the same layout as Wigram's plan but a mirror image of it. It is possible that the cottage was built the other way on for reasons dictated by its location.

[49] Spring, *Landed Estate,* p.177.

[50] Keele University (hereafter KU) S3186/59.

[51] KU S3184/190; KU S3184/192; TNA MAF 66/30/296.

[52] KU S3186/60.

[53] KU S3186/222.

[54] T. W. Beastall, *A North Country Estate: The Lumleys and Saundersons as Landowners 1600-1900* (Chichester, 1975), passim.

[55] In 1770 Christopher Sykes of Sledmere, E. Yorks, married Elizabeth Egerton of Tatton whose inheritance of £17,000 from her father was hugely augmented by her inheriting her brother's Cheshire estates and another £60,000 from her aunt in 1780. Christopher Sykes sold off shipping interests and government stock and he and his wife expanded and improved the Sledmere estate. http://www.hull.ac.uk/arc/collection/landedfamilyan-destatepapers/sykes.html Accessed 22.10.10.

[56] TNA MAF 66/25/192; TNA MAF 66/25/193. The spelling of the parish name is 'Northcotes' in these documents.

[57] TNA MAF 66/26/99; TNA MAF 66/26/101.

[58] TNA MAF 66/26/104.

[59] *White's 1856 Lincolnshire* (repr., New York, 1969), p.559.

[60] TNA MAF 66/25/260; TNA MAF 66/25/278.

[61] TNA MAF 66/35/30; TNA MAF 66/35/288; LAO MGA 622.

[62] S. Daniels and S. Seymour, 'Landscape design and the idea of improvement 1730-1914', in *An Historical Geography of England and Wales,* edited by R. A. Dodgshon and R. A. Butlin (2nd edn., 1990), p.487.

[63] It should be noted that the permission of the owner should be sought before entering private land to visit old farm buildings. My gratitude is extended to the owners of all the buildings I have had permission to visit and record.

CHAPTER 7

FAIRS AND MARKETS
Challenging encounters between the urban and rural in Lincolnshire c.1840-1920
Andrew Walker

Introduction

Over the past half century, a recurring feature of Dennis Mills's work has been his interest in the interaction between the urban and the rural in past societies. His publications, for instance, have explored migration from rural areas; the impact urban growth has had upon the nature of surrounding rural villages; the economic significance of agricultural customers to small-town tradespeople; and the ways in which edgelands between the rural and urban have been developed over time.[1] A characteristic feature of all of this work is its engagement with the quantifiable in order to gauge the nature of the relationship between the rural and the urban.

A significant amount of attention has been paid in recent decades by cultural historians to the ways in which it is claimed the rural has been romanticised, largely by those who have made their livings in the city. It has been noted that the championing of all things bucolic can be discerned in key cultural movements including the Pre-Raphaelites and the Arts and Crafts movement. The enduring popularity of William Morris, the floral prints of Laura Ashley and the success of the long-running radio series 'The Archers' are all in part evidence, it is claimed, of the cultural potency of an idealised rural England, largely consumed by urban dwellers.[2] Indeed, one line of argument has suggested that this predilection for the rural, especially amongst the middle classes, when mixed with an associated anti-industrial attitude, was partially responsible for the decline of the entrepreneurial spirit in twentieth-century Britain.[3]

This chapter takes issue with romanticised notions of the rural being the norm during the later-nineteenth and early-twentieth centuries. Like Dennis Mills's consideration of past rural and urban interactions, this chapter explores specific local examples. In an examination of encounters between the rural and the urban in a medium-sized town, Lincoln, the chapter suggests that, far from having romanticised views of the rural, leading townspeople sought to guard against some rustic aspects which regularly threatened their hard-won urban orderliness and control. By examining a number of set-piece events in Lincoln's calendar, the sometimes problematic relationship between urban and rural sensibilities will be examined in the later-nineteenth and early-twentieth centuries. Two annual events will be considered, the hiring fair and the horse fair, and then a more regular economic and social urban-rural encounter will be scrutinised in the form of the weekly livestock market.

Lincolnshire hiring fairs, c. 1850-1920

One particular type of fair, the hiring fair, was the subject of much 'respectable' concern, especially during the mid-Victorian period. Before examining the nature of the hiring fair, the reasons for the moral outrage often surrounding it, and the causes of its demise by the early twentieth century, it is pertinent to consider why the hiring fair continued to prevail in Lincolnshire when in many parts of England this form of securing agricultural labour had ceased some one hundred or more years earlier.

Throughout much of England, until at least the end of the eighteenth century, agricultural labour was hired on a twelve-month or a six-month basis, usually with contracts ending in the Spring often on or near to May Day or 'Old' May Day - May 14.[4] However, by the early nineteenth century, in many arable parts of England, annual hiring was in decline as farmers began to employ labourers on a weekly or daily basis, thus giving them much more flexibility. The payment in kind, usually by means of providing accommodation, was also becoming less common as the relationships between farmer and labourer were becoming defined increasingly by the cash nexus in a capitalised system of production. This was especially the case in intensively-farmed arable areas such as East Anglia.

In some agricultural districts, especially those where pastoral farming prevailed, or where population was sparse, and therefore labour difficult to obtain, the annual hiring system of obtaining living-in farm servants continued. Arthur Wilson-Fox, the Assistant Commissioner, noted in his Lincolnshire report published in the Royal Commission on Agriculture in 1895 that:

> In Lincolnshire, the system of the yearly hiring prevails in the case of foremen and men in charge of animals; that is shepherds, horsemen, waggoners and stockmen. They are called confined men. Ordinary labourers are engaged by the week or day. There appeared to be more confined men in North Lincolnshire than in the South because in the north the farms are larger and require the supervision of foremen and also more sheep and cattle are kept on them which necessitates the attendance of confined men. Moreover, many of the farms on the Wolds are a long distance from villages and it is consequently both for the convenience of the master and the men that the latter should live with them.[5]

By 1901, still some 16.1 per cent of agricultural workers in Lincolnshire were living-in and being hired annually.[6] As Wilson-Fox indicated in his report, the cycle of annual hirings did vary: he noted that married men were usually hired in February and left for their new situations on April 6, but in some districts, particularly in the north of the county, new jobs began on May 14, when single men were also usually hired.[7] As one farm labourer, Fred Brader, from Belchford, near Horncastle explained:

> There's a rason for it being the 14th of May. When you was a hoss chap, you'd got all the hard work done wi' the horses then. You'd drilled all your spring corn, and a lot o' your roots, and you'd turned your horses out to grass. So that was the best time to leave. Because if another waggoner came when the horses was living in the stables, his feeding would be different to yours, and so therefore it'd throw the horses wrong. But if there was out at grass, they could be changed over when they was brought back in October.[8]

The Statute Fairs - usually known as the 'Stattis' or 'Statters' - took place in many Lincolnshire market towns. Wilson-Fox identifies the principal ones occurring in Louth, Horncastle and Boston, with less significant ones still being staged at the end of the nineteenth century at Sleaford, Spalding and Gainsborough.[9] In 1886, the hiring fair at Brigg was sufficiently significant to be reported in the national agricultural paper, the *Mark Lane Express*. It noted that the wages obtained were head waggoners £14 19s 0d; second waggoners, £9 12s 0d; lads £4 7s 0d. The report concluded that farm servants were more eagerly sought after and the wages were 'fully as high as last year'.[10] It is important to note that the hiring fair was a labour market both for males and females: women were hired at such events as farm servants (often for instance working as dairy maids, or overseeing poultry), or as domestic servants. The opportunities for interaction between the sexes at the hiring fairs was a particular cause for concern amongst members of 'respectable' society.

The hiring fair itself was an event freighted with ritual: an evocative description of one custom associated with Brigg hiring fair was collected by Ethel Rudkin in Lincolnshire Folklore (1936):

> It was once the custom at Brigg May-week hirings to give the first man into Brigg (who was in search of a 'place') a pint of beer. There was great competition to get there first and some arrived there as early as five o'clock in the morning. The men used to go to the 'Staties' in their best clothes, with buttons up the bottom part of their trousers and frills on their waistcoats.[11]

Laurence Elvin's account of the Lincoln hiring fairs also indicates the colourful nature of the occasion:

> 'On the first Friday following the fourteenth of May, Lincoln's High Street was chock-a-block with farm workers and servants seeking fresh employment. The waggoners with their flowing ribbons, the shepherds, garthmen and others with their distinctive badges stood on the edge of the pavement and many hundreds of bargains for 'places' for the following year were cemented by a 'fastening penny' (about 1/6 or 2/6) and a pint of ale in the nearest hostelry. A multi-coloured ribbon worn in the cap or the hat showed that the wearer was bound for another year.[12]

For both employee and employer there were advantages to be enjoyed through the use of the hiring fair. Captain Philip Bicknell, chief constable for Lincolnshire, summarised the benefits of the statute fair to the agricultural investigator, Edward Stanhope in 1867:

> One advantage of statutes is that it enables the farmer to see the class of men and women whom

he is about to hire; the health and strength being very important as they are going to be bound to him for a year. Besides this, it gives the servants the chance of getting clear away into fresh service, away from a bad set, or from bad masters.[13]

Stanhope himself identified a number of other key advantages associated with the hiring fair in his 1867 report, published in the Second Report of the Commissioners on the Employment of Children, Young Persons and Women in Agriculture, 1869:

> One of the principal hardships affecting the agricultural population is uncertainty of employment and anything which tends to mitigate this is to be welcomed. Yearly hiring secures to the labourer regular work at a rate to which he himself has agreed and a maintenance if sick … To the employer also it serves a certainty of labour at all times of the year.[14]

Some agricultural servants relished the opportunity to move on regularly, as one of Laurence Elvin's respondents noted: 'I mooastly packed me piller case an lucked for a fresh place each maider. I larnt more in shiftin' about.'[15] The hiring fair also gave the chance to agricultural servants to exchange information about the nature of employers - wages were just one consideration: the quality of accommodation and the quality of the meals provided were also major factors that needed to be taken into consideration before accepting the Fessen Penny.

For many agricultural servants, a disproportionately high number of whom were young males, the statute fair offered them an element of economic power. This was the only point in the year when they enjoyed the opportunity to negotiate with their eventual employer. They could warn colleagues about bad employers; and they could organise against them. At the 1853 Binbrook statute fair, for instance, a disturbance arose when a farmer hired a lad for what the boy's uncle considered an unfair and inadequate wage. The farmer found himself surrounded by an angry crowd and had to take refuge in the police station.[16]

However, during the nineteenth century, increasing opposition to the hiring fair was expressed, especially by those who professed to represent 'respectable society'. In 1832, the *Lincoln, Rutland and Stamford Mercury* reported upon the 'multitude of villainous looking adventurers who thronged the streets' of Lincoln during the city's hiring fair.[17] Sixteen years later, whilst acknowledging some improvement in behaviour at the Lincoln statute fair, the *Lincoln, Rutland and Stamford Mercury* noted how it was usually 'a scene of fiddling, dancing and disorder, as if a day's plenary indulgence in dissipation was necessary to compensate for the past twelve month's hard work and restriction.'[18]

Amongst the most outspoken critics of hiring fairs were the clergy. In 1852, the Vicar of Scopwick, the Rev. Dr Oliver, declared that:

> These fairs are the Saturnalia of servants and every kind of licence is indulged with impunity. The young men appear like sailors on shore after a long voyage, to have no idea of order or propriety … Drinking, dancing, fighting and every other irregularity prevail; and practical jokes without regard to personal consequences are played off to an unlimited extent. Removing the linch pins from carts full of female passengers that they may be overturned is very common …[19]

Concerns were expressed by those in authority about the criteria used by farmers in selecting men at hirings: it was invariably the physique of the young man rather than his education and moral character which was the chief factor in the recruitment process. A pamphlet published anonymously by a clergyman in Market Rasen in 1859-60, immediately prior to a hiring fair, emphasised the Church's concerns about the immorality of the young agricultural servants. He criticised farmers who were disinclined to encourage their servants to pursue Christian ways. He urged farmers to make a habit of 'requiring a character' whenever a servant was hired. He asked his readers: 'Is it nothing to you whether you bring into your houses men … who will not scruple to gratify their uncontrolled passion by attempting to rob your female servants, nay perhaps your very daughters, of their virtue?'[21]

In parish magazines, too, complaints about the hiring fairs were advanced during the 1860s. As one correspondent in the *South Cliff Parish Magazine* observed in May 1868: 'To take a servant from a fair is the same as to say that you care nothing for character; and if employers do not, is it likely the servants will? Of course they will think "whether I am good or bad, steady or unsteady doesn't matter at all"'[21] Another correspondent in the same

Lincolnshire parish magazine, signing herself 'Martha Motherly' declared dramatically: 'Statute fairs are a curse to the country. I have had two daughters ruined going to them and I find some of my neighbours could say the same.' This writer concluded her letter using a recurring motif in much of the oppositional literature: 'It stands to reason that to be chosen like a beast in a fair isn't the right thing for a modest girl.'[22] Rowland Winn in his criticisms of the hiring fairs in 1867 commented on the degrading habits of men and women standing in the street waiting to be judged 'like horses by their points'.[23] The following year, again in the *South Cliff Parish Magazine*, antipathy to the hiring fair was expressed by a correspondent - though even more strongly than before: 'No statute servants, Sir for me. They have done away with slave markets in America and I think it is quite time they did away with servants' fairs in England.'[24]

Some attempts were made to replace the hiring fairs with other means of contracting agricultural employees, which took account of the characters of workers as well as their physical qualities. Often orchestrated by clergymen, campaigns were launched to persuade farmers to give every servant leaving their employment a character reference. In many places these were to be administered by registration societies. As was noted in the First Report of the Commission on Employment of Children, Young Persons and Women in Agriculture (1867): 'At Doncaster and in its neighbourhood, great efforts have been made by the Dr Rev. Vaughan and by others of the clergy to establish a system of register offices for the farm servants.'[25]
Other Agricultural Servant Registration Societies were established in Worcestershire, Gloucestershire, Warwickshire and Herefordshire.[26] In Lincolnshire, the Lincolnshire General Servants' Amelioration Society was founded in 1858 with the main aim of abolishing hiring fairs and establishing employment offices. The Society, however, was not a success: by 1860, it was in debt and its annual meeting was attended by only six people. In 1867, the president of the Society, Col. Amcotts, a landowner and magistrate of Hackthorn, was unable to recall accurately the name of the organisation to the Royal Commission. He noted that 'we have nominally at least register offices in every town in the county and it has done good by keeping some women away from the statutes; but the institution is I might almost say, moribund.'[27]

The inconvenience of having to attend such offices and the need to write references for departing staff deterred many employers from engaging with this alternative process of recruitment. The 1860 report of the Secretary of the Lincolnshire General Servants' Amelioration Society indicated the problems 'respectable' female agricultural servants were confronted with when their former employers declined to write references, 'though having no adequate grounds for such refusal'. The Secretary stated he knew several instances in which 'female servants had been totally ruined and driven on the streets through their mistresses refusing to give them a character.'[28]

With the general failure of such registration societies to remove the hiring fair from the streets, other less radical measures were taken to tame what were considered the excesses of these events. One frequently-tried strategy was to segregate the sexes at hiring fairs. The work of historians Gary Moses and Stephen Caunce indicate that this was adopted with moderate success north of the Humber in the East Riding.[29] In 1873, a Yorkshire clergyman wrote of his success in segregating the sexes at Pocklington hiring fair, where he 'hired the largest room in the place for the female servants … thus separating them for a few hours from the farm lads standing in the market place. It has answered perfectly well as far as it goes, the room being always crowded to excess, though holding 200 to 300 people.'[30]

According to the *Lincolnshire Chronicle,* the segregation of the sexes at the Lincoln hiring fair occurred in 1872 when the city's mayor made the Guildhall available free of charge for the hiring of female servants. The aim, the report stated, was 'to remove some of the many serious objections to the Statute Fairs. Several ladies have taken the matter in hand [and have been] induced to attend in that building instead of loitering upon the High Street.'[31] The increasing respectability of the hiring fairs, no doubt facilitated by these initiatives, was commented upon favourably by the Rev. Reginald Langley of Scampton in a letter, published in the *Lincolnshire Chronicle* in May 1872.[32]

As the heart of urban centres became increasingly dedicated to retailing, with consumption triumphing over production in these spaces, they became increasingly feminised districts, especially during the daytime. The incursion of the hiring fair into this

sphere, with its capacity for 'contamination' and its threat to 'good manners' thus became increasingly inappropriate and unwelcome. By the end of the nineteenth century, urban sensibilities were also extending beyond the boundaries of the town: just as farmers and their families were, on occasion, taken to task for their increasing materialism, so too were their employees. By the beginning of the twentieth century, the impact of urban fashions and attitudes within the rural population was the subject of much comment. As some of Laurence Elvin's respondents made clear, the week of the Lincoln hiring fair became a busy one for the city's retailers.
He comments that during the hiring fair week, 'A visit to Bainbridge's [department store] was a "must" for lads and lasses alike in search of new suits, hats and dresses and this enterprising firm at one time presented a watch to all who bought a new suit, as well as a ticket for a free lunch of cold roast beef and beer.'[33]

The increasing sophistication of female servants presenting themselves for hire at the fairs caught the attention of the magazine *Boston Society* in 1900 where a journalist reportedly overheard the following exchange at Boston's May Hiring between a female servant and her prospective employer. Wages had been agreed upon and the only question remaining was the 'day out'. The girl asked for Wednesday afternoons, but the mistress pointed out that this would be inconvenient as it was market day. Would not another afternoon do equally well? The domestic promptly replied, 'I'm afraid not ma'am as that is the day I have arranged to take my music lesson'. The report concluded with the following poetical flourish:

The Evolution of Mary

Once the honest raw-boned Mary,
Though in beauty not a fairy
Was a lesson even to the busy bee
Now she flouts the farm and dairy
And her manners are contrary
A triumph of Board-schooling now is she.

She's descended from a Viking
For fine arts she's a liking
For her 'toilette' off to Paris straight she goes
If we check her golf and biking
She will jolly soon be striking
And where we'll get another, goodness knows![34]

In some accounts of the later nineteenth century, then, it seems that the Lincolnshire hiring fairs were becoming somewhat less troublesome affairs than had earlier been the case, partly through attempts to regulate and segregate on the side of the authorities, but also as a consequence of the changing sensibilities of at least some of the fairs' participants.

By the end of the nineteenth and early twentieth centuries, the hiring fairs of Lincolnshire were in receipt of rather more national press coverage than had been the case before. This was largely due to the increasing rarity of these events at the national level. Whilst within the county there seemed to be some sense that the hiring fairs had become more orderly, this was not how they were reported in the national press. In both 1909 and 1911, the *Mark Lane Express* noted Lincolnshire's May hiring fairs and 'Pag rag day', May 14, when the agricultural servants left their 'places' with their belongings and 'pagged' (or carried) their clothes home in white bags.[35] The *Mark Lane Express's* 1909 report observed that:

> The annual May hirings have been held in all the more important towns in Lincolnshire this week and some of the sights witnessed were truly reminiscent of a day on Epsom Downs … The trains to Boston from all the surrounding districts on Wednesday were crowded to suffocation and some of the ploughboys behaved as though they had escaped from a lunatic asylum. Even the more staid farm servants jostled and pushed among the crowds as though they had just awoke after a sleep of twenty years and did not know here to put themselves.[36]

The report continued to outline the bad behaviour of farm servants caused in large part by excessive drinking. However, it is interesting to note the blurring of urban and rural cultural practices: the account notes how 'towards evening, snatches of comic songs were sung'. These were most likely to be popular music hall songs which permeated both urban and rural society. These were performed in the towns' streets, it was reported critically, 'as though the singers were in some country lane'. As the reporter declared: 'It does seem a pity that these young fellows - and females too - should work hard for twelve months in order to acquire possession of a few pounds and then to foolishly throw their money away on intoxicate and cigars.'[37]

By the early twentieth century, however, some of the excessive consumption that marked the hiring fair weeks, in which farm lads in particular staggered from one town's hiring fair to another to enjoy the bacchanalian revelries, was being effectively diluted by another means. As the *Mark Lane Express* noted in 1911, farm servants had rather less cash at their disposal at hiring fairs since they were increasingly drawing upon account the money owing to them from their employers through the year so that 'instead of £15 or £20 owing to them when Pag-rag day arrives, a balance of less than £5 stands in their favour.'[38]

Certainly, by 1911, within the county it was not the excessively rowdy behaviour of agricultural servants at the hiring fairs which preoccupied those in authority. Instead, the high levels of mobility caused by the hiring system came under critical scrutiny. The *Mark Lane Express* reporter in 1911 observed that in Lincolnshire 'There are many male and female servants who have been out at service ten or fifteen years and lived in as many as a dozen old farmhouses and districts during that time. Some of these apparently believe in the old saying that "a change is as good as a rest."'[39]

In 1913, the Bishop of Lincoln, Edward Lee Hicks, expressed his concern at such a practice. Whilst he acknowledged that for the young and unmarried men 'it is usually a good thing for them to move about for some years and see different people, places and things, it is a form of education and training for life.' However, he expressed reservations at the mobility of the older farmworkers and their families. He noticed that:

> Our clergy on all sides complain of the system which discourages and often baffles their pastoral zeal: for no sooner have parents and children settled down to church and school and the relations of pastor and flock are becoming intimate and helpful than the whole business is broken up and all is begun over again. The teachers everywhere make a similar complaint.[40]

The demise of the hiring fair, though, in the end had little to do with the social, cultural and moralistic concerns of its opponents. It was economic change which brought about the decline of the fair as a site of hiring. Changes in the organisation of agriculture prompted by the Great War, which involved much more state involvement than before, were the principal factor. Reports in *The Times* in the early inter-war period underline this point. In an account headlined 'Yorkshire hiring fair deserted', the paper recorded in 1919 that no farmers attended the Driffield hiring fair as a consequence of the Corn Production Act, 'with its schedule of minimum weekly wages which may result in the total extinction of the hiring fairs which have been a recognised institution for generations.'[41]

Two years later, in May 1921, a similar report in *The Times* noted the decline of the hiring fair in Lincoln. Under the heading 'Hiring fair's lost glories', the account explained that:

> The revolution caused by the wages boards in the agricultural industry was strikingly illustrated at Lincoln yesterday when at the May statutory hiring fair, in place of the hundreds and even thousands of hirings of bygone years, not a single hiring was reported … Almost all farm labourers now work for weekly wages without board, the living-in system having been abolished.[42]

Instead of farm servants negotiating individually with employers, under the Wages Boards, at a county level representatives of farmers and farmworkers, together with 'independent members', set a county rate which was ratified by the Agricultural Wages Board in London.[43] *The Times* may have overstated the extent of the decline, however: the *Lincolnshire Echo* reported in 1922 of hiring fairs that had taken place in Sleaford where there was 'a large attendance of farm hands' and at Scunthorpe where there was little hiring done'.[44] In Lincoln in the same year, 1922, whilst there was little mention of the hiring of male labour, that of female domestic staff continued, though in a rather more genteel manner than before. Indeed, the Lincoln Savings Bank on Bank Street was allowing its large Board Room to be used free of charge by 'country girls or their mothers during Statute Day … Newspapers and writing materials will be provided…'[45]

Whilst undoubtedly the hiring fair as a site of labour exchange was in decline, nevertheless, the social and cultural dimensions, which were such a central part of the lives of many of the county's farmworkers, ensured that some of the May fairs continued. The *Lincolnshire Echo* reported in 1922 of the Spilsby hiring fair, which it declared was a 'Mecca for East Lincolnshire people' with its extensive pleasure rides. As it noted succinctly, 'Business was a secondary consideration and not a great deal of hiring was done.'[46]

The Lincoln Horse Fair

Another event which brought together the urban and rural in problematic fashion was Lincoln's annual April Horse Fair, at the conclusion of which, according to one commentator, 'the city's streets looked and smelt like a farm yard.'[47] For much of the nineteenth century, the Horse Fair injected a substantial amount of income into the local economy, not least through the city's various inns and hotels which did a brisk trade during the week of the fair. In 1869, some 5000 animals were shown during the week[48], the majority of them displayed on the city's streets, most notably the High Street and those adjoining it. The 1882 report of the fair, in the local newspaper, reveals a certain pride in the event: It noted that:

> By Monday morning there was a great influx into our city of breeders and dealers, several of the latter being from France, Germany, Austria and Belgium while the Irish breeders and dealers were largely represented. The various hotels and inns in the central part of the city were thronged with guests.[49]

However, the same report also drew attention to the cultural clashes experienced in the city centre during the Horse Fair, when, it noted, 'as usual the men in charge [of the horses] have made these neighbourhoods particularly unpleasant to the occupants by reason of their unearthly yells and rough conduct.'[50] In addition to the offence caused to the urbane citizens of Lincoln by the influx of horse breeders and dealers, very real dangers presented themselves to passers-by as horses were put through their paces on the city's streets. Various accounts of accidents underline this point. In 1907, a newspaper account detailed how 'a horse which was being run along the street developed temper, threw its rider who entangled in the stirrups was dragged a little distance but not seriously hurt. The horse broke the window of [a confectioner's shop] and then galloped along Newland and up the Avenue where it was stopped.'[51]

By the beginning of the twentieth century, concerns about the Horse Fair and the way in which it took over the city were becoming much more conspicuous. Whilst pride continued to be expressed

Figure 7.1
The April Horse Fair on Lincoln's High Street, looking south, c.1905.

(Courtesy of Maurice Hodson)

in the event's significance, the uneasy disjunction between the rustic, dangerous, masculine, and relatively lawless world of the horse trader and the increasingly regulated, retail-orientated and feminized High Street became the subject of discussion. In 1903, for instance, the *Lincolnshire Chronicle* reported that there were enough horses at the fair 'to seriously interfere with vehicular traffic, to stop the trams … and to cause anxiety to nervous pedestrians who look askance at the business-like appearance of the hind-quarters of the hundreds of heavy animals backed up against the pavement.'[52] The 'nerves of timid pedestrians' were again referred to in a report of 1907 which also remarked upon 'the boisterous display on the part of the dealers.'[53]

By the end of the nineteenth century, discussions took place within the town council about the fuller regulation of the event. In 1898, for instance, it was

Figure 7.2
The April Horse Fair on Lincoln's High Street, looking north, c.1905.
(Courtesy of Maurice Hodson)

suggested that tolls should be charged for horses attending the fair; that the horses should be enclosed in one space; and that the Horse Fair should be removed from the High Street.[54] However, no action was taken - perhaps owing in part to the increasing success with which the event was policed. Surviving police officer journals, scrutinised during fair weeks, reveal much vigilance: in 1866, for instance, it was noted that 'it being Lincoln fair, a great number of suspicious characters was about.'[54]

Newspaper reports at the end of the nineteenth century and early twentieth century regularly commended the Lincoln police for their handling of the Horse Fair and associated pleasure fair, when the town's population was swelled with the arrival of substantial numbers of rural visitors. The *Lincolnshire Chronicle's* report of 1882 is fairly typical: 'Several members of the force have done good service during the week ... as "plain clothes" men and these, together with the placing of men in uniform... have succeeded in maintaining order under, in many instances, trying and difficult circumstances.'[56]

Repeatedly, reports in the local press at the time of the fair make reference to cases of drunkenness, with associated violence occurring during the fair. One of the worst such cases resulted in a serious charge of assault being brought before the City Police Court in 1882 following the breakdown of order in a public house, the Spread Eagle, which was frequented by many grooms and drovers. The report noted that a disturbance resulted in a fight and that 'the female in charge lost all presence of mind and that the servant locked herself up in the kitchen so that not only the house but the drink was at the mercy of the people assembled ...'[57]

To ameliorate the situation during fair week, gospel temperance meetings for the 'wandering people who annually visit our great April Fair', complete with a 'Fair Sunday free tea' were laid on by city philanthropists during the 1880s.[58] By 1893, the Rev. H. Joy, on behalf of the Committee of the Church of England Temperance Society, was arranging for the supply of non-intoxicating refreshments to the herdsmen and others who attended the fair in the cattle market.[59]

Within Lincolnshire urban centres, therefore, although there remained an awareness that economic benefit was derived from the close links with the rural hinterland, in the eyes of many law-abiding citizens, the incursion of the rural population into the urban centre was a mixed blessing. Far from the idyllic bucolic imagery which attracted the eye of the metropolitan sophisticate, to many inhabitants of smaller towns, the 'rural' denoted inconvenience, disorder, lawlessness and the unwelcome smell of the farmyard.

Lincoln cattle market and abattoir

In his consideration of the English townscape, W. G. Hoskins placed much emphasis upon the significance of the market. As he noted in *The Making of the English Landscape,* 'The market-place was the growing point of most towns, and they have taken their shape around it. Standing in the market-place we are - not always but very often - at the origin of things.'[60] Markets and fairs have, in recent times, again been the subject of considerable research by historians. In work by writers such as Patrick Joyce and James Schmiechen, particular attention is paid to the symbolic significance of the market and its location within the urban landscape.[61] Both writers emphasise the liminality of the market and the uneasiness later nineteenth-century corporations had in dealing with markets, especially beast markets.

Patrick Joyce describes markets as being intermediary spaces - locations of transition, places which occupy a place on a boundary, marking off buyers and sellers, and particularly country and town.[62] The market place was the location in which the rules of the moral economy could be applied, where from time to time, crowds enacted customary law to secure 'fair' prices for goods.[63] James Schmiechen identified that during the late eighteenth century and early nineteenth century, the market place became particularly associated with 'fraud, crime, adulteration, street fighting and ... food riots ... The public market in short was seen as promoting bad habits, low morals, public disorder and an interruption in the town's food supply.'[64]

As the process of urbanisation gathered pace in nineteenth-century Britain, increasing attention was

Figure 7.3
The April Horse Fair, Cornhill, Lincoln, c.1905.

(Courtesy of Maurice Hodson)

paid to the regulation of public space. Within many towns and cities, such as the rapidly growing industrial centres of Sheffield and Manchester, marked social segregation occurred, with the middle classes fleeing to the suburbs as authorities struggled to regulate and control the centres of such towns and cities. As town authorities increased their powers, following the 1835 Municipal Corporations Act, increased efforts were made to tame and order urban public space.

Although in many ways, Lincoln's urban form in the early and mid-nineteenth century remained largely pre-industrial, with members of the various social classes continuing to live cheek by jowl in the older parts, it seems that with regard to the reordering of market provision, the city was uncharacteristically progressive. In 1846, a cattle and sheep market was opened in Monks Lane, on the eastern periphery of the city.[65] A site was acquired, partly owned by the Corporation and partly by the Ecclesiastical Commissioners. The site comprised an enclosure of three acres. It was described as being 'fitted up with pens etc and having a commodious inn at the entrance.'[67] According to White's 1856 directory, before the opening of the new, enclosed (and therefore implicitly 'controlled') market place, the cattle markets and fairs were held in St Swithin's Square, off Broadgate, an open and therefore difficult-to-control space.[67] Padley's 1842 map reveals that a sheep market was located immediately to the east of St Swithin's church and west of Broad Street, a pig market was located to the north east of the sheep market, on the other side of Broadgate, and a separate 'beast market' was situated next to the City Gaol at the intersection of Broad Street, New Road, Clasketgate and Monks Lane. This former home of the beast market was marked by the continued existence of public houses named the Bull's Head on the corner of Clasketgate and Silver Street, and the Brown Cow virtually opposite, a little further south on the east side of Broad Street.[68]

The fear of unrest, not to mention the concerns over traffic flows, encouraged the Corporation to find an alternative site for the markets. They were supported in this task by the Lincolnshire Agricultural Association which demanded an improved and enlarged cattle market, not least because of the damage the existing accommodation was allegedly causing to livestock.[69] It was commented, too, that removal of the cattle market from the city's streets was needed because it had outgrown its site. According to the *Lincoln, Rutland and Stamford Mercury*, on 5 May 1844, 'the site of the beast fair was bitterly complained of last Friday, it being so small that the cattle were strewed about far and wide from the top of the New Road down into Silver St.'[70] The report went on to consider other benefits associated with the removal of the event from the city's streets: 'the high roads and streets of the city would then be left free and the pushing and driving and swearing now so prevalent would be prevented.'[71] Memorials from cattle dealers, butchers and 226 citizens persuaded the Corporation to develop the new site despite the opposition of some tradespeople who were anxious that the relocation of the market would impact upon their business.[72] As Francis Hill notes, the new market scheme was complete by 1849.[73] The site of the pig market was rebranded 'Unity Square'; and the former sheep market made way for the construction of a new church, St Swithin's, built between 1869 and 1887, designed by James Fowler in a High Victorian Gothic style.[74]

The Marrat plan of 1848 indicates clearly how relatively isolated the new cattle market was, located to the east of the old friary, to the west of a parcel of land referred to as a vineyard.[75] Though the newly-constructed railway line to Market Rasen passed relatively close by, there seems to have been little concerted effort at the outset to maximise this potential transport benefit. In moving the market to its new site on what was to become Monks Road, the Corporation sought to exercise control of the market in a way which had not been possible before. Whilst the market took place on a public thoroughfare, control and regulation of the transactions conducted were problematic. This changed with the development of a new purpose-built market. The Corporation leased the cattle market to a series of individuals who had responsibility for ensuring the orderly transaction of business on the site. Various trade directories give some information regarding the lessees who invariably also leased the Cattle Market Hotel, which was constructed as part of the development.

The market lessees' autonomy appeared to diminish in the final decades of the nineteenth century. In part, this was due to the increasing intervention by the local corporation, but also as a consequence of the growth in central government-driven regulation.

Central government legislation, such as the Contagious Diseases Act (Animals) of 1884, relating to the attempts to prevent the spread of disease, foot-and-mouth, or swine fever was keenly felt at the local level. However, as part of the ongoing process of regulating the sale of goods, various pieces of legislation and the recruitment of a battery of inspectors also determined the actions of market lessees. In 1882, for instance, following a complaint made by the Privy Council Inspector, the whole of the cattle pens had to be 'effectively paved and drained'.[76] More than £350 was spent on this.[77] Although the Lincoln cattle market had installed a five-ton weighing machine in 1888, Board of Agriculture officials subsequently inspected the machine three years later, following the introduction of the new Markets and Fairs (Weighing of Cattle) Act.[78] They found the machine to be sub-standard. The Corporation was instructed to move the machine to a more suitable site within the market, though the Corporation protested at this decision.[79] Ultimately, it was agreed to install railings around the machine, as suggested by the Inspector of the Board of Agriculture.[80]

Concerns were expressed about the lessee's oversight of the cattle market. The Corporation viewed seriously any contravention of the market regulations. The sale of inappropriate goods was a recurring subject within the Markets and Fairs Committee of the Corporation. In 1889, Mr Giles, the Corporation-appointed market inspector was instructed to report on any sales held in the cattle market which were 'in opposition to the terms of the lease'.[81] In November 1889, it was noted that 'the sale of hardware, ironmongery goods, also of harnesses, rugs, lines and brushes etc are now held … are hereby forgiven.'[82] At several points, the Markets and Fairs Committee threatened to take court action against the lessee, though very rarely followed these through. This prompted one councillor, Mr Page, to declare that 'there appeared to be no backbone to the Markets Committee.'[83]

Other forms of bad behaviour in the cattle market also prompted actions by the Corporation as it sought to ensure that the lessee discharged his duties conscientiously. One of the benefits of the move to a semi-public site was to be that the market could be effectively policed. However, on a number

Figure 7.4
Lincoln's cattle market accommodating a sheep sale c.1905. The city's abattoir is located next to the market in the centre of the picture.

(Courtesy of Maurice Hodson)

Animals	1894-5	1896-7	1898-9	1900-1	1902-3	1904-5	1906-7	1908-9
Beasts	10,258	8130	7836	8561	10,040	9819	10,234	10,749
Sheep	68,115	66,984	66,772	55,624	65,412	62,547	60,532	59,395
Swine	7805	14,291	10,952	13,162	12,166	20,079	13,905	20,805
Calves	---	---	---	---	---	1093	1088	1694
Rams	---	---	---	---	---	379	353	403
Horses	---	---	---	---	---	84	212	203
Totals	**86,178**	**89,405**	**85,560**	**77,347**	**87,618**	**94,001**	**86,324**	**93,249**

Table 7.1
Animals entering the Lincoln cattle market
(Source: City of Lincoln Urban Sanitary Authority: Annual Reports of City Surveyor, R. A. MacBrair)

of occasions, it was noted that gates were not closed when the market was not in use and that, as a consequence, it tended to be used for unsuitable purposes. In 1889, Mr Percy was informed that 'complaints have been made of boys using the pens and markets as a playground and that this, in his own interests, being liable to repairs, should be prevented.'[84]

Zealous policing of the market was also called for on market days. The Chief Constable was instructed to take action against those who sold unbranded pigs outside the cattle market.[85] Concerns were also expressed at the treatment of animals bound for market. Patrick Joyce refers to the increasing sensitivities felt towards animals during the nineteenth century. (The RSPCA was founded in 1824, for instance.) In the 1850s and 1860s, when animals were still driven through London's streets, horror at their treatment was widely expressed: 'the daily sight of sheep being pushed down the steps into basement abattoirs close to St James's church in Piccadilly was a cause of great upset at the time.'[86] In Lincoln, the Chief Constable, Mr Mansell, was requested to direct the attention of the Police Constable on duty near the market to the loading and unloading of sheep and as to their mode of treatment.[87]

This prompts some questions about how the animals were sent to market. Clearly, the instructions to the Police Constable suggest that some livestock was brought in by wagons. In 1893, the Markets and Fairs Committee discussed the possible purchase of a 'float on wheels' for the purpose of 'unloading cattle from carts and waggons'[88] In the event, a cheaper option was preferred - two floats without wheels were ordered instead of one with wheels.[89]

Clearly, then, substantial numbers of beasts were conveyed to market in wheeled vehicles - such expense would not otherwise have been undertaken. In the middle years of the nineteenth century, though, many beasts were still being led into the city by drovers. Francis Hill in *Victorian Lincoln* draws attention to Edward Peacock, a countryman and farmer, who wrote in 1857 of the 'numerous droves of ... cattle [which] pass daily through the streets leaving behind them unmistakable traces of their presence.'[90]

Much use, however, was being made of the railway as a means of bringing livestock to market. In 1849, the *Lincoln, Rutland and Stamford Mercury* reported that many of the sheep brought into the city of Lincoln for the April Fair were conveyed by rail: the last train into to Lincoln on 25 April 1849 comprised 30 Great Northern carriages full of sheep.[91] In 1887, the Market and Fairs Committee appointed Mr Howse as the Veterinary Inspector under the Contagious Diseases (Animals) Act of 1869. His weekly fee of £1 1s. was to be paid on his inspection of the cattle market twice weekly, all cattle and sheep fairs held within the city, and the railway docks and pens once weekly.[92]

By the end of the nineteenth century, attempts were being made to increase the use of the railway as a means of transporting livestock to market and thereby to reduce the inconvenience of processions of cattle through the city's streets. Lengthy discussions were conducted at both the Markets and Fairs Committee and at full council about the desirability of relocating the cattle market.
By 1890, the site of the cattle market was deemed unsatisfactory. Besides requiring a site which was to be 'easily connected to the railway'[93], it was made

clear by the Markets and Fairs Committee that the existing site, containing an area of under two acres was too small, particularly as future plans were to remove the city's annual horse fair from the streets and locate it within the market.

Despite a lengthy search, no suitable alternative site was found, however. Instead, the cattle market continued to take place on its existing site and incremental improvements to the facilities were undertaken. The most significant addition to the cattle market site was the erection of an abattoir. In his recent work, Christopher Otter identifies the growth of the public abattoir, replacing the often 'insanitary, uncivilized, private slaughterhouses'[94] with the public abattoir, which was represented as 'a machine for silent and salubrious killing, where noxious industries were concentrated and technology enlisted to deodorize and cleanse.'[95] The first public abattoir in Britain was opened in Edinburgh in 1851. In 1895, there were fifty-four public abattoirs in Britain; by 1908, there were 135.[96] Lincoln's public abattoir was opened in 1903. As the city's population expanded, so its need for slaughterhouses necessarily grew. The Council had sought to establish a temporary slaughterhouse in St Rumbolds Lane in 1894, but objections had been raised by the neighbouring Wesleyan Day School.[97] Plans for a corporation slaughter-house in the cattle market were drawn up by the City Engineer in April 1903 and this was constructed at the rear of the cattle market site, where it seems considerable earthworks were needed to accommodate the building.
An abattoir is mentioned in Ruddock's directory for 1903, though it doesn't appear in the accompanying map of the town.[98]

The location of the abattoir was significant. Previously, the Butchery had been located in the heart of the city on a road unambiguously named Butchery Street. This had been a relatively open site and no attempt appeared to have been made to conceal it. Alongside the corporation slaughter house on the cattle market site, several retail butchers had premises. Such spatial arrangements associated with the wholesale and retail meat trades had been common in the pre-industrial period, as W. G. Hoskins has noted in *Local History in England*.[99] However, these were becoming relatively unusual by the end of the nineteenth century. According to one anthropologist, Noelle Vialles, by the end of the nineteenth century, the slaughterhouse became a 'place that was no place'.[100] As Patrick Joyce identifies, 'Slaughter now took place in anonymous buildings.' Slaughter had become monitored, controlled and punished if it did not measure up to its new science. Slaughter also became humane, large scale and industrial.'[101] As Joyce indicates, something of the invisibility of the slaughterhouse is conveyed in the use of the euphemism for slaughterhouse - abattoir, which in French means 'to cause to fall, as trees are caused to fall.'[102] Interestingly, in Lincoln, with the removal of the butcheries to the margins of the city centre (ironically next to an ornamental collection of trees, the Arboretum), Butchery Street was removed from the streetscape. By 1909, in both Ruddock's and Kelly's directories, whilst entries for Butchery Street still exist, the reader is instructed to 'see Clasketgate.'[103]

Despite the attempt to impose control and orderliness in the cattle market, necessarily some aspects were beyond human control. Attempts were continually made, it seems, to keep the premises clean, to such an extent that there were repeated critical comments recorded in the minutes of the Markets and Fairs Committee regarding the considerable amounts of water (and their associated costs) used for cleansing purposes. Helpful resolutions were passed that 'no more water is to be

Animals	1905-6	1906-7	1907-8	1908-9	1909-10	1910-11
Beasts	1486	1495	1181	1325	1690	1771
Sheep	9198	9466	6750	7226	11,384	10,776
Calves	34	64	14	16	55	14
Pigs	2329	2605	2636	3202	2884	2785
Totals	**13,047**	**13,630**	**10,581**	**11,769**	**16,013**	**15,346**

Table 7.2
Abbatoir: animals slaughtered

(Source: City of Lincoln Urban Sanitary Authority: Annual Reports of City Surveyor, R. A. MacBrair)

used than is absolutely necessary.'[104] References to the instatement of brick manure pits to accommodate 'sweepings and droppings' alluded to the constant battle to enforce order within the confines of the market.[105]

At first sight, it seems that, to an extent, some of the Lincoln Corporation's efforts to emphasise the regimented organisation of the market were undermined by the decision to use it as a location for the city's pleasure fairs, particularly that associated with the April horse and beast fair. Objections were made to this development, not least from a Mr Tennant, on behalf of the Privy Council. It was noted that markets being used as pleasure fairs 'brought a number of persons into contact with livestock which might have the effect of spreading disease and that it tended to prevent the cleansing of the market.'[106] Despite such reservations, and with the considerable compensation offered by the rents received from the stallholders, the Corporation succumbed to the pressures applied from, amongst others, the local press and accommodated the fair on the cattle market site from the mid-1890s onwards.

By 1907, the April pleasure fair appeared to be well-established on the cattle market site. According to the *Lincolnshire Chronicle*, 'the pleasure fair was again situated on the usual spot on Monks Road and here citizens of all ages enjoyed themselves to the full.'[107] Interestingly, prior to its move to the cattle market site, much of the reporting of the pleasure fair refers to the lawlessness, or potential lawlessness associated with the event. Two-thirds of the *Lincoln, Rutland and Stamford Mercury's* 1861 report of the April pleasure fair, for instance, is dedicated to the crimes and policing associated with the event - with detectives being called upon from Manchester, Stoke, Birmingham, Leeds, Nottingham and Sheffield and reports of well-known thieves arriving for the event from Nottingham.[108] By 1907, the report of the fair is given over almost entirely to a description of its attractions. As a postscript, it was added that the 'street traffic has been admirably controlled by the police under Chief Constable Coleman and his able staff…'[109]

Conclusion

The increasing determination to regulate and to control *rus in urbe* in the form of the hiring fair, the horse fair and the livestock market needs to be seen in a wider context. Much has been written about the later nineteenth-century attempts to romanticise the rural, often emanating from metropolitan cultural opinion-formers, through for instance the arts and crafts movement, the work of William Morris and, in the early twentieth-century, the garden city movement.[110] However, perhaps rather less acknowledged is the conspicuous efforts of small and medium-sized urban societies and their authorities to repel the rural, or at least those aspects of country life which had the capacity to endanger what middle-class society within the town deemed to be its most civilised and urbane elements.

By the early twentieth century, Lincoln's cattle market appeared to be a relatively well-ordered space. Because of the sustained efforts to police and regulate the space it occupied, through the implementation of government measures, local byelaws and self-regulation, the orderly terrain offered to the city by the cattle market was used to stage other events potentially challenging to the social order. By the beginning of the twentieth century, therefore, the threats to the city's economy and society, which had been perceived by many in association with the mid-nineteenth century cattle market, detailed by historians such as Joyce and Schmiechen, had been removed.[111] Although constant vigilance was required, Lincoln's Monks Road cattle market could now be regarded not as a site of social disruption, but one of regulation, hygiene and order. Whereas the relocation of the market in the mid-century had sought to marginalise it, by the beginning of the twentieth century Lincoln's cattle market was at the heart of a burgeoning, largely newly-built, part of the city.

Another reason why events such as the hiring fair, horse fair and livestock market seemed less threatening to urban society was because of the changing cultural nature of the visiting country folk associated with these events. Arguably, by the beginning of the twentieth century, rural visitors were becoming increasingly accommodated to urban sensibilities. By the turn of the twentieth century, the penetration of urban patterns of behaviour and consumption into rural districts was commented upon increasingly in the reports of these calendrical events. As the *Mark Lane Express* noted in its 1911 report of Lincolnshire's pag rag day:

> Even the men who 'speed the plough' are moving with the times and are becoming up to date in some of their habits. They have now adopted the

more fashionable means of locomotion and ride bicycles ... some of the better paid servants - especially head waggoners - ride bicycles which would do credit to even a City clerk.[112]

The bicycle's role in linking the rural worker to the urban world prompted much comment and no little concern. The *Sleaford Journal* in 1908 mocked a recent report in the *Mark Lane Express* on the subject. The *Sleaford Journal* declared:

> now we learn, says the *Mark Lane Express*, that at recent May hirings, a number of servants arrived at the fair on their bicycles and report has it that certain people asked what the world was coming to in consequence. Why in the name of all that is reasonable should not a farm servant, male or female, ride a bicycle if he or she cares to and can afford to buy one?[113]

By the early twentieth century, it seems that improvements in communication had a considerable impact upon the modes of interaction between the rural and the urban. The bicycle certainly enabled the agricultural labourers to become more regular visitors to neighbouring urban centres and facilitated their consumption of an increasingly urbanised, commercial popular culture, which was much lamented by an army of middle-class folklorists decrying the demise of rural superstition, dialect and folksong. In Lincolnshire, the work of pioneering folklorists such as Mabel Gutch and Mrs Peacock and, rather later, Ethel Rudkin, sought to record selectively the fast-disappearing remnants of this old 'prior culture'.[114]

As the twentieth century advanced, as Dennis Mills's work on population trends in the Lincoln area reveals, the blurring of urban and rural intensified with the growth of what arguably became dormitory settlements. He noted that 'commuting has effectively extended the residential areas of all towns far out into the countryside. This has led to crises of identity for many rapidly expanding villages which have clung to their historically separate and self-sufficient image in the face of absorption into the economy of the nearby town.'[115] As Dennis Mills notes, therefore, by the mid-twentieth century, local social commentators' anxieties were not of the incursion of the rural into the city, but of the reverse, though it seems that urban sensibilities may have moved into these rural communities some time before the commuters did so.

Notes

[1] Dennis Mills's many works which examine connections between the rural and the urban include: Dennis Mills and Kevin Schurer, *Local Communities in the Victorian Census Enumerators' Books* (Oxford, 1996); Dennis Mills and Ruth Tinley, 'Population turnover in an eighteenth-century Lincolnshire parish in comparative context', *Local Population Studies,* 52 (1994), pp.30-38; Dennis Mills, *People and Places in the Victorian Census: A Review and Bibliography of Publications Based Substantially on the Manuscript Census Enumerators' Books, 1841-1911* (Bristol, 1989); Dennis Mills, 'The revolution in workplace and home', in *Twentieth Century Lincolnshire,* edited by Dennis Mills, History of Lincolnshire 12 (Lincoln, 1989), pp.18-36; Dennis Mills, *Rural Community History from Trade Directories* (Aldenham, 2001); and Dennis Mills, 'An "edge-land": the development of the Witham Valley east of Canwick Road', in *Aspects of Lincoln,* edited by Andrew Walker (Barnsley, 2001), pp.134-46.

[2] See for instance: Jan Marsh, *Back to the Land: The Pastoral Impulse in England from 1800 to 1914* (1982) and *The English Rural Community: Image and Analysis,* edited by Brian Short (Cambridge, 1992). For a critical consideration of this debate, see Jeremy Burchardt, *Paradise Lost: Rural Idyll and Social Change Since 1800* (2002).

[3] See especially: Martin Wiener, English *Culture and the Decline of the Industrial Spirit* (Cambridge, 1981).

[4] After the calendar reform of 1752 when England belatedly switched from the Julian to the Gregorian calendar, eleven days were 'lost': Wednesday 2 September 1752 was followed by Thursday 14 September 1752. See Robert Poole, '"Give us our eleven days!": Calendar reform in eighteenth-century England', *Past and Present,* 149 (1995), pp.95-139.

[5] *Report by Arthur Wilson-Fox, the Assistant Commissioner, on the County of Lincolnshire (Excepting in the Isle of Axholme),* published in the Royal Commission on Agriculture (1895), p.84.

[6] Stephen Caunce, *Amongst Farm Horses: The Horse Lads of East Yorkshire* (Stroud, 1991), p.2.

[7] Wilson-Fox, *Lincolnshire Report,* p.84.

[8] Fred Brader, b. 1916, Belchford, a farm labourer, waggoner and shepherd, quoted in Charles Kightly, *Country Voices: Life and Lore in Farm and Village* (1984), p.31.

[9] Wilson-Fox, *Lincolnshire Report,* p.84.

[10] *Mark Lane Express* (hereafter *MLE*), 10 May 1886.

[11] Ethel Rudkin, *Lincolnshire Folklore* (Gainsborough, 1936), p.46.

[12] Lawrence Elvin, 'The May hirings', *Fireside Magazine,* 8.2 (1965), p.4.

[13] *First Report of the Commission on Employment of Children, Young Persons and Women in Agriculture* (1867), p.287.

[14] *Parliamentary Papers: The Second Report of the Commissioners on the Employment of Children, Young Persons and Women in Agriculture* (1869), para. 199, p.30.

[15] Elvin, 'May hirings', p.3.

[16] *Labouring Life on the Lincolnshire Wolds: A Study of Binbrook in the Mid Nineteenth Century,* edited by R. J. Olney (Nottingham, 1975).

[17] *Lincoln, Rutland and Stamford Mercury* (hereafter *LRSM*), 4 May 1832.

[18] *LRSM*, 19 May 1848.

[19] Oliver, 'May Day statutes in Lincolnshire', in W and B. Brooke, *Companion to the Almanack* (Lincoln 1852).

[20] Lincolnshire Archives (hereafter LAO), Dixon, 21/5/6/3.

[21] *South Cliff Parish Magazine,* May 1868.

[22] *Ibid.*

[23] *First Report of the Commission on Employment of Children, Young Persons and Women in Agriculture* (1867), p.287.

[24] *South Cliff Parish Magazine,* May 1869.

[25] *First Report of the Commission on Employment,* p.99.

[26] Sermon reprinted in *South Cliff Parish Magazine,* June 1872.

[27] *First Report of the Commission on Employment,* p.287.

[28] Rex Russell, *From Cock-Fighting to Chapel Building: Changes in Popular Culture in Eighteenth and Nineteenth Century Lincolnshire* (Sleaford, 2002), p.100.

[29] See for instance: Stephen Caunce, *Amongst Farm Horses: The Horse Lads of East Yorkshire* (1991); Stephen Caunce, '"Does tha' want hiring?" Hiring fairs in northern England, 1870-1930', *Ancestors,* 27 (2004); Gary Moses, '"Rustic and rude": hiring fairs and their critics in East Yorkshire, c.1850-75', *Rural History,* 7 (1996), pp.151-175; Gary Moses, 'Reshaping rural culture? The Church of England and hiring fairs in the East Riding of Yorkshire, c.1850-1880', *Rural History,* 13.1 (2002), pp.61-84; Gary Moses, *Rural Moral Reform in Nineteenth-Century England: The Crusade Against Adolescent Farm Servants and Hiring Fairs* (Lampeter, 2007); and Susan Parrott, 'The decline of hiring fairs in the East Riding of Yorkshire: Driffield, 1874-1939', *Journal of Regional and Local Studies,* 16.2 (1996), pp.19-31.

[30] *South Cliff Parish Magazine,* May 1873.

[31] *Lincolnshire Chronicle* (hereafter *LC*), 19 April 1872.

[32] *LC,* 17 May 1872.

[33] Elvin, 'May hirings', p.4.

[34] *Boston Society,* 2 May 1900, p.176.

[35] Rudkin, *Lincolnshire Folklore,* pp.45 and 46.

[36] *MLE,* 24 May 1909.

[37] *MLE,* 24 May 1909.

[38] *MLE,* 8 May 1911.

[39] *MLE,* 22 May 1911.

[40] *LC,* 4 July 1913.

[41] *The Times,* 11 November 1919, p.11, col. B.

[42] *The Times,* 18 May 1921, p.5, col. E.

[43] Alun Howkins, *The Death of Rural England: A Social History of the Countryside Since 1900* (2003), p.35.

[44] *Lincolnshire Echo* (hereafter *LE*), 16 May 1922.

[45] *LE,* 13 May 1922.

[46] *LE,* 16 May 1922.

[47] Elvin, 'May hirings', p.7.

[48] *LC,* 30 April 1869.

[49] *LC,* 28 April 1882.

[50] *LC,* 28 April 1882.

[51] *LC,* 26 April 1907.

[52] *LC,* 24 April 1903.

[53] *LC,* 26 April 1907.

[54] *LC,* 6 May 1898.

[55] LAO, Police Officers' Journals and Pocket Books CONSTAB 2/1/2/2/1, 23/4/66.

[56] *LC,* 28 April 1882.

[57] *LC,* 5 May 1882.

[58] *LC,* 27 April 1883.

[59] *Minutes of the Markets and Fairs Committee of the Corporation of the City of Lincoln,* 10 March 1893 and 14 April 1893.

[60] W. G. Hoskins, *The Making of the English Landscape* (1955), p.289.

[61] Patrick Joyce, *The Rule of Freedom: Liberalism and the Modern City* (2003); and James Schmiechen, 'The nineteenth-century British townscape and the return of the market place to Victorian history', in *Splendidly Victorian,* edited by Michael Shirley and Todd Larson (2001).

[62] Joyce, *Rule of Freedom,* p.81.

[63] E. P. Thompson, *Customs in Common* (1991), p.323.

[64] Schmiechen, 'Return of the market place', p.189.

[65] However, the *Post Office Directories of Lincolnshire* of 1855, (p.114) and 1876, (p.229), and *Kelly's Directory of Lincolnshire* (1889), p.288 all insist on 1848 as the date of opening.

[66] *White's Directory of Lincolnshire* (1856), p.104; *White's Directory of Lincolnshire* (1872), p.88.

[67] *White's Directory of Lincolnshire* (1852), p.104.

[68] *Historic Town Plans of Lincoln, 1610-1920,* edited by D. R. Mills and R. C. Wheeler, Lincoln Record Society, 92 (Woodbridge, 2004). See especially the Padley plans of 1842 and 1851, pp.50 and 64.

[69] Francis Hill, *Victorian Lincoln* (Cambridge, 1974), p.49.

[70] *LC,* 3 May 1844.

[71] *LRSM,* 3 May 1844.

[72] *LC,* 8 May 1846.

[73] Hill, *Victorian Lincoln,* p.50.

[74] Arthur Ward, 'The "Clayton and Shuttleworth" churches: St Swithin's and All Saints', in *Monks Road: Lincoln's East End Through Time,* edited by Andrew Walker, Survey of Lincoln (Lincoln, 2006), p.35.

[75] Mills and Wheeler, *Historic Town Plans,* Marrat plan, 1848, p39.

[76] *Minutes of the Markets and Fairs Committee of the Corporation of the City of Lincoln,* 21 December 1883.

[77] *Markets and Fairs Committee,* 6 May 1884.

[78] *Ibid.,* 11 January 1888.

[79] *Ibid.,* 14 April 1893.

[80] *Ibid.,* 13 June 1893.

[81] *Ibid.,* 13 September 1889.

[82] *Ibid.,* 18 November 1889.

[83] *LC,* 20 June 1890.

[84] *Markets and Fairs Committee,* 9 August 1889.

[85] *Ibid.,* 3 September 1885.

[86] Joyce, *Rule of Freedom,* p.78.

[87] *Markets and Fairs Committee,* 6 July 1885.

[88] *Ibid.,* 14 February 1893.

[89] *Ibid.,* 14 March 1893.

[90] Hill, *Victorian Lincoln,* p.2.

[91] *LRSM,* 4 May 1849.

[92] *Markets and Fairs Committee,* 5 December 1887.

[93] *Ibid.,* 18 June 1890.

[94] Christopher Otter, 'Civilizing slaughter: the development of the British public abattoir, 1850-1910', *Food and History* 3.2 (2005), p.49.

[95] *Ibid.,* p.50.

[96] *Ibid.,* p.50.

[97] *Markets and Fairs Committee,* 20 August 1894.

[98] *Ruddock's Lincoln City Directory* (1903).

[99] W. G. Hoskins, *Local History in England,* 3rd edn (1984), p.117.

[100] N. Vialles, *Animal to Edible* (Cambridge, 1984), ch. 15 cited in Joyce, *Rule of Freedom,* p.77.

[101] Joyce, *Rule of Freedom,* p.77.

[102] *Ibid.,* p.77.

[103] *Ruddock's Lincoln City Directory* (1907), p.18 ; *Kelly's Directory of Lincolnshire* (1907), p.378.

[104] *Markets and Fairs Committee,* 10 March 1893.

[105] *Ibid.,* 14 February 1893.

[106] *Ibid.,* 1 August 1888.

[107] *LC,* 26 April 1907.

[108] *LRSM,* 26 April 1861.

[109] *LC,* 26 April 1907.

[110] See for instance: Martin Wiener, *English Culture and the Decline of the Industrial Spirit;* Jan Marsh, *Back to the Land;* Jeremy Burchardt, *Paradise Lost;* Peter Gould, *Early Green Politics: Back to Nature, Back to the Land and Socialism in Britain, 1880-1900* (Brighton, 1988); Peter Hall and Colin Ward, *Sociable Cities: the Legacy of Ebenezer Howard* (Chichester, 1998); and Mark Freeman, *Social Investigation and Rural England* (2003).

[111] Joyce, *Rule of Freedom* and Schmiechen, 'Return of the market place'.

[112] *MLE,* 22 May 1911.

[113] *Sleaford Journal,* 27 June 1908.

[114] Mabel Peacock and Mrs Gutch, *County Folklore, Vol. V. Examples of Printed Folk-Lore Concerning Lincolnshire* (1908); Rudkin, *Lincolnshire Folklore.*

[115] Dennis Mills, 'The revolution in workplace and home', pp.25-26.

CHAPTER 8

VISIONS OF VICTORIAN LINCOLN
The production of an urban image 1846-1900

Denise McHugh

Introduction

This chapter considers the 'production' or interpretation of city space and the development of an urban image for the railway tourist in Victorian Lincoln.[1] It examines the impact of railway tourism from the 1840s, the presentation of the city to visitors and how they consumed the urban space. Lincoln organisations, trades and elites reacted to visitor crowds in various ways. Visitors produced commercial opportunities but also exposed disunity within the city and brought a critical external gaze to the urban environment. The impact of the tourist gaze has been shown to be powerful in moulding places.[2] Tourists consumed places, buildings and features with their gaze but this was not a passive process; the tourist gaze could remake or re-evaluate places and spaces. In Victorian Lincoln the tourists' gaze was directed to certain urban spaces and buildings and a clear city image was created and cultivated. Using evidence from local and national print media, this chapter explores how local institutions, iconic buildings and 'special' events, including Queen Victoria's Diamond Jubilee celebrations and a memorial to a famous poet, formed part of a constructed spatial experience of the city which conveyed a unified narrative and image of Lincoln to both visitors and inhabitants.

Victorian Lincoln was a city undergoing 'late' but intense industrialisation; its society became profoundly affected by industry and the city environment moved from that of a traditional or even pre-modern city to an industrialised, urban environment and economy.[3] Between 1851 and 1901, the population grew from 17,536 to 48,784; an increase of over 170 per cent and, during the same period, the city's economy moved from a broad-based artisan manufacturing and dealing centre to a modern industrial manufacturing centre dominated by a single industry.[4] The scale, space and townscape of Lincoln were altered irrevocably and it could be said to have become a truly 'urban' city in this period. Changes in the space and character of Victorian townscapes created new forms of social experience and interactions but did not always sweep away the heritage of the past which sometimes came to be understood and appreciated in new ways. The development of the railway network from the 1840s onwards brought a new phenomenon to Lincoln; the railway tourist. With tourism came new opportunities, not only to sell and to market but also to see and evaluate the city from a fresh perspective. In Lincoln, early struggles over the accessibility and presentation of the city's heritage evolved into a dynamic and modern cultural representation of place to the growing tourist trade. Lincoln citizens developed new ways of identifying and presenting their city and were motivated by both external and internal factors to construct a historic and consumable urban landscape from the shifting environment of Victorian Lincoln.[5]

The railway visitor to Victorian Lincoln

As a county town and cathedral city Lincoln had always attracted visitors; writers and diarists Daniel Defoe, John Evelyn and Celia Fiennes all visited Lincoln, Defoe describing it as 'an ancient, ragged, decayed and still decaying city'.[6] Despite this image of stagnation and although not on a major coaching route, Lincoln was a county town and administrative centre and enjoyed significant urban status in the early modern period. The number of substantial seventeenth- and eighteenth-century inns testified to its role as a local transport and communications 'hub'.[7] Early modern tourists were affluent travellers who visited Lincoln as part of a 'tour' of the country; they travelled in small groups, or individually, and were few in number. Once in Lincoln they were joined occasionally and seasonally by the regional gentry and aristocracy who came into the city for the assizes, races or annual 'Stuff Ball'. Middle-class and working-class visitors to Lincoln often came from smaller local centres such as country towns and visited for business, trade and employment functions such as markets and hiring fairs rather than for leisure purposes (although entertainment was often involved).

The mobility of travellers was 'transformed' in Lincoln between 1846 and 1849 with the building of two railways.[8] The opening of the Midland Railway in 1846 connected Lincoln to Newark and Nottingham and linked Lincoln to the larger midland rail network via Nottingham. This line, followed by the arrival of the Manchester, Sheffield and Lincolnshire Railway (MSL) in 1848, dubbed the 'mucky, slow and late' by Lincoln citizens,[9] tightened regional urban links and allowed greater flows of traffic between cities. In 1848, the Great Northern Railway (GNR) opened its 'loop' line from the GNR main line which connected Lincoln via Boston and Spalding to the main line at Peterborough and on to London.[10] By 1849, Lincoln had two passenger stations, the Midland and the Great Northern, and flourishing passenger traffic. In 1855, *The Post Office Directory of Lincolnshire* claimed that: 'The facilities for communication in travelling and traffic which the railways have offered everywhere have been nowhere more beneficial, or produced more marked and important results upon the prosperity and commerce of individual localities, than in this ancient and now flourishing and increasing city ...'[11]

The immediate difference produced by the rail network was the scale of visitor numbers to Lincoln. Despite Lincoln's branch line location 'mass tourism' arrived with the railways bringing middle-class and working-class visitors from other urban centres across the Midlands.[12] Railway companies adapted rapidly to the day trip or excursion market and by 1844 *The Railway Chronicle* claimed that railway excursions were 'becoming our chief national amusement'.[13] The proliferation of railway companies and chartered or 'special' trains in the region enabled large parties to visit Lincoln for day trips, particularly in the summer months. Railway historian Jack Simmons has described the difficulty of assessing tourist numbers travelling by train in the Victorian period, considering the sources of information as 'unsatisfactory'.[14] We do not know exactly how many tourists visited Lincoln, but the local press gives an impression of the level of such traffic. Local newspapers both reported crowds of visitors, such as the '700 visitors from Birmingham and Sheffield' in June 1848 and gave Lincoln traders and residents advance notice (or warning) of expected crowds.[15] In June 1849, the *Lincoln, Rutland and Stamford Mercury (LRSM)* announced that '... 3,000 people are to come from Birmingham on the 25th ...'[16] In 1860, a special train from Sheffield pulled nineteen carriages of visitors, while special trains ran from Hull, Peterborough, London, Manchester and Sheffield for Lincoln race meetings.[17] Where visitors came from was significant, not only because it enabled readers of the local press to assess which railway carrier was producing profitable passenger traffic but also because it gave an indication of the social class of the tourists. Increased leisure hours, savings clubs and commercial organisation meant that the railway tourists were of a different class to their predecessors. It is clear from the press reports that the majority of these visitors were 'excursionists' or day trippers, a new type of tourist made possible by railways and encouraged by railway companies.[18]

Railway tourism sometimes grew in unexpected ways: rail travel was adopted rapidly by existing social networks and this promoted the growth in passenger numbers. In Lincoln, temperance was an important factor in leisure activities; the Lincoln Temperance Society had formed by 1835 and the commons were used for large temperance meetings.[19] This movement was supported by the high levels of non-conformity, particularly Wesleyan Methodists, in the city and surroundings but spread across denominations.[20] Victorian Lincoln's reputation as a centre of temperance combined with the 'educational' aspect of a visit to the city attracted many such visitors. In August 1848: 'About 700 of the Derby teetotallers visited Lincoln by special train...and spent the greater part of the day in rambling about the city, and in inspecting the cathedral and other objects of note.'[21] The Derby teetotallers' experience of 'consuming' the urban environment was typical of the type of temperance day out enjoyed in Lincoln and the city was a popular alternative to more rowdy or intoxicating venues. In 1849 the British Association for the Promotion of Temperance held its annual conference in Lincoln and from the first decade of railway travel a tradition of temperance visiting was established; in 1890 this movement was still attracting visitors as a temperance festival in the Arboretum showed.[22]

Institutions also played an important role in attracting railway visitors to Lincoln and in promoting the image of the city. As early as 1848, the Archaeological Institute of Great Britain and

Ireland held their annual meeting at Lincoln; the meeting was well attended and created a great deal of interest locally.[23] The subsequent reports and publications boosted interest in Lincoln among Victorian archaeologists and medievalists.[24] Institutions and professionals were already clustered in Victorian Lincoln as a result of its traditional county town function and a conscious development and reform of these resources, including the schools, hospital and asylum, throughout the period brought visitors in. In 1848, visitors were reported as 'inspecting' all 'the chief objects of interest in the city ... including the Cathedral, the Asylum and the Mechanics Institute'.[25] The Mechanics' Institute with its library and museum was a draw in the 1840s and continued to support the development of arts and educational amenities in Lincoln. The city became a venue for conferences, exhibitions and festivals: the *Lincoln, Rutland and Stamford Mercury* lists numerous such meetings, including the choral festival of 1868, the international health exhibition of 1884 and the art exhibition of 1887.[26] Lincoln's agricultural machinery industry also drew visitors for industrial exhibitions and it became a centre for showing new patented products; the summer meeting of the Institution of Mechanical Engineers held at Lincoln in August 1885 and the industrial and loan exhibition of 1891 were two examples of technological displays attracting visitors.[27]

Railway tourists tended to arrive in Lincoln in their hundreds rather than their thousands and even then only at the height of summer: the city's experience of the visitor crowd was in no way comparable with the scale of numbers descending on Victorian seaside resorts, however railway visitors did make an impact and Lincoln was quick to respond to commercial tourism. There seems to have been little concern raised about the behaviour of these large groups. Victorian Lincoln was not the seaside: it was often closed and sleepy, on Sundays in particular, and visiting groups tended towards the respectable end of the social spectrum.[28] There is little evidence regarding the reception of such railway excursionists in Lincoln although a newspaper report of an excursion from Lincoln in June 1848 offers some insight: '... not less than 30,000 persons visited the Arboretum at Derby ... The shops were closed, and the public places thrown open for inspection; thus furnishing a grateful example, which it is hoped will in future be reciprocated in Lincoln, instead of strangers being looked upon as pigeons who may be plucked.'[29] The railways were blamed for an increase in crime in Lincoln. In 1848 it was claimed that: 'Pickpockets now take advantage of the opportunity afforded by the railways for visiting the different markets: and almost every Friday brings a tribe of light-fingered gentry from Derby and Nottingham who mix with the crowds in Lincoln and frequently render pockets lighter'.[30] On the whole increased railway passenger traffic to Lincoln was considered to be good for the city and elite anxieties about crowds in Lincoln generally focused on the markets, annual hiring fairs and on the large numbers of resident young male foundry labourers.[31] The ignorance of visitors, however, was considered to be an issue: in 1848 the *Lincoln, Rutland and Stamford Mercury* claimed that visitors were 'confused' by 'the Old Palace, the Cathedral, the Deanery and their occupants' and a debate about signage began. It was claimed that Lincoln tourists were often unsure of what they should see or indeed what they were looking at.[32]

Tourists' confusion was rapidly turned to local commercial opportunity and Lincoln printers began to produce affordable guides to the city. Early national and local directories such as Pigot's had always included a 'historical sketch' outlining the importance of Roman Lincoln and stressing the city's relative decline in recent centuries, along with a brief architectural guide to the cathedral.[33] These descriptive sections of the directories grew ever more extensive and detailed across the second half of the nineteenth century but they also became less portable. In addition to directories, there were some specialist historical publications, mainly in pamphlet form, such as *A Sketch Historical and Descriptive of the Minster and Antiquities of the City of Lincoln* published in 1831, or antiquarian descriptions in national publications like *Winkles Architectural and Picturesque Illustrations of the Cathedral Churches of England and Wales.*[34] From the late 1840s onwards, there was an initiative by Lincoln printers to produce accessible and comprehensive local guides aimed specifically at the railway tourist.

Guidebooks for travellers had been in existence since the Roman period but for many centuries were large, heavy and mainly designed as 'armchair' reading for elites.[35] Smaller handbooks for portable guides were in use in England from the late eighteenth century and were largely focussed on travellers undertaking 'picturesque' tours of remote landscapes such as the Lake District.[36] Individual guides to English towns and cities pre-dated railway tourism but were clearly connected to tourist traffic and to the urban leisure functions of specific places: resorts, gentry centres and capitals produced early guide books for visitors including *The Stranger's Assistant and Guide to Bath* (1789), *The Chester Guide* (1781) and *The London Adviser and Guide* (1790).[37] These were frequently aimed at gentry tourists who were planning extended stays 'in town' or at the spa. In Lincoln, like many provincial towns and cities, consumer demand for such products arrived with the railway excursionists in the mid-nineteenth century.

The traveller's handbook or guidebook has been largely overlooked by historians but they are a valuable source for local and urban history.[38] Their form, cheapness and accessibility were part of the 'print capitalism' of the Victorian period and as such they are interesting consumer artefacts in themselves.[39] For the local historian, guidebooks offer an insight into the development of the publishing and tourism industries as well as the commercial and cultural aspects of urban life. These guides provide a selective portrait of towns and cities but give a wealth of local detail; through them we can 'walk' the streets of the city, be directed to historic sites and novel innovations and occasionally receive guidance as to certain local customs and an indication of costs and services.

In Lincoln guides were clearly aimed at introducing non-resident strangers to the city. Volumes such as *Drury's Handbook for Lincoln Cathedral: Containing every information necessary for visitors* (Lincoln, 1849), Lockyer's *The Stranger's Illustrated Guide through Lincoln* (in its eighth edition by 1855), *The Handbook Guide to Lincoln and Business Intelligencer* (Lincoln, 1853) and *The Pocket Guide to Lincoln* published from the 1850s onwards were typical of the type of local guide books produced.[40] By the 1860s, *Lincoln as it is! What there is to see!* (Lincoln, 1862) had appeared, and later local printer Charles Akrill started producing *Akrill's Visitors' Guide to Lincoln*.[41] Lincoln printers and publishers commissioned, compiled and produced these handbooks for sale alongside other types of print media designed for both visitors and inhabitants, for example George Lockyer produced and sold engravings depicting Lincoln Cathedral, Lincoln buildings and local scenes from his premises at the Stonebow. Printing and publishing were well established in Lincoln; *Pigot's Directory* of 1828 listed six printers in the city, a later directory of 1868 listed seven.[42] The local guide books they published were designed to be carried and to become an integral part of the city visit; both a filter for, and a part of, the experience of Victorian Lincoln for the outsider.

Lincoln visitors' guides created in text a virtual 'heritage trail' approach to the city, its topography and architecture, with an approved method of navigating the Lincoln streets which 'took in' all the key sights for visitors.[43] The texts of these guides typically started the visitor from the railway stations, taking them along the High Street, through the Stonebow and toiling up Steep Hill before touring the castle and the cathedral close with great thoroughness. This development dated from the arrival of railway tourists, the pre-railway (1838) *Winkles Architectural and Picturesque Illustrations of the Cathedral Churches* began with a detailed tour of Lincoln Cathedral but offered no practical advice on how to reach or approach the minster; the text began by 'planting' the reader at the front porch. Guides for railway visitors focussed on the Roman, medieval and architectural heritage of the city en-route to the cathedral.

The presentation of built heritage and the past is often highly selective in nature, guiding visitors or consumers towards aspects of the past which are highly valued while ignoring others.[44] Visitors to Victorian Lincoln were directed to just such a selective and edited experience of the city's history; the Roman and medieval periods were privileged above others, the Danish town or the Civil War, for example, were barely mentioned. The texts directed readers to 'see' particular buildings, such as the 'Jew's House', in detail, but large geographical features such as the Brayford Pool or the cliff were constructed as little more than pedestrian inconveniences. Like medieval pilgrims, the tourists focussed on reaching and experiencing Lincoln Cathedral where they were expected to invest some time. A ground plan of the cathedral was key in most guides and they contained a high level of architectural and historic detail about the fabric of the cathedral, including information about the bells and the early Victorian restorations. This format remained standard across the late Victorian period. The set nature of the visitor's itinerary and the

Figure 8.1
Engraving showing a Lincoln High Street scene of the 1830s
Image courtesy of the Illustrations Index, Lincolnshire County Council Cultural Collections (Ref. LCL2458 [8900])

formalised and structured walking route around the city was further reinforced by the visit of Prince Albert to Lincoln in 1849.

The Prince Consort arrived by train and was conveyed to the new Corn Exchange, with great ceremony, to receive a welcoming address before touring the cathedral. *The Times* reported that: 'After inspecting the Cathedral his Royal Highness returned to the railway station and proceeded at once, by special train ...' He was actually on his way to lay the foundation stone of the new dock at Grimsby but was tact itself: 'I have availed myself of this opportunity to visit Lincolnshire for the first time, and could not do so without visiting also the capital city and the great cathedral with which it is adorned'.[45] The method of navigating and 'seeing' Lincoln was established. While the proportion of text in guide books devoted to Roman remains or modern conveniences varied, the route and text were to remain essentially fixed from the decade of the railways' arrival until the First World War.

The development of implicitly approved or didactic visitor routes for traversing and exploring Lincoln in both the 'virtual' city of the guide books and in 'real' physical travels are interesting examples of 'produced' or 'constructed' social space during this period.[46] City space became differentiated not just by activity, such as work spaces and leisure spaces, but also by the attribution of abstract social and cultural values. Some streets and buildings were deemed 'worth' looking at, or spending time on, while others were not. Visitors had city space interpreted for them and marketed to them as part of the experience of visiting Lincoln. The progression routes between the railway stations and the cathedral negotiated and selected the urban landscape of Lincoln for the visitor's gaze; some buildings, details and views were flagged as significant, to be 'seen', while others were to be passed unnoticed, urban spaces which were literally blanks in the visit. That is not to say that this was how Lincoln's railway visitors actually experienced the urban landscape of the city and using, moving and 'seeing' cities in unexpected ways has been seen as a form of resistance and self-assertion on the part of the user of urban space.[47] Between the arrival of the railway and railway tourists in the 1840s and the end of the century, Lincoln's influential elites engaged in the production and presentation of a coherent consumable urban narrative which both represented, and was recognised by, Lincoln inhabitants.

What to 'see' in Victorian Lincoln and what not to see

A visit to Lincoln Minster lay at the heart of the Victorian visitor's experience as the Lincoln guides indicated. The railway companies made the cathedral the centrepiece of their marketing from an early point and an 'inspection' was the rationale behind many chartered train trips and group visits. Tourism to the minster grew throughout the nineteenth century from an uncertain start however. In the early Victorian period Lincoln Cathedral, its dean and chapter could be said to have been in a phase of decay.[48] The cathedral was largely deserted, was locked for the majority of the time and, even when open during services, remained unlit.[49] The public were largely confined to viewing the exterior from the close, a situation which had impeded visitor growth to the point where in 1848, *The Gentleman's Magazine* suggested that Lincoln Cathedral and the Bishop's Palace might be of interest to readers who were already visiting Tattershall.[50] This inaccessibility was a cause of controversy locally from the 1840s. The *Lincoln, Rutland and Stamford Mercury* newspaper, whose Lincoln correspondent tended towards a radical representation of the 'trade' interest in the city, argued for open and free public access '... to a building which is public property'.[51] The paper claimed that the dean and chapter were only 'trustees' of the cathedral for the public. Pressure to open the cathedral came from sources as diverse as Downing Street and the Lincoln Mechanics Institute. Charles Seely the Lincoln MP, speaking at a soiree for the Mechanics Institute in 1848, explicitly linked access to the cathedral with morally improving leisure, arguing for its opening and claiming that: 'the pleasures of the working classes were too few'. This was a situation which, he said, led to drink.[52]

Railway tourists had exacerbated the local tension over access as it became apparent that the cathedral authorities were willing to unlock the doors for a financial consideration. In June 1849, reports of a large group of holiday visitors prompted the chapter to confirm that '... a contract was made to admit the lot at 10s. Those who wished to feast their eyes with a peep at the famous GREAT TOM (sic) were ... charged 3d each.'[53] In the same report the newspaper noted that other local institutions such as the Lincoln Mechanics Museum were to be 'thrown open cost free' on the following holiday when large crowds were expected. The directors of these institutions, representing both local gentry and commercial interests wished to 'benefit all classes regardless of social scale' it was argued and the clergy should follow their example. The difficulties of public access continued though the 1850s but by the 1860s the Dean and Chapter were experiencing both renewal in membership and reform.[54]

By the end of the 1860s, Lincoln Cathedral was well-established as a visitor destination and any problems of access for tourists caused local objections and were reported in the press.[55]

Beyond the cathedral close the production of the city space of Lincoln as 'historical' narrative to be consumed in the space of a day trip was problematic. It was obvious to the most casual observer that the environment was fragmented and the historical temporal narrative disrupted by the constant intrusion of modernity, particularly in the form of industrial activity. Spatially and socially Lincoln did not represent a coherent experience; the townscape was characterised by contrast and disruption; a gazetteer of 1894 explained how:

> The upper or north section, locally designated 'up-hill' or 'above-hill', spreads over slopes and plateau to a height of 210 feet above the river; about a mile long and 1,000 yards wide, and contains the Cathedral, the castle, the lunatic asylum, some of the other public buildings, and many of the best private houses. 'Below-hill' presents an appearance much inferior to that of the upper section, and contains the principal shops and inns, the markets, the least prominent of the public buildings, and most of the abodes of the working population.[56]

The image of Lincoln in the mid-Victorian period was one riddled with dichotomies: uphill and downhill, town and close, history and modernity. The quiet, ancient and medieval heritage contrasted with the huge, noisy foundries. In 'downhill'

Lincoln the agricultural engineering foundries occupied a growing and significant share of the central urban space, these and other works clustered around the railway lines and waterways. The larger employers and their works dominated the landscape of the lower town especially and, as Francis Hill noted, 'crept uphill' across the late Victorian period.[57] Clayton and Shuttleworth's Stamp End Works, Robey and Co.'s Perseverance Iron Works, Ruston and Co.'s Sheaf Iron Works and Foster's Wellington Foundry shaped the town space, culture and economy.[58] The scale of the foundries was comparable to that of major factories in larger British industrial cities of the same period: the Stamp End Works covered eleven acres and employed 1300, Robey and Co., was described as covering 'an area of about seven acres of land [having] a frontage of 200 yards towards the Canwick Road and gives employment to about 700 hands'.[59] These firms employed around a thousand men in the early 1860s, by 1885, this number had risen to 5000. Large scale agricultural engineering production had become synonymous with the name of Lincoln.

In many places, and to a large part, the physical urban environment of Victorian Lincoln was that of an intensively industrial town, but these industrial activities were absent from the earlier visitors' guides. Invisible by their omission and usually at one remove from the recommended walking routes, they rarely merited comment. John Urry has noted how the tourist gaze focuses on places 'not directly connected with paid work and [these places] normally offer some distinct contrasts with work'[60] suggesting that workplaces and visitors' interests were not compatible. Yet Victorian visitors did gaze upon industrial sights and sites, visiting factories, mills, quarries and docks. The enclosed worlds of the iron foundries with their high walls and gated entrances, their hot, noisy and dirty masculine environments may not have seemed especially enticing to the respectable Victorian visitor yet some did attract tourists. Bedford's Britannia Ironworks owned by the Howard family also produced agricultural machinery and was considered to be a 'model' of its kind. The ironworks were visited frequently, mentioned in local guides and received Garibaldi in 1864.[61] For those who did not wish to experience the environment directly, a publication entitled *A Visit to Bedford,* produced in 1883, gave three pages of description of the works and its

processes, emphasising the 'busy scene', 'rich sight' and 'something like magic' of manufacturing.[62] Local directories carried bird's-eye illustrations of the works. This suggests that there was some public appetite for the leisurely consumption of the viewed manufacturing process but there is no evidence of this occurring in Lincoln where the works were walled and closed. It is possible that part of the reason for this was temporal; holidays in Lincoln were, by definition, days when the foundries were closed and it is clear from the actions of the cathedral clergy that Lincoln did not expect a tourist trade beyond these defined times. Another very pragmatic reason was that the Lincoln foundries were involved in fierce global market competition and guarded their innovations well; visitors could be a threat.

In the last quarter of the nineteenth century Lincoln's industrial development had the potential to undermine the city's romantic appeal and historical status as iron works expanded beyond the 'downhill' waterside area. It was no longer possible to ignore the presence of industry; a unified image needed to be presented to the visitor. The urban industrial economy needed to be portrayed in a positive manner and new images and identities had to be found to combine the disparate elements of Lincoln in a coherent spatial narrative. *The Times* had attempted to convey both aspects of the city to its readers on the occasion of Prince Albert's visit in 1849:

> The spirit of commercial enterprise has in modern times so generally deserted our old cathedral cities that most of them have fallen into a species of obscurity which it requires some love of antiquarian lore and architectural beauty to penetrate ... The eye of the stranger glances with wonder from the silent streets to guide-books, which tell how in times gone by kings, and nobles, and prelates, contended for their possession as the great prizes of the state. Lincoln has been, to a great extent, rescued from the obscurity and decay of its fellows by the vast agricultural improvements.[63]

It was, it emerged, possible to make a virtue of a necessity and by 1890, *Williamson's Guide through Lincoln* asserted:

> Any description of Lincoln as it is, would be incomplete that failed to call attention to the extensive engineering works, foundries etc. which,

though of very recent date, have familiarized almost every country in Europe, as well as our distant colonies, with the name of the old city, and the great firms that have so largely contributed to its celebrity and prosperity.[64]

At the end of the guide book there is a description of 'four very extensive establishments': the Stamp End Works, the Sheaf Iron Works, the Globe Works and the Wellington Foundry.[65] Industry was integrated into the urban narrative and the exteriors, at least of the more renowned works, were to be 'seen' as part of the visit to Lincoln.

With industry came modernity and in the last quarter of the nineteenth century new buildings started to appear in the spatial construction of Lincoln for tourists. Illustrations became more important to guide books as printing technology allowed them to proliferate even in low cost publications and new architecture was represented in the guides. In the 1850s, early editions of *The Stranger's Illustrated Guide through Lincoln,* in common with other contemporary guides, mainly presented images of the ecclesiastical and medieval buildings but later guides showed modern Lincoln represented by lithographs of institutions, including the County Hospital and the Penitent Females' Home. Guides from the last quarter of the nineteenth century were keen to draw the visitors' gaze to reformed, educational and modern establishments in the townscape; as well as showing Lincoln as a progressive and dynamic city it is possible that the emphasis on the prison, hospital and female penitents would have enabled the visitor to feel reassured and safe in a strange urban environment.

Representing the city

There is evidence that the coming of 'mass' commercial tourism changed the perceptions of Lincoln residents and the elite with regard to the city. External opinions became more important and the local understanding of the significance of urban reputation grew; both the cathedral authorities and the corporation were keen to emphasize their concern for the historic fabric of the city. The Dean and Chapter became very anxious to be seen as active in preservation; they were under constant fire (and rather a cloud) from the *Lincoln, Rutland and Stamford Mercury* which had exposed the defacing and sale of portions of illuminated manuscripts in 1848 when it had found that visitors were 'permitted' to cut out the illuminated capitals 'in return for a gratuity'.[66] The cathedral authorities had reduced access and said that they had been unaware of this practice among the library staff, but the newspaper thundered: 'Theft and destruction do not take place at the British Museum, and the local collection ought to be as accessible as the national one.'[67] Issues of access and heritage were becoming political and the paper kept up both its scrutiny and criticism reporting on 'bad restoration work' in 1867.[68]

There was growing investment in the historic urban fabric and buildings of Lincoln both within the Close and outside. The Dean and Chapter spent increasing amounts of their income on maintaining the fabric of the cathedral and were anxious to show that they were following advice from the Archaeological Institute in their restorations.[69] The Corporation of Lincoln were also concerned to maintain the heritage aspects of the city and, in 1885, *The Times* reported urban improvements in Lincoln, including street widening and the construction of a new street to:

> ... greatly relieve the ancient gateway known as the 'Stonebow' and will do much to secure the preservation of this most interesting historic monument. The Corporation are fully alive to the value of this memorial of past ages and have called in Mr Pearson RA to advise them how best to maintain its ancient character and at the same time adapt it to the necessities of modern commerce.[70]

In addition to maintaining the historic buildings it was noted that visitors preferred a clean and orderly urban environment as part of their leisure experience. As early as 1848, the *Lincoln, Rutland and Stamford Mercury* claimed that: 'By accounts given in the newspapers, a stranger would suppose Lincoln to be the dirtiest city in England'.[71]
In Lincoln it was understood that there should not be a conflict between the reputation of the city and the visitor experience and nor should potential tourists be deterred from visiting. The struggle to control and improve Lincoln's physical environment is well documented.[72] Lincoln's road towards the production of a satisfactory sanitary and hygienic environment (even by Victorian standards) was a complex and contested one, nevertheless such an environment was increasingly expected and indeed assumed by visitors prior to arrival. The visibility and

accessibility of various aspects of the townscape were contested but resolved in the interests of the tourist consumer. The overall narrative was more complex; it took an occasion of national celebration for Lincoln to unify its medieval, ecclesiastical and technological elements into a coherent 'readable' whole. For Queen Victoria's Golden Jubilee of 1887 the city celebrated by illuminating the cathedral and other historical monuments in the city.[73] This lighting aspect of the jubilee celebrations was significant as, for the first time, the city's modern industrial and technological strengths were allied to the historical fabric.

It was not the first time that the industrial and ecclesiastical elements in Lincoln had co-operated;[74] there had been a gradual and tentative drawing together from the 1870s onwards. In 1880, leading industrialists Clayton and Shuttleworth had donated new bells 'formally signalling the completion of the difficult and anxious work of cathedral restoration'.[75] Yet this was the most public display of modernity and status. In 1887 the city had no civic electrical supply (companies and local authorities could have applied for such from 1882) although some of the foundries both manufactured and used electrical equipment. It was still considered acceptable, indeed notable, to illuminate the Newport Arch and other historic buildings with candle light but the central tower of the cathedral was illuminated by electricity powered by generators provided by Robey and Company.[76] Industrial and ecclesiastical elites combined to provide a memorable spectacle for visitors and residents which was reported widely both before and after the jubilee by local and national newspapers. This event was so successful that it was repeated at the 1897 Diamond Jubilee when *The Times* reported that: 'Lincoln Cathedral is to be specially illuminated on Jubilee Day, and a large signal rocket will be fired from the top of the Central Tower at 10 o'clock as a sign for the setting ablaze of all the bonfires in the county.'[77] The role of the cathedral in signalling the start of the county-wide celebrations was significant in reinforcing the status of the minster in the city, as was the grand civic procession to the cathedral which started from the Great Northern station.[78]

Figure 8.2
Photograph of the unveiling of the Tennyson Statue
(Courtesy of Maurice Hodson)

Following the Local Government Act of 1888 Lincoln became a county borough and there was a new confidence and a new enthusiasm to assert dominance over the county hinterland or at least over the area of Lincolnshire, Lindsey, administered from, although not by, Lincoln. The Lindsey County Council was based formally in the city from 1888 and the townscape was once again linked to the county elite as in the eighteenth century. In the last two decades of the nineteenth century new Lincoln institutions were 'county' rather than 'city'. The city was reinforced at the heart of Lincolnshire and the cathedral at the heart of the city, Lincoln was portrayed as the leading (although not the largest) urban centre in the shire. No opportunity to connect Lincoln with its sprawling and diverse county was to be missed, as the erection of the Tennyson memorial in 1899 showed.

Alfred, Lord Tennyson (1809-1892), the poet laureate, was born in Somersby in the Lincolnshire Wolds and educated at Louth Grammar School but had no direct connection with the city of Lincoln. In the late Victorian period, Lincoln had only one contemporary non-ecclesiastical statue, that of Dr Charlesworth which stood outside the Lawn Lunatic Asylum, erected by subscription in 1854. In contrast, Grantham had erected a statue of Isaac Newton in 1876 and one honouring their former MP F. J. Tollemache in 1891.[79] Grimsby had installed a statute of the late Prince Consort at the docks, unveiled by the Prince and Princess of Wales in 1879.[80] In 1898, Lord Brownlow proposed the erection of a statue of Tennyson in Lincoln at a county meeting saying that 'Lord Tennyson, having been born in Lincolnshire, and having been one of the most distinguished men of the century, it seemed extraordinary that Lincolnshire had not desired to erect some memorial of him.' Lord Brownlow suggested that he had only met a single objection to this plan:

> ... and that was that he [Tennyson] had now been dead some time; but this did not appear to be any real objection. In the neighbouring town of Grantham, for instance, a fine statue of Newton had been erected more than a 100 years after his death, and therefore Lincoln would not be at all too late in now erecting a statue of Tennyson.[81]

Lord Brownlow's proposal was seconded by the Bishop of Lincoln who expressed his opinion that the memorial should take the form of a statue in the open air where it 'might exert a wholesome influence'. Moral improvement and civic pride assured and urban competition invoked, a public meeting in Lincoln followed the same evening, presided over by the Mayor. Lord Brownlow was present and the meeting was addressed by his wife Countess Brownlow and various members of the Corporation including 'Mr Councillor Turner' who '... spoke on behalf of the working classes of the city, and observed that they ought undoubtedly to have some suitable memorial for a great Lincolnshire man, of whom they were all proud'. The meeting is reported to have closed in unanimous agreement. While the report may suggest a heavily and clumsily orchestrated campaign, there is no doubt that local feeling intended to appropriate the memory of Tennyson for Lincoln's townscape and heritage. The decision also demonstrates the alliances built between the cathedral close, the municipal elite and the industrial workforce in the name of civic pride and local identity. It is also interesting to note that the statue was considered to be for the benefit of the inhabitants of the city rather than a visitor attraction although Tennyson was already a literary and tourism 'industry' in his own lifetime.[82] What was Lincolnshire's was appropriated for Lincoln and become part of the city's image and identity.

Conclusion

The arrival of the railway in Lincoln is generally considered in relation to the ending of comparative urban isolation or the development of heavy industry, but the arrival of the railway tourist, in particular the day trip excursionist, had a clear impact on the city, its development and its identity. The growth of railway excursion visiting provided trade for the print and publishing industry and gave impetus to the re-evaluation and opening up of the built heritage. The lure of Lincoln Cathedral, the value of the historic fabric of the city and the importance of the streetscape were all discovered or rediscovered in the decades following railway development. Influential groups in the city found themselves at odds over issues of access, usage and custody of urban spaces and places, yet commercial forces, including competition with other towns and cities, drove them into alliances. The industrial and commercial urban middle class of Victorian Lincoln with their vested interests in technology and industry, their assertion of the value of modernity, reformed institutions and improving leisure, forged a coalition with 'traditional' authorities of the clergy and county gentry. Together they formed an urban elite adroit enough to adapt and 'embed' diverse events and icons such as royal jubilees and dead poets into a consumable narrative of space, power and civic identity.

The represented or imagined urban scene produced for the tourist gaze in late Victorian Lincoln changed from one of contrasts and potential conflicts in the early period of railway tourism to a more integrated, fluid picture of a progressive and evolving urbanity to be consumed in a safe sanitized environment. The tourist gaze, a particular form of use or consumption of some aspects of this space, came to 'see' industry in the townscape which was predominantly marketed as 'ancient' and 'historic'. The produced space of Lincoln and the town narrative offered to the railway visitor shifted across the late Victorian period from one of historic relic to that of a dynamic multi-layered temporal narrative which moved the visitors' gaze from Roman remains to a modern global industry.

Notes

[1] 'Production' here refers to the assigning of differential social values to spaces using the concepts of Henri Lefebvre from *The Production of Space* (Oxford, 1991). This chapter explores three key ideas from Lefebvre: spatial practice; the representation of space and representational spaces, *The Production of Space*, p.33. The aim is to combine two of Dennis Mills's intellectual enthusiasms; geography (in its broadest sense) and the local history of Lincoln, to produce a fresh perspective.

[2] John Urry, *The Tourist Gaze: Leisure and Travel in Contemporary Societies* (2002); John Urry, *Consuming Places* (1995).

[3] J. V. Beckett and J. E. Heath, 'When was the industrial revolution in the East Midlands?' *Midland History,* 13 (1988); Neil R. Wright, *Lincolnshire Towns and Industry 1700-1914* (Lincoln, 1982).

[4] Parliamentary Papers, *Census of England and Wales 1851, Vol. I,* (1852), p. CLXXXV; *Census of England and Wales 1901 County of Lincoln* (1902), p.14.

[5] Lefebvre, *The Production of Space;* Urry, *The Tourist Gaze;* Urry, *Consuming Places.*

[6] Quoted in Wright, *Lincolnshire Towns and Industry,* p.14.

[7] Francis Hill, *Tudor and Stuart Lincoln* (Lincoln, 1956), p.4.

[8] J. G. Ruddock and R. E. Pearson, *The Railway History of Lincoln* (Lincoln, 1985), p.185.

[9] A. Williamson, *Guide through Lincoln* (Lincoln, 1890), p.17.

[10] *The Oxford Companion to British Railway History from 1603 - the 1990s,* edited by Jack Simmons and Gordon Biddle (Oxford, 1997), p.121.

[11] *The Lincolnshire Post Office Directory 1855* (Lincoln, 1855), p.145.

[12] Here the term 'mass tourism' is used in its loosest and most popular sense although it is recognised that this is not unproblematic; for a discussion see *Histories of Tourism: Representation, Identity and Conflict,* edited by John K. Walton (Clevedon, 2005), p.4.

[13] Quoted in *Oxford Companion to British Railway History,* edited by Simmons and Biddle, p.150.

[14] Jack Simmons, 'Railways, Hotels and Tourism in Great Britain 1839-1914', *Journal of Contemporary History,* 19.2 (1984), p.216.

[15] *Lincoln, Rutland and Stamford Mercury* (hereafter *LRSM*), 23 June 1848, p3.

[16] *LRSM,* 15 June 1849, p.3.

[17] Ruddock and Pearson, *Railway History,* p.218.

[18] Simmons, 'Railways, Hotels and Tourism in Great Britain 1839-1914', p.209.

[19] Wright, *Lincolnshire Towns and Industry,* pp.107,108.

[20] Francis Hill, *Victorian Lincoln* (Cambridge, 1974), p.139.

[21] *LRSM,* 1 September 1848, p.3.

[22] *LRSM,* 30 May 1890, p.5.

[23] Neville Birch, 'The "Archaeologians" visit Lincoln' in *Lincolnshire People and Places: Essays in memory of of Terence R. Leach 1937-1994,* edited by Christopher Sturman (Lincoln, 1996), p.174.

[24] For example, *The Archaeological Journal,* 25 (1868), pp.1-20.

[25] *LRSM,* 23 June 1848, p.4.

[26] *LRSM,* 6 August 1868, p.5; Miscellaneous Printed Papers, Lincolnshire Archives (hereafter LAO) Lincoln City Parcels, Box 25, No. 84; *LRSM,* 5 August, 1887, p.5.

[27] *Proceedings Institution of Mechanical Engineers,* 46.1-2, p. 304; *LRSM,* 17 April, 1891, p.5.

[28] Hill, *Victorian Lincoln,* p.303.

[29] *LRSM,* 30 June 1848, p.4.

[30] *LRSM,* 15 December 1848, p.3.

[31] Rex C. Russell, *From Cock Fighting to Chapel Building: Changes in Popular Culture in Eighteenth and Nineteenth Century Lincolnshire* (Sleaford, 2002), pp.24-25.

[32] *LRSM,* 2 June 1848, p.3.

[33] *Pigot and Co.'s Directory for Cheshire, Cumberland...Lincolnshire and Northumberland 1828-29* (London and Manchester, 1828-29), pp.505-506.

[34] *A Sketch Historical and Descriptive of the Minster and Antiquities of the City of Lincoln* (Lincoln, 1831), LAO Scorer Collection, pamphlet; Benjamin Winkles, Thomas Moule, *Winkles's Architectural and Picturesque Illustrations of the Cathedral Churches of England and Wales* (1838).

[35] Loykie Lomine, 'Tourism in Augustan Society (44BC - AD69)' in *Histories of Tourism,* edited by Walton, p.82.

[36] Simmons, 'Railways, Hotels and Tourism in Great Britain 1839-1914', p.212.

[37] *The Stranger's Assistant and Guide to Bath* (Bath, 1789); P. Broster, *The Chester Guide* (Chester, 1781); John Trusler, *The London Adviser and Guide* (1790).

[38] John M. Mackenzie, 'Empires of travel: British guidebooks and cultural imperialism in the 19th and 20th centuries' in *Histories of Tourism*, edited by Walton, p.21, 34.

[39] *Ibid.*, p. 21.

[40] Drury's *Handbook for Lincoln Cathedral: Containing every information necessary for visitors* (Lincoln, 1849); George J. Lockyer, *The Stranger's Illustrated Guide through Lincoln* (Lincoln, 1855); *The Pocket Guide to Lincoln* (1874) LAO R. Box, L. Linc 910; *The Handbook Guide to Lincoln and Business Intelligencer* (Lincoln, 1853).

[41] Leary's *Lincoln as it is! What there is to see or the Illustrated Handbook Guide* (Lincoln, 1862); Charles Akrill, *Akrill's Visitors' Guide to Lincoln* (Lincoln, 1882).

[42] *Pigot's Directory for Cheshire, Cumberland,....Lincolnshire*, p.542; E. R Kelly, *The Post Office Directory of Lincolnshire 1868* (1868) p.470.

[43] Stephen V. Ward, *Selling Places: The Marketing and Promotion of Towns and Cities* (1998), p.190, notes 'possibly the first' actual heritage trail was created with signage in Boston, Massachusetts 1951.

[44] Ward, *Selling Places*, p.210; Robert Hewison, *The Heritage Industry: Britain in a climate of decline* (1987).

[45] *The Times*, 18 April, 1849, p.8.

[46] Lefebvre, *Production of Space*, p.17.

[47] Michel De Certeau, 'Walking in the city', in *The Cultural Studies Reader*, edited by Simon During (1999), pp.126-133.

[48] Wright, *Lincolnshire Towns and Industry*, p.14.

[49] Hill, *Victorian Lincoln*, p.262.

[50] *The Gentleman's Magazine*, 30 (1848), p.292.

[51] *LRSM*, 15 June, 1849, p.3.

[52] *LRSM*, 28 January 1848, p.4.

[53] *LRSM*, 15 June, 1849 p.3. "Great Tom" was a large cathedral bell.

[54] David M. Thompson, 'Historical survey 1750-1949' in *A History of Lincoln Minster*, edited by Dorothy Owen (Cambridge, 1994), pp.213, 246-7.

[55] *LRSM*, 8 November 1867, p.6.

[56] *The Comprehensive Gazetteer of England and Wales*, edited by J. F. H. Brabner (1894), p.15.

[57] Hill, *Victorian Lincoln*, p.304.

[58] Denise McHugh, 'Remaking the Victorian County Town 1860-1910' unpublished Ph.D. thesis (University of Leicester, 2002).

[59] *White's Directory of Lincolnshire* (1882), p.498.

[60] Urry, *The Tourist Gaze* (2002), p.3.

[61] J. Hamson, *Bedford Town and Townsmen* (Bedford, 1896).

[62] *A Visit to Bedford* (1883), pp.11-14.

[63] *The Times*, 18 April, 1849, p.8.

[64] James Williamson, *Guide Through Lincoln* (Lincoln, 1890) p.147.

[65] *Ibid.*, p.148.

[66] *LRSM*, 19 March, 1848, p.3.

[67] *Ibid.*

[68] *LRSM*, 8 November 1867, p.6.

[69] *A History of Lincoln Minster*, edited by Owen, p.243.

[70] *The Times*, 20 November, 1885, p.7.

[71] *LRSM*, 21 June 1848, p3.

[72] Dennis Mills, 'Public health, environment and surveying' in *Social History of Medicine* 22.1 (Oxford, 2009), pp. 153-163.

[73] *LRSM*, 17 June 1887, p.5.

[74] Thompson, 'Historical Survey 1750-1949', pp. 212-213.

[75] *The Times*, 14 December 1880, p.5.

[76] Wright, *Lincolnshire Towns and Industry*, p.250.

[77] *The Times*, 16 June 1897, p.8.

[78] Official Programme of the Celebration in Lincoln, the Diamond Jubilee 1897, LAO Miscellaneous deposit, Hill/16/3.

[79] *LRSM*, 2 January 1891, p.4.

[80] Ceremony of Opening the New Dock at Grimsby, and of the Unveiling of the Statue of the late Prince Consort, by their Royal Highnesses the Prince and Princess of Wales on the 22nd July 1879, North East Lincolnshire Archives, George Moody Papers, 1028/10.

[81] *The New York Times*, 18 June 1898.

[82] Phillip J. Waller, *Writers, Readers and Reputations: Literary Life in Britain 1870-1918* (Oxford, 2006), p.376; Helen Groth, *Victorian Photography and Literary Nostalgia* (Oxford, 2003), p.148.

CHAPTER 9

TOWARDS THE LATE TWENTIETH CENTURY AND BEYOND
Rural and urban change and the task of the historian

Andrew J. H. Jackson

Introduction

The work of Dennis Mills is of great significance for historians of Lincolnshire and indeed elsewhere. Some of his thoughts and findings have achieved both an enduring relevance and a general appeal. These include his accessible reflections on the evolution of the concept of 'community' and how it might be approached by historians in practical terms.[1] There is also his creation, adaptation and application of the 'open' and 'closed' settlement 'model'.[2] In addition, he extended understanding of, and modes of exploiting, key sources, such as census enumerators' books and commercial directories.[3] These important contributions, and in fact much of Mills's research, shed considerable light on our knowledge and comprehension of the nineteenth century. However, it is apparent as well that his published output is of value for historical and geographical investigations of the twentieth and early twenty-first centuries. After all, Mills edited one of the first county histories of the twentieth century, for Lincolnshire, compiled a decade before the turning of the Millennium.[4] The encouragement that he gave to local historians to engage with the contemporary history of the county has a prophetic quality about it.[5]

This chapter considers aspects of Mills's work that can assist with histories of the later twentieth century up to the present. Open and closed settlements, rural and urban planning, community identity, case studies in Lincolnshire and Devon, and the task of the local historian today, are among the perspectives featuring in this appreciation.[6] The body of literature that Mills has created is considerable. Here two pieces of writing are taken as starting points and texts upon which to reflect: a concluding chapter of a publication of 1980, and a journal article of 1994.[7] They open up, or rather reopen up here, some interesting lines of enquiry for those examining change in Britain over the last two or three decades, and those considering what the craft of the local historian has to offer.

Rural and urban change and the open-closed settlement model

In an epilogue of 1980 entitled 'Lord and peasant today', concluding his study of nineteenth-century Britain, Mills commenced:

A title of this kind relating to modern Britain will strike the reader at first sight as totally discordant. Yet I am often asked what happened to the peasants? Moreover, there are still some very large estates and crofting still going on in north-west Scotland. So, on a very speculative, intentionally provocative basis, some thoughts are offered which may help to link the foregoing study of nineteenth-century society with later developments.[8]

Mills's 'foregoing study' was a further extension and application of his work on the open and closed settlement model. The epilogue is understandably a fairly short one. However, he sought to project well into the twentieth century some of the themes that he had been investigating in relation to the preceding century. The open-closed model explored the connecting up of explanatory and predictive linkages between the ownership of property and other dimensions of local life, including: population size and growth trends, housing supply, pauperism, poor rate levels, economic activity and diversity, farm size, resident labour levels, religious provision, leisure and welfare services, and political culture. In closed settlements, a product of the 'estate system', there was monopoly holding of landed property, development was relatively more prescribed and contained, life more regulated, and the social-economy more narrowly agrarian in its focus. In open settlements, an outcome of the 'peasant system', property holding was more dispersed, development less restricted, life less controlled, and the social-economy dynamic, more diverse and expansive. Open and closed settlements comprised a dichotomy or, perhaps better, formed part of a looser continuum of settlement types ranging between the open and closed extremes - from the 'wide open' to the 'firmly shut'.[9]

This spectrum also included the 'absentee' settlements, with no resident or local squire. The dichotomy or continuum could be applied spatially and analytically 'on the ground'. This contextualising of the model could illuminate settlement differences, and the internal and external relations existing within and between settlements.[10]

Mills drew attention to a number of continuities and the relevance that the open-closed conceptualisation might have for the study of the twentieth century:

> Taking the estate system first, it exerts one of two influences on rural community development ... In the areas remoter from towns, the estate village tends, at least outwardly, to be a museum of itself, especially where property has remained in the hands of a few people ... By virtue of recent and current planning policies, housing developments have been channelled into the bigger villages, i.e. mainly those which were open villages in the nineteenth century. Although this policy has been evolved on the basis of providing adequate services in a limited number of places, the result is much the same as could have been predicted on the basis of the open-closed model.[11]

There are various studies that have explored the fortunes of closed villages that have remained part of landed estates - 'under the wing' or 'under the shadow' of 'the big house'. The sustainability of such communities is an important concern. 'Museumification' or 'fossilisation' is a possible scenario for some closed villages. For others opportunities for diversification may be offered up under the mixed agrarian regime of the traditional landed estate. These alternative courses are among the themes assessed in investigations of estate villages in the later twentieth century.[12] Mills also turned to another direction adopted by closed villages:

> where the once model village has found itself in the path of strong development pressures for suburban or 'dormitory' development and has succumbed. It has usually done this on a totally different basis from the former open village. Instead of large numbers of three bedroom semi-detached houses, there will be limited numbers of individually-designed detached houses, enhanced in desirability by the leafy environment surviving from estate days. Sometimes the big house has gone and smaller houses have been built on the site, sometimes it remains as a block of flats, with new houses in the grounds. Stable blocks, laundries, servants' quarters, gardeners' cottages, barns and granaries have all acquired a status which would have made the former inhabitants smile. And this status is protected by planning policies which prevent developments not in keeping with the character of the locality.[13]

This trajectory is one that Mills illustrated in his studies of Canwick, just south of Lincoln.[14] The village has mutated through the later twentieth and early twenty-first centuries, as land and property have changed hands and demands for redevelopment have pressed upon the place. The owners of the Canwick estate, the Sibthorps, sold up to Jesus College, Cambridge, in 1940. Jesus College, subsequently, sold much of the estate, allowing for further local development. However, the estate, through its legacy of buildings and designed landscapes, has continued to act as a cultural factor influencing the manner of change.

The negotiation between property owners, developers and local authorites that has brought contrasting development trajectories for settlements is quite apparent in the rural studies literature. By the early 1990s geographers had observed that diversification within the agrarian economy and intensifying and competing use demands upon a 'contested' countryside were contributing to uneven development and local and regional difference. If the mid-twentieth century 'community studies' tradition had fallen into some disfavour by the 1970s, it found a form of revival in local investigations ofrestructuring and divergence in the countryside of the 1990s.[15] Even if researchers of the post-war countryside have not explicitly employed Mills's open-closed model, the perpetuation of tendencies towards 'closedness' and 'openness', or some state between the two, is much in evidence in findings.[16]

In some of the relatively more 'open' villages north of Lincoln various and successive rounds of development have been permitted and accommodated.[17] Inter-war development in 'ribbons', small blocks of post-war local authority accommodation, sinuous lines of bungalows, and housing in many variants and degrees of the 'modernist', 'quasi-neo-vernacular' or 'executive' *(Figures 9.1 and 9.2)*, have all added to the expansion and appearance of places like Nettleham, Dunholme and Welton. Landownership patterns,

Figure 9.1
A house in Welton
(Ken Redmore, 2011)

Figure 9.2
Housing infill near the ford at Dunholme
(Andrew J H Jackson, 2010)

existing development tendencies and proximity to Lincoln are to the fore of decisive factors bringing about the evolution of such places.

Elsewhere, former RAF 'estate' settlements offer historians and geographers something of a Lincolnshire speciality, given the concentration of airbases in the county and the rate of their decommissioning in recent decades.[18] The contrasting life courses of places like Hemswell and Nocton will make for interesting studies in the present and in decades ahead. The functional and visual compartmentalisation of Hemswell is heavily determined by the architecture and infrastructure of its life as an RAF base. At its heart now is an out-of-town antiques retail park. In Nocton, meanwhile, its accommodation of a military hospital complex led to one of a number of distinctive phases of development. The preceding phase was its life as the centre of a landed estate, and the one succeeding is its current and most prominent incarnation, as a dormitory suburb. The socio-spatial composition of Nocton is quite an entanglement of rounds of redevelopment, re-segregation and identity reforming.[19]

Turning from the rural to the urban, Mills continued his reflection on the ongoing relevance of the open-closed model and in particular the estate system. He suggested that:

> [It] has had the greatest influence on our present living conditions in the urban areas where most people still live. This is because a continuous thread can be traced from the English estate village and the Scottish planned village through various factory villages and company towns down to the garden city movement, post-1918 suburbia and the New Towns ... Town planning outside the New Towns also owes something to the ideals of the estate village transmitted through the garden city movement.[20]

In Lincolnshire the local authorities, in partnership with landowners and developers, responded with varying levels of haste and enthusiasm to the calls for large-scale housing schemes for the twentieth century.[21] Local and national demands for larger numbers, and a better quality, of housing were met with the introduction of new planning legislation; while design was cultivated by the ideals of the garden city and suburb movements, with their promotion of overall visual and functional coherence, generous allowance for open spaces, verges and trees, and differing degrees of commitment towards self containment. Lincoln was quick off the mark in setting out the St Giles' estate to the north east of the city. The laying out of housing began in a suitably neo-vernacular manner along Wragby Road, just after the First World War, although building styles would become relatively more utilitarian as the estate unfolded further to the north and east.[22] The estate has a powerful visual and morphological coherence. Its roads, laid out in a grid system, are boulevard-like: heavily tree lined and with ample verges. Prominent as well is a central core, the location for shops, churches, chapels and schools. The commitment to large-scale local authority housing provision did not lessen in Lincoln through the middle decades of the twentieth century, following the construction of the St Giles' estate. Elsewhere, the city's council would assume a wider role as major landed proprietor and landlord, with its paternalist charge reaching further still as estates would be developed at Hartsholme, Boultham and on the Ermine.[23]

History, heritage and the task of the local historian

In 1994 Dennis Mills tackled the uneasy relationship that exists between history and heritage, and what part the local historian should play. He observed that:

> 'Academic local history' and the requirements of the heritage industry may appear to be so far apart, that there is no point in the professional historian bothering with the industry. How wrong this could be is demonstrated by the thinking about how the average person becomes conscious of the importance of the local past. It must be mainly through visiting museums, historic sites and ancient buildings; random browsing in local libraries and bookshops; and going to events replicating the life and times of the civil war soldier, iron age man, the Armada and so on. For the majority, it is not through local history classes or the activities of local history societies.[24]

Mills's consideration of history and heritage, and their interrelationship, gave emphasis to possibilities rather than pitfalls. He was concerned at the lack of engagement of local historians with the statutory planning process, or rather the lack of structures and mechanisms that would allow for such engagement. Local historians seemed to feature little in debates over building preservation, or in the production of planning documents relating to historical contexts. Mills went on to urge local historians to contribute to the process of developing good quality historical guides, or at least to collate, in an accessible form, key primary source material that would provide an insight into the past of localities.[25]

The nature of history and heritage and how they interrelate has been a subject of much discussion and debate.[26] At one end of the extreme there is an antipathy among academic historians towards heritage, as Mills observed. Heritage is often understood by the professional historian as meaning no more than heritage industry, that is, the use and abuse of the past to serve the demands of contemporary consumerism. History, meanwhile, is a nobler pursuit, determined by the worthy and well-considered agenda of the academic establishment. In this rather adversarial context some have argued that local history ought to be aligned clearly and outwardly with the practice of history and not heritage. Furthermore, its output should be judged in terms of a narrowly-defined end product, that is, the high-quality local history publication, authoritative and convention bound. At the other end of the extreme is a position favouring a history and heritage more harmoniously accommodated, or at least co-operative and co-dependent: a state of affairs, it seems, welcomed by Mills. Here there is an appreciation that heritage is highly varied and multifaceted, more than merely an industrial or commercial process. It is also, like history, all the time evolving as a cultural force.[27] In this context local historians can be seen engaging with the past in such a diverse and dynamic way that discerning whether their activity is history or heritage is futile. Local historians are involved in the saving of historical artefacts and recollections for the future, lobbying for the protection of the historic environment, mounting exhibitions and events, promoting the enjoyment of historic places, as well as publishing traditional local histories.[28]

Heritage is associated with the requirements of the statutory planning of the historic environment, and also with the provision of a necessary heritage leisure and tourism industry. Equally, heritage over the last decade has become greatly preoccupied with the nature and creation of community identity. There is a fuller realisation of the role that local heritage plays in empowering and enriching the lives of places through engagement initiatives. This is of course what the work of local historians has long participated in, to some extent, either directly or indirectly. Moreover, the structures of adult education, until fairly recently, provided a framework for bringing this about.[29] However, the turning of the Millennium, the operation of heritage lottery funding, and shifts towards a relatively more people-focussed planning philosophy, have given a considerable new impetus to the outreach dimension of local history. There has been a stepping up of the activity of the local historians in their work with local communities and their heritage.[30]

In Lincoln there has been a great deal of activity that has seen a positive and fruitful coming together of history and heritage, a professional and popular engagement with the past, and an involvement of statutory planning processes with 'lay' history. Such developments are a realisation of what Mills was calling for in 1994, and indeed he has been a contributor to their advancement. The Survey of Lincoln series is approaching the sixth volume in its neighbourhood booklet series.[31] The volumes that comprise the series form an historical record and a model of good local historical practice, consolidating, extending and enhancing knowledge and understanding of the history of Lincoln. In addition they are a medium through which the built heritage of the city can be appreciated, expressed and promoted. The work of the Survey of Lincoln parallels the creation of the Lincoln Townscape Assessment (LTA), the product of a partnership between the City of Lincoln Council, English Heritage and the Heritage Lottery Fund, as well as with, essentially if less formally, the people of Lincoln itself.[32] The Assessment has aimed to document the history and heritage of 108 Character Areas of the city in order to provide an information base to support the processes of statutory planning. The content of the LTA is also enriched, informed and given added validity and authenticity by the inclusion of the perceptions, recollections, testimonies and artefacts of the inhabitants of the Character Areas themselves. The input of local planners and the people has been brought together in an electronic and interactive repository, 'Heritage Connect Lincoln', a web resource serving local government officers, schools, professional researchers and enthusiasts.[33] A further feature of the LTA is to extend the knowledge and recognition of areas of twentieth century and later development, including those that have been neglected by published local histories, fall outside the 'tourist trail', or have attracted derogatory associations. The steady programme of history writing under the auspices of the Survey of Lincoln is also assisting with such shortcomings.

A short history of the Ermine council estate was produced in 2008-9 for the Survey of Lincoln. This arose from a fortuitous coinciding of two sets of circumstances: the formation of a partnership connecting professional historical research with community archiving on the Ermine, and the engagement of local planners with the people through the LTA.[34] The history of the Ermine drew on the then draft Landscape Character Assessments for Ermine East and West produced by the City of Lincoln Council.[35] The historical account also made valuable use of the community archive gathered by the estate. The collection is held at the parish church of St John the Baptist, and much of it has since been digitised and made available through the church's website.[35] Both the Assessments and the history for the Survey of Lincoln achieved certain primary aims of local historical activity broadly defined, that is, the writing of local histories as well as the recognition and representation of local heritage.

The Ermine estate, comprising its two portions of Ermine East and West, forms a substantial part of north-west Lincoln, and indeed the city as a whole. The estate is the location of two Lincoln landmarks, 'classics' of their age, the 1960s. These are the tower block of Trent View in Ermine West and, in Ermine East, the church of St. John by the architect Sam Scorer, with its reverse hyberbolic paraboloid roof and semi-abstract, coloured-glass east window by Keith New *(Figure 9.3)*.

Figure 9.3
St. John the Baptist Parish Church, Ermine East
(Andrew J H Jackson, 2010)

The estate is both a model and historical legacy of large scale 1950s local authority urban planning. The architecture is low rise, and noticeably plainer in its form and decorative detail than in the 'garden suburb' inspired, earlier local authority estate of St. Giles to the east. This said, in the Ermine East section most clearly, the designed landscape is more sinuous in its flow and more open in its feel, prefiguring the private housing estates that would become such a feature of the two decades to follow. Domestic buildings, though fairly homogeneous in appearance and aesthetic, incorporate a diversity intended to meet the needs of the incoming settlers: yellow-brick apartments *(Figure 9.4)*, 'pre-fab' 'semis' *(Figure 9.5)*, and red-brick terraces and bungalows *(Figure 9.6)*. Public and commercial buildings are dispersed through the estate, with the provision of a single main centre a conspicuous omission. Churches, chapels, shops, schools and community centres are generally in large plots, either surrounded by housing or at the meeting points of through-roads.[37]

In the Ermine, in the 1950s, there was a fulfilment of the historical processes descending from the estate village to twentieth-century town planning, as Mills was of the view:

> the ideals of the town-planning movement have probably been most strongly felt on municipal housing estates which now provide accommodation for perhaps one third of the population. It is not merely the spacious layouts and the provision of amenities which seem so redolent of the estate village. It could also be argued that on the council estate the housing department has taken over the role of the old time landowner, regulating not only the properties but also the inhabitants, limiting lodgers, disallowing huts and preventing businesses from being run from council houses. Such rules and regulations go well beyond normal planning regulations, which in themselves are also a powerful aspect of paternal control by the state.[38]

However, it is evident in the genesis of the Ermine estate there is to be discerned the presence of a paternalist hand of more ancient descent, not entirely rendered relict, the Anglican church. The church was an essential agent in the fostering of a sense of community identity among the new inhabitants of the developing estate. The estate would become an ecclesiastical parish, served by a combined church and community hall of 1957. This would be replaced by the new Sam Scorer church of 1963. Meanwhile, the estate would also come to accommodate an Anglican building on Ermine West, and chapels for the United Reformed and Methodist churches on the East and West respectively. The Anglican church's community newspaper, the *Ermine News*, reported upon, and sought to stimulate the formation of, new social, cultural and economic networks across the estate. Monthly, from 1957 to 1965, it published a wide range of articles, calendars and advertisements aiming to inform and encourage.[39] Editorials also called for enhancements to the estate's design, charted the church's support for planning applications, and promoted ways of optimising the facilities emerging across the estate. The *Ermine News*, and indeed the estate archive as a whole, offer a rich resource for exploring the nature of community. Mills outlined tasks for the community historian: seeking out the meaning and sense of community, searching out the relationships that exist both within and beyond communities, as well as

Figure 9.4
An apartment block on Ermine East. Sale signs highlight flats now passing through private ownership
(Andrew J H Jackson, 2010)

Figure 9.5
A 'gentrified' 'semi' on Ermine East, near Waitrose supermarket
(Andrew J H Jackson, 2010)

Figure 9.6
Bungalows on Ermine East
(Ken Redmore, 2010)

revealing the dynamics operating among and across the groups existing within those communities.[40] The Ermine estate archive enabled such an approach to community history to be undertaken.

Conclusion: beyond the epilogue

This offering can only partially explore some of the applications of the research of Dennis Mills in historical and historical-geographical investigations of the later twentieth and early twenty-first centuries, within Lincolnshire and beyond. Various perspectives and their relevance are not reached here. In his epilogue to *Lord and Peasant*, for example, he also asked: 'But what of the peasantry and their values in this day and age?'.[41] Despite the agrarian change of the second half of the twentieth century, Mills continued:

> the careful observer will find examples of dual occupationists which appear to be in direct line of descent from the nineteenth-century peasantry ... [In addition] Moonlighters must be very close in attitude to the less respectable elements of the nineteenth-century peasantry - able to combine the use of their own labour with small amounts of capital, willing to seek out custom, sometimes dual occupationists, sometimes ignoring the paternalistic rules of the modern state ... Is there a link between this line of thinking and the drive towards a property-owning democracy? DIY enthusiasts at least have more scope and more incentive when they live not as tenants, but in the hope of being the outright owners of their houses ... Finally, it is necessary to say a word about self-sufficiency perhaps the ultimate in DIY ... There has, of course, been a continuous tradition of digging the back garden and allotment ... However, there is a more serious, even intellectual following for self-sufficiency, not only at the family level, but at the national level ... A revival then, in some suitably modernised form, of the peasant system seems to be most desirable to complement our large-scale monoculture.[42]

The work of Mills - some artful, some social scientific, and some a skilful blending of the two - will continue to promote, provoke and predict. His contribution also underlines the significant role that the past can play in the service of both the present and the future. Regularly his thoughts and findings bring him, and us, to the conclusion that in many local landscapes and among many local societies: *'Tout ça change, tout c'est la même chose'*.[43]

Notes

[1] Dennis Mills, 'Community and nation in the past: perception and reality', in, *Time, Family and Community: Perspectives on Family and Community History*, edited by Michael Drake (Oxford, 1994), pp.261-85; Dennis Mills, 'Defining community: a critical review of 'community' in Family and Community History', *Family and Community History*, 7.1 (2004), pp.5-12.

[2] D. R. Mills, 'Has historical geography changed?', *New Trends in Geography*, D281 (Milton Keynes, 1972), pp.58-75; and Dennis R. Mills, *Lord and Peasant in Nineteenth Century Britain* (1980).

[3] Dennis R. Mills, *Rural Community History from Trade Directories* (Aldenham, 2001); Dennis Mills and Michael Drake, 'The census, 1801-1991', in *Studying Family and Community History, Nineteenth and Twentieth Centuries, 4, Sources and Methods: A Handbook*, edited by Michael Drake and Ruth Finnegan (2nd edn, Oxford, 1997). pp.25-56

[4] Dennis R. Mills (ed.), *Twentieth Century Lincolnshire*, History of Lincolnshire, 12 (Lincoln, 1989).

[5] Dennis R. Mills, 'Introduction', in *Twentieth Century Lincolnshire*, edited by Mills, pp.12-15. The study of the later twentieth and early twenty-first centuries by local historians has been followed up since, for example, by Kate Tiller in 'Practising twentieth-century local history', for *Researching and Writing Local Histories of the Twentieth Century*, Conference of the British Association of Local History and the Society for Lincolnshire History and Archaeology (Lincoln, 2010, 23 April).

[6] These particular set of perspectives were explored first in Andrew J. H. Jackson, 'Rural property rights and the survival of historic landed estates in the late twentieth century', unpublished PhD thesis (1988); and most recently in Andrew J. H. Jackson, 'Rural Lincolnshire from the mid-twentieth century: landscapes and settlements', for *A Century of Lincolnshire's Past: a Conference to Mark the Centenary of the Lincoln Record Society* (Lincoln, 2010, 22 May).

[7] Mills, *Lord and Peasant*, pp.223-8; and Dennis Mills, 'Heritage and historians', *Local Historian*, 24.4 (1994), p.226.

[8] Mills, *Lord and Peasant*, p.223.

[9] Dennis R. Mills and Brian Short, 'Social change and social conflict in nineteenth-century England', *Journal of Peasant Studies*, 10.4 (1983), p.254.

[10] On the development and application of the open and closed model, see also: D. R. Mills, 'The geographical effects of the Laws of Settlement in Nottinghamshire: an analysis of Francis Howell's report, 1948', *East Midlands Geographer*, 5 (1970), pp.31-8; Mills, 'Has historical geography changed?'; D. R. Mills, 'The development of rural settlement around Lincoln, with special reference to the eighteenth and nineteenth centuries', in *English Rural Communities: The Impact of a Specialist Economy*, edited by Dennis R. Mills (1973), pp.83-97.

[11] Mills, *Lord and Peasant*, p.223.

[12] For example, on Powderham in Devon, Jackson, 'Rural property rights', and Andrew J. H. Jackson, 'A landed estate and parish in the mid-20th century: insights from the 1941-43 National Farm Survey of England and Wales', *Family and Community History*, 8.1 (2005), pp.5-20. See also Lockinge in Berkshire, M. A. Havinden, *Estate Villages: A Study of the Berkshire Villages of Ardington and Lockinge* (1966).

[13] Mills, *Lord and Peasant*, p.223.

[14] Dennis Mills, *A Walk round Canwick: The Lincolnshire Estate Village of the Sibthorps with the Enclosure Award Map of 1787* (Lincoln, 2003); Dennis Mills, 'Canwick (Lincolnshire) and Melbourn (Cambridgeshire) in comparative perspective within the open-closed village model', *Rural History*, 17.1 (2006), pp.1-22.

[15] Colin Bell and Howard Newby, *Community Studies* (1971), pp.1-20; Terry Marsden, Jonathan Murdoch, Philip Lowe, Richard Munton and Andrew Flynn, *Constructing the Countryside* (1993); Jonathan Murdoch and Terry Marsden, *Reconstituting Rurality* (1994).

[16] In Lincolnshire, see David I. A. Steel, *A Lincolnshire Village: The Parish of Corby Glen in its Historical Context* (1979); Bill Goodhand, 'Changes in the quality of rural life: a case study of Welbourn', in *Twentieth Century Lincolnshire*, edited by Mills, pp.181-211. On Kenton and Powderham in Devon, Jackson, 'Rural property rights'; and on the Devon villages of Poltimore and Stoke Canon, Andrew J. H. Jackson, 'Published parish and community histories - a starting point in adult learning and the retheorising of local history', *Local Historian*, 36.1 (2006), pp.42-50.

[17] The rapid growth of villages around Lincoln was among the more conspicuous of the county's demographic trends through the first three quarters of the twentieth century; see Dennis Mills, 'The revolution in workplace and home', in *Twentieth Century Lincolnshire*, edited by Mills, pp.23-6.

[18] Barry Holliss, 'The impact of the Royal Air Force', in *Twentieth Century Lincolnshire*, edited by Mills, pp.151-4.

[19] Jackson, 'Rural Lincolnshire'.

[20] Mills, *Lord and Peasant*, pp.223-4.

[21] Sally Scott, 'The early days of planning', in *Twentieth Century Lincolnshire*, edited by Mills, pp.181-211.

[22] Andrew J. H. Jackson, 'Twentieth-century residential development: the St Giles' estate', in *Uphill Lincoln II: The North Eastern Suburbs*, edited by Andrew Walker (Lincoln, 2010) pp.58-61; Scott, 'The early days', pp.204-5.

[23] Nigel Horner, 'Castle Ward: contemporary impressions', in *Uphill Lincoln I: Burton Road, Newport, and the Ermine Estate*, edited by Andrew Walker (Lincoln, 2009), pp.68-71; and Andrew J. H. Jackson, 'The development of the Ermine Estate in the 1950s and 1960s', in Walker, *Uphill Lincoln I*, pp.65-7.

[24] Mills, 'Heritage and historians', p.226.

[25] Mills, 'Heritage and historians', p.225-8. Mills's views found material realisation in, for example: Mills, *A Walk around Canwick*.

[26] Andrew J. H. Jackson, 'Local and regional history as heritage: the heritage process and conceptualising the purpose and practice of local historians', *International Journal of Heritage Studies*, 14.4 (2008), pp.362-79.

[27] Andrew J. H. Jackson, 'Process and synthesis in the rethinking of local history: perspectives in essays for a county history society', *International Journal of Regional and Local Studies*, 2.1 (2006), pp.5-19.

[28] A sense of this dynamism is captured in Kate Tiller, 'Local historians can do this for themselves' - a personal view of 2008-9', *Local Historian*, 39.4 (2009), pp.324-9.

[29] Maurice Barley, 'Postscript', in *Twentieth Century Lincolnshire*, edited by Mills, pp. 355-61. For a specific example see: *Kirkby Green and Scopwick: Historical Sketches of two Lincolnshire Parishes*, edited by Peter Baumber and Dennis Mills (Scopwick, 1993).

[30] Andrew J. H. Jackson, 'Local history and local history education in the early twenty-first century: organisational and intellectual challenges', *Local Historian*, 38.4 (2008), pp.266-73.

[31] Walker, *Uphill Lincoln II*.

[32] David Walsh, 'Post-war suburbs and the new urbanism: Lincoln's Ermine estates', *Conservation Bulletin*, 56 (2007), pp.7-9; David Walsh and Adam Partington, 'The Lincoln Townscape Assessment: valuing places', *Conservation Bulletin*, 63 (2010), pp.39-40.

[33] City of Lincoln Council, 'Heritage Connect Lincoln' (Lincoln, 2010), available online at: http://www.heritageconnectlincoln.com.

[34] Jackson, 'The development of the Ermine Estate'.

[35] City of Lincoln Council, 'Lincoln Townscape Assessment. Character Area: Ermine West Estate. Draft' (Lincoln, 2007); 'Lincoln Townscape Assessment. Ermine East Character Area. Draft 1.0'. (Lincoln, 2008).

[36] St John the Baptist, Ermine, Lincoln, 'eArchive' (Lincoln, 2010), available online at: http://www.stjohnthebaptistparishchurch.org.uk/eArchive/index.php.

[37] City of Lincoln Council, 'Ermine West' and 'Ermine East'; Jackson, 'The development of the Ermine Estate', pp.65-6.

[38] Mills, *Lord and Peasant*, p.224.

[39] John Hodgkinson, *The Creation of a Parish and the Building of its Church 1956-64* (Lincoln, 2010); Andrew J. H. Jackson, 'A community history of the 1950s and '60s: the Ermine East estate, Lincoln', for *Researching and Writing Local Histories;* and Jackson, 'The development of the Ermine Estate, pp.66-7.

[40] Mills, 'Community and nation in the past', pp.281-4.

[41] Mills, *Lord and Peasant*, p.225.

[42] Mills, *Lord and Peasant*, pp.225-7.

[43] Mills, *Lord and Peasant*, p.223.